Hedonistic Utilitarianism

Torbjörn Tännsjö

Edinburgh University Press

© Torbjörn Tännsjö, 1998

Transferred to digital print 2012

Edinburgh University Press
22 George Square, Edinburgh

Typeset in Bembo
by Hewer Text Composition Services, Edinburgh,
**printed and bound by CPI Group (UK) Ltd
Croydon, CR0 4YY**

A CIP record for this book is
available from the British Library

ISBN 0 7486 1042 1

Contents

Acknowledgements

This book presents a defence of hedonistic utilitarianism. It covers the entire field relevant to the defence, but it does not penetrate all the parts of it equally deeply. This is due to the fact that the core of the book is several previously and separately published articles. These articles reflect my thinking on the subject over some twenty years. These articles have been rethought, revised and put together, but they have also been supplemented with much new material, to form a book. So while it is true that some crucial questions are elaborated thoroughly, such as the problems of a paradox-free statement of the utilitarian criterion of rightness, of measurement and interpersonal comparisons of happiness, and of the relative merits of hedonism as compared to competing ideas about intrinsic value, other questions are dismissed rather quickly. The most obvious point is my treatment of rule utilitarianism. In my treatment of it I have focused entirely on what I consider the strongest argument for it (even if people conform to act utilitarianism the outcome may be sub-optimal, it has been claimed, while general conformance to rule utilitarianism guarantees an optimal outcome) and I show (in Chapter 4) that, if collective action is taken into proper account, the argument is flawed (general conformance to act utilitarianism guarantees optimality as well). Rather than going into the extensive literature on rule utilitarianism, where I feel I have little to contribute, I have referred the reader to the relevant literature and left the problem at that.

Moreover, not only are there aspects of the defence of hedonistic utilitarianism that are glossed over, there are also parts of the book that treat problems of a general character, problems facing anyone wanting to defend any kind of utilitarian theory. This is true in particular of my Chapter 2 defending theory in ethics, and of my Chapter 10 treating the problem of free will and moral responsibility, but also, to some extent, of my Chapter 11, defending utilitarianism against criticisms from common sense morality.

All this means that the book should not be seen as an introduction to its subject. Yet, for all that, I feel confident that it should interest anyone already somewhat familiar with the subject and prepared to think hard about some of the

v

more difficult and crucial aspects of it. The book is intended for advanced courses in moral philosophy.

Chapter 1 is new. The core of the argument of Chapter 2 appeared in *Canadian Journal of Philosophy*, Vol. 25,1995, but important additions have been made to it. Chapter 3 is new, but it is based on ideas put forward in my book *The Relevance of Metaethics to Ethics*, and the papers 'The Morality of Abstract Entities', which appeared in *Theoria*, Vol. XLIV, 1978, and 'Moral Conflict and Moral Realism', which appeared in the *Journal of Philosophy*, Vol. LXXXI, 1985. Chapter 4 is entirely new. Chapter 5 is based on 'Classical Hedonistic Utilitarianism', published in *Philosophical Studies*, Vol. 81, 1996. Chapter 6 is based on 'Welfare Economics and the Meaning of Life', in *In So Many Words*, a Festschrift for Sven Danielsson. Chapter 7 is based on 'Against Personal Autonomy', which was published in the *International Journal of Applied Philosophy*, Vol. 4, 1989. Chapter 8 is entirely new. Chapter 9 is based on 'Blameless Wrongdoing', published in *Ethics*, Vol. 105, 1995, and Chapter 10 is based on 'Soft Determinism and How We Become Responsible for the Past', which was published in *Philosophical Papers*, Vol. XVIII, 1989. It also contains some material from 'Morality and Modality', which was published in *Philosophical Papers*, Vol. XX, 1991. Chapter 11 and Chapter 12 are new.

Many people have made helpful comments on the manuscript of this book, or on particular chapters of it. Earlier versions of the entire book have been read and commented upon by Hans Mathlein, Christian Munthe, Ragnar Ohlsson, Jack Smart and Folke Tersman. Drafts of Chapter 2 have been read and commented upon by Jonathan Dancy. Chapter 5 has been read and commented upon by David Copp, Michael R. DePaul, Wlodek Rabinowicz, Donald Regan and Derek Parfit. Drafts of Chapter 6 have been commented upon by Bengt Brülde. Drafts of Chapter 7 have been read and commented upon by Elliot Cohen, G. A. Cohen, Jonathan Glover and H. J. McCloskey. Drafts of Chapter 9 have been read and commented upon by David Copp, Jonathan Dancy and Derek Parfit. Drafts of Chapter 10 have been read and commented upon by Sven Danielsson, Michael Dummett, David Lewis and Wlodek Rabinowicz. I thank all these commentators for their most helpful criticism.

I initiated the work on this book when I held a position as senior researcher at the Swedish Council for Research in the Humanities and Social Sciences. The Council has also supported the publication of the book. For all this I am thankful.

Chapter 1

Introduction

When Bernard Williams some twenty years ago strongly repudiated the utilitarian doctrine, he also conjectured that the 'day cannot be too far off in which we hear no more of it'.[1] This prophecy has not come true. The discussions about the doctrine over the last decades have been extensive and more sophisticated than ever. Yet, there was some grain of truth in the prophecy put forward by Williams. Utilitarianism is today not a view that is in vogue, nor has it been so the last decades. This is true in particular of its classical, hedonistic form. Even among those who discuss utilitarianism, and add new dimensions to our understanding of it, few profess adherence to it. Why is this so?

Superficially, at least, philosophy is a very serious business. People doing philosophy are people of a critical bent of mind, obsessed with an earnest pursuit of deep truths. Yet, for all that, philosophy is also a place where fashion is of great importance. Some ideas become fashionable at a time but, later on, they fall into oblivion. However, we do not forget about them for ever; they tend to come back. The reason that they do is that there are no knock-down arguments in philosophy, which once and for all show that one theory is really any better than another. This is true of all genuine philosophical positions. When a philosophical doctrine falls into disrepute it is often because the philosophers are, at the time, fed up with it. They rarely find new, strong arguments against it, arguments that they feel compel them to give it up. It is rather the case that, unconsciously (or subconsciously), they lower their criteria of acceptance, when dealing with some well-known crucial arguments. Arguments that were at one time considered of little importance come, at once, to convince.

Classical hedonistic utilitarianism is a theory that has nowadays fallen, if not completely into oblivion, at least into disrepute. Hence it gets dismissed in the opening chapters of many contemporary books in moral and political philosophy on very poor grounds. The authors do not feel any need to give strong arguments. They know that, in order to persuade, they need not do that. They know that few are prepared to accept the doctrine, anyway. However, hedonistic utilitarianism is a viable option for anyone in pursuit of truth in normative ethics. It is as viable today as it was, say, when Henry Sidgwick wrote

1

his *Methods of Ethics*. Classical hedonistic utilitarianism deserves to be taken seriously.

In particular, John Rawls's criticism of utilitarianism has been extremely influential. People who work in the tradition of Rawls seem simply to take for granted that utilitarianism has been rebutted, once and for all, by Rawls's saying (echoed by Robert Nozick) that utilitarianism does not take seriously the distinction between persons.[2] However, upon closer inspection it is far from clear whether Rawls's own theory really is in any practical conflict with utilitarianism. I am referring not only to the fact that his contractual apparatus has been thought by some to yield utilitarianism (such as J. C. Harsanyi),[3] but also to the much more surprising fact that it is far from clear whether his difference principle as such is inconsistent with utilitarianism.

On Rawls's difference principle, social and economic inequalities are to be arranged so that they are to the greatest benefit of the least advantaged. This may be thought to be, in an obvious manner, at variance with utilitarianism. However, it is far from clear that utilitarians cannot argue from the principle of diminishing marginal utility that it is a good investment in utilitarian terms to concentrate scarce resources on those who are worst off. A sum of money can do more for a poor person than for a rich one. To this it might be retorted that, if we bring into consideration persons who are really in a weak position, such as the very sick or disabled, concentrating scarce resources on them may mean a waste of resources. For we can always improve their lot a little bit, by allocating more resources to them, resources we take from those who are better off. And this will mean that those who are better off will have to sacrifice, in the end, much more than is gained by those who are worst off.

Now, this may well be so. However, it should be noticed that Rawls himself does not recommend, under these circumstances, that his difference principle be followed! He explicitly excludes severely sick or disabled persons from the class of those who are worst off in society.[4] In this Ronald Dworkin, for example, follows suit. Rawls does not say anything himself about when we should refrain from spending more resources on those who are really worst off. Ronald Dworkin constructs a special contractual apparatus to resolve this problem.[5] However, none of these authors seems prepared to apply the difference principle in these cases. But these are the very cases, and perhaps the only ones, where the difference principle and the utilitarian formula come into practical conflict. In the circumstances, not only the utilitarian but Rawls himself hesitate to take seriously the distinction between persons.

If this argument is correct it seems to be quite possible that Rawls (and Dworkin) and the utilitarian would make exactly the same prescriptions about particular cases. If this is so, however, I suggest that utilitarianism gives the best (moral) explanation of the truth of these prescriptions. What counts against the claim that Rawls's difference principle provides us with good moral explanations is its lack of generality (I suggest, then, that we must follow Rawls when he hesitates to apply the difference principle in dealing with people who are really worst off).

Irrespective of how this argument be assessed, I think it clear that, when we realise that not even John Rawls's theory of justice is obviously in any practical conflict with utilitarianism, we should at least be prepared to take utilitarianism seriously.

In the present book (hedonistic) utilitarianism is taken seriously. My hope is that the book and the rethinking of hedonistic utilitarianism that it provides will revive a general interest in utilitarian theory. The principal aim of the book is to give a clear, simple, comprehensive and yet plausible statement of the doctrine. But my aim is also to defend it.

The defence is undertaken in the consciousness that there exist no knock-down arguments either in defence of, or against, the doctrine. But a conjecture made in the book (in the spirit of Henry Sidgwick) is that hedonistic utilitarianism is a true doctrine, capable of explaining (the truth of) particular moral judgements. My belief is that hedonistic utilitarianism gives the best explanation of these judgements. It is beyond the scope of the present book to show that this is a fact. I attempt to show, however, that hedonistic utilitarianism gives at least a good explanation of these judgements. This is the reason why it should be taken seriously.

Of course, hedonistic utilitarianism cannot explain all particular judgements that contemporary moralists should want to make. No theory can do this, since these judgements often contradict each other. However, on the whole, hedonistic utilitarianism gives the best explanation of the part of our common sense morality that, after a process of careful reflection and critical examination, we should be prepared to retain. Or so I believe. And at least it gives a good explanation of them. This is the claim defended in the book. Futhermore, when hard practical cases must be decided, and common sense morality fails us (is silent or equivocal), utilitarianism helps us to fill in the gaps, showing what kinds of consideration are morally relevant and explaining why these considerations have the weight they have.

Recent treatments of the subject

Classical hedonistic utilitarianism was first stated by Jeremy Bentham in *Introduction to the Principles of Morals and Legislation*. It was Bentham who coined the word 'utilitarianism'.[6] A concise statement of the doctrine can be found in J. S. Mill's *Utilitarianism*. The first subtle discussion of it is in Henry Sidgwick's *The Methods of Ethics*.

The most influential, brief and modern statement of utilitarianism is J. J. C.

Smart's 'An Outline of a System of Utilitarian Ethics'. Instructive overviews of the modern general discussion of utilitarianism (including contributions from the sixties such as David Lyons's *Forms and Limits of Utilitarianism*, David Hodgson's *Consequences of Utilitarianism* and Jan Narveson's *Morality and Utility*, all representing a sympathetic interest in utilitarianism during that period, an interest which seems now to be gone) are found in Dan Brock, 'Recent Work in Utilitarianism', and in James Griffin, 'Modern Utilitarianism'. A recent discussion of hedonistic utilitarianism is found in J. J. C. Smart, 'Hedonistic and Ideal Utilitarianism'.

Lars Bergström, in his book *The Alternatives and Consequences of Actions*, which was also a good example of the widespread sympathetic interest in utilitarianism during the sixties, opened up a new field in the discussion of utilitarianism. He showed that many statements of the doctrine lead to deontic paradoxes, due to problematic aspects of the concepts of alternatives and consequences. This discussion is reviewed in Erik Carlson's book *Some Basic Problems of Consequentialism*.

Two themes have been recurring in the normative discussion of utilitarianism. On the one hand, utilitarianism has been considered to require from moral agents that, in some circumstances, they perform actions that are inherently wrong, such as rape, murder and torture. On the other hand, utilitarianism has been considered to make too heavy demands on moral agents, requiring of them that they give up their own favoured life projects and become pure do-gooders. On both these counts, utilitarianism has been considered to be at variance with common sense morality.

The former kind of criticism is legion in all attempts to state and defend a basic moral principle that can serve as an alternative to the utilitarian one. It is also a recurring theme in various attempts to state an anti-theoretical, commonsensical moral position. It is not meaningful to give references here to this abundantly rich literature. It must suffice to refer the reader to books such as John Rawls's *A Theory of Justice* (with a defence of equalitarianism), Robert Nozick's *Anarchy, State, and Utopia* (with a defence of rights as absolute constraints), David Gauthier's *Morals by Agreement* (with a defence of moral contractualism), and Jonathan Dancy's *Moral Reasons* (with a defence of an anti-theoretical particularism).

The latter kind of criticism, according to which utilitarianism makes too heavy demands on moral agents, is discussed in Shelly Kagan's book *The Limits of Morality*, and reviewed in Björn Eriksson's *Heavy Duty*.

Two recent collections of articles critical of utilitarian thought are *Consequentialism and its Critics*, edited by Samuel Scheffler, and *Utilitarianism and Beyond*, edited by Amartya Sen and Bernard Williams.

Plan of the book

The book opens up with a defence of theory in ethics. In this chapter I try to rebut particularism and to show that it is sound moral methodology to search for true moral principles that can explain those judgements about particular cases that, upon critical examination, we want to stick to. In this chapter I defend, then, a certain moral methodology, coherentism.

In this book I take moral realism for granted. I do not defend it, however. I have done so elsewhere, mainly in my book *Moral Realism*. If the moral methodology I defend, coherentism, be accepted, it is not a very controversial claim to make that moral judgements about particular cases, as well as moral principles, are 'true' or 'false'. After all, even such anti-realists or quasi-realists as J. J. C. Smart and Simon Blackburn avail themselves of moral truth and falsehood.[7]

In Chapter 3 I give a more precise statement of the utilitarian formula, leaving the problem of value open, however. I make clear that I am looking for criteria of rightness rather than a decision method, for criteria of objective rightness rather than of subjective rightness, and for criteria of objective rightness of concrete actions (I ascribe rightness *de re*) rather than criteria of objective rightness of abstract actions (i.e., I do not ascribe rightness *de dicto*), and that I distinguish act utilitarianism from rule utilitarianism. I show in this chapter that my statement of utilitarianism is not open to the problems discussed by Lars Bergström in his aforementioned book. My statement of utilitarianism does not give rise to any deontic paradoxes.

In Chapter 4 I defend the claim that there are collective actions and I hold that the utilitarian formula should also be applied to these. This prepares the ground for the claim that, if all agents (individual as well as collective) perform their utilitarian duty, the outcome is optimal.

In Chapter 5 I state and rethink the hedonistic version of utilitarianism. I argue that subjective time rather than objective time is what matters in the moral assessment of actions, and I defend the view that interpersonal comparisons of well-being are meaningful. I argue that on hedonistic utilitarianism we must take sub-noticeable differences of well-being into moral account. In a manner of speaking, I 'split' what has been considered the hedonistic atom, the hedon. On my view, the hedonistic unit is the least sub-noticeable difference of well-being.

My discussion of sub-noticeable differences of well-being leads me to what I will call the ultra repugnant conclusion of hedonistic utilitarianism that, in order to increase the well-being in a sub-noticeable manner for many already very happy persons, we may have to torture one person. It is argued that this conclusion, even if unsought, is compatible with hedonistic utilitarianism. In spite of this conclusion, and as a matter of overall plausibility, hedonistic utilitarianism remains preferable to other moral theories.

In Chapter 6 and Chapter 7 I confront hedonism with two alternative theories of intrinsic value, preferentialism (that which has intrinsic value is the satisfaction of preferences) and perfectionism (that which has intrinsic value is to achieve some objective goal, set independently of what the person achieving it wants or feels about it).

In Chapter 6 I argue that preferentialism is inherently unstable and I claim that a strong argument tells against its acceptability.

In Chapter 7 I try to rebut the idea that personal autonomy has intrinsic value; in my opinion, this is the most plausible form of perfectionism. In Chapter 7 I also discuss and reject the 'experience machine' objection to hedonism put forward by Robert Nozick, and I reject also in this chapter J. S. Mill's proposal that some pleasures are of a more valuable kind than others.

In Chapter 8 I defend the claim, taken for granted in Chapter 6 and Chapter 7, that intrinsic value is personal, and I state my reasons for rejecting what G. E. Moore has called 'ideal' utilitarianism. I call the evaluative part of this theory 'idealism' for short.

A special comment should be made about Chapters 6–8. The aim of my defence of hedonistic utilitarianism in the main parts (the rest) of my book is limited. I want to show that the utilitarian doctrine is worthy of our attention, I want to clarify it, I want to trace its main problematic consequences, and I want to indicate how these consequences should be handled. I do not attempt to show, however, that the utilitarian doctrine is superior to all other competing ethical doctrines. In Chapters 6–8, though, I go somewhat further. In these chapters, where I follow up my discussion of the hedonistic utilitarian view of intrinsic value (the hedonistic doctrine), I do attempt to defeat competing doctrines.

In doing so, in arguing against preferentialism, perfectionism and idealism, I realise that adherents of these competing views may not always be convinced by my arguments. I indicate what sorts of considerations have moved me in the direction of hedonism and I show that at least some arguments in defence of competing views are flawed. The nature of the subject is such that more should not be attempted (since more cannot be achieved). However, I note here that the rest of the book is relevant to most readers, even to most of them who are not convinced by my argument in Chapters 6–8. My general defence of hedonistic utilitarianism is relevant also to those who believe that while pleasure and displeasure are not the only things possessing (positive and negative) intrinsic value, these things are at least among those possessing such value. I take it for granted that most readers share that belief with me.

A problem for utilitarianism is that it cannot be applied in any direct manner. We can never know of an action whether it is right or wrong. But our accepting the utilitarian criterion of rightness may inform our choice of decision procedure. In some situations, it seems to me, the utilitarian needs a method of responsible decision making where subjective probabilities and subjective assessments of value are brought together in a rational fashion. I touch upon this subject in many places in this book, mainly in Chapter 2 and Chapter 3. But the utilitarian must also have recourse to what R. M. Hare has called (in *Moral Thinking*) an 'intuitive' level of morality; we must go for what Peter Railton has called (in 'Alienation, Consequentialism, and the Demands of Morality') 'sophisticated' consequentialism. If utilitarianism is true, then it would not be wise always to try to do one's utilitarian duty, not even to try to perform subjectively right actions, or so I will argue, at any rate. Consistent utilitarians must be prepared to foster in themselves and others certain habits and traits of character that are, from a utilitarian point of view, optimal, but which are such that, when acting on them, we sometimes act wrongly. This is considered by the utilitarian to be blameless wrongdoing. This utilitarian idea has come into disrepute, however. In Chapter 9 I defend it against a recent criticism put forward by Jonathan Dancy.

In Chapter 10 I raise the difficult question of utilitarianism, free will and determinism. I defend a certain conception of free will and I defend soft determinism. However, in this chapter I end up with another very unexpected conclusion. If utilitarianism is true, and if our universe is, in all aspects relevant to moral action, deterministic, then we become morally responsible not only for the future but also for what went on in the past.

In Chapter 11 I defend the claim that hedonistic utilitarianism really provides us with a good explanation of those common sense moral judgements that, upon closer inspection, we should be prepared to hold on to. In this chapter I address the feminist critique of mainstream moral theory and practice. I claim that, when the core of a recent feminist criticism is taken into account and given due weight, i.e., when 'common sense morality' is viewed from its perspective, then it turns out that utilitarianism explains what should be explained (to wit, those common sense moral judgements that we want to retain when we have filtered our common sense beliefs through this criticism) better than standard competing views do. I think not only of views such as Kantianism and theories of rights, but also of moral particularism and virtue ethics of an Aristotelian bent.

In the concluding Chapter 12 I review the main results of the book and indicate some remaining concerns, points in my argument that I feel are weak and in need of further elaboration.

Notes

1 J. J. C. Smart and B. Williams (eds), *Utilitarianism: For and Against*, p. 150.
2 J. Rawls, *A Theory of Justice*, p. 27.
3 Cf. J. C. Harsanyi, 'Rule Utilitarianism and Decision Theory'.
4 It is clear from *A Theory of Justice* that Rawls would not acknowledge the class of

severely handicapped people as constituting a relevant stratum in his theory. However, it is not crystal clear how he would want to deal with the problem that severely handicapped people may have very expensive needs. The difference principle does not require society to try to even out handicaps, he says (since that would be impossible, I suppose), but it does not even require society fully to compensate handicapped people to the point where there is no way further to improve their lot. They should be given some help, in order to 'improve the long-term expectation of the least favored' (p. 101), but there is no saying when to stop allocating resources to them.

5 R. Dworkin, 'What is Equality? Part I: Equality of Welfare; Part II: Equality of Resources'.

6 According to Mary Warnock, he first used it in a letter dated 1781. Cf. her preface to J. S. Mill, *Utilitarianism*, p. 9, n. 1.

7 Cf. J. J. C. Smart, *Ethics, Persuasion and Truth*, p. 97, and S. Blackburn, *Spreading the Word*, p. 196. So did, by the way, C. L. Stevenson before them, in his later writings. Cf. Stevenson, *Facts and Values*, p. 216, about this. In my 'The Expressivist Theory of Truth' I myself give a fuller explanation of truth in irrealist contexts.

Chapter 2

In defence of theory in ethics

Particularism is today in vogue in ethics. Particularism is sometimes described as the idea that what is a sufficient moral reason in one situation need not be a sufficient moral reason in another situation. Indeed, it has been held on particularism that what is a reason for an action in one situation might be a reason against the same type of action, or might not be a reason at all, in another situation.[1] However, this description is insufficient. Even a generalist, such as a utilitarian, may admit that what is in one situation a sufficient reason for the rightness of an action may in another situation be a sufficient reason for its wrongness. For example, the fact that if I shoot at a certain person I kill him may, in one situation, be a sufficient reason not to shoot at him. It is sufficient for the wrongness of shooting at him if, in the situation, shooting at him suffices to guarantee that welfare does not get maximised. He is killed, say, and deprived of future pleasure, with no positive 'side-effects' whatever. However, the fact that if I shoot at him then I kill him is sufficient (in another situation) for the rightness of shooting at him, if, in that situation, my shooting at him suffices to guarantee that welfare is maximised (if I had not shot him and hence killed him he would have killed several other persons). We have to strengthen our characterisation of particularism, then. What should be added to it is the claim that there exists no empirical characterisation whatever (however complex or general) of any situation which is sufficient to guarantee the same moral conclusion in all similar situations. This is tantamount to saying that there exist no plausible moral principles that explain our particular moral obligations. We can never reach a correct moral conclusion about a particular situation by bringing relevant and correct moral principles to it. There exist no correct moral principles.

What if we have a complete description of a situation, then? Must not the particularist agree that, if two situations are exactly similar in all empirical respects, they must also be similar in moral respects? Or should the particularist deny that moral properties supervene on empirical ones and claim that two situations that are similar in all empirical respects may differ morally? I do not think that this would be wise. It would probably be a better strategy for the particularist to hold on to some idea of supervenience, stated, however, without reference to the idea of a complete description of a situation. The particularist could reject the very idea of such a description as incoherent. He or she could claim that there does not exist any definite list of empirical characteristics. The idea of supervenience could be stated instead by the particularist in the following way: if two situations differ in moral respects, then they must differ in some empirical respects as well. This is compatible with particularism.[2]

Perhaps the difference between particularism and generalism is a matter of degree rather than kind. Ideally, the generalist would like to assert that there are true and deterministic principles that explain our particular moral obligations, but he or she may well have to rest content with something less definite. After all, not even in science is there any unanimity about a deterministic outlook. It might seem quixotic therefore to aspire to such an outlook in ethics. On the other hand, the particularist may hope to show that there exist no law-like moral generalisations whatever, not even of a *prima facie* kind. In the final analysis, however, he or she may have to admit that at least some natural characteristics tend to bring with them certain moral ones.

In my discussion I will simplify and concentrate on the most extreme versions of particularism and generalism. Prototypes of these are, on the one hand, the kind of stance taken up by Jonathan Dancy,[3] who rejects even the idea of principles of *prima facie* moral duties as incoherent (pure particularism) and, on the other hand, the kind of hedonistic utilitarianism that will be defended in this book, which insists that there exists a deterministic empirical criterion of rightness of particular actions (pure generalism).[4]

I know of no good positive arguments in defence of particularism. However, particularism has been seen to be a natural default position to take up once one has found that no suggested moral principle seems to be fully plausible. I will argue, however, that particularism ought to be only our very last resort in ethics. The intellectual price we have to pay if we take this stance is considerable. Rather than having resort to particularism if we find that all known moral principles seem to be flawed, we ought to continue to look for better principles. We ought to persist in our search for principles that do account for, and explain, those among our moral intuitions that, even upon careful and critical reflection, we want to retain.

One obvious aspect of this price of particularism is lack of simplicity. A more important – although less obvious aspect of it – is moral scepticism. I concentrate on the latter aspect. To be sure, if there are no (true) moral principles (of either an absolute form, like the utilitarian formula, or a *prima facie* form, such as the one put forward and defended by W. D. Ross),[5] then, trivially, we cannot have moral knowledge of them. But – and this is not trivial – nor can we have moral knowledge about particular cases, if particularism is true. If particularism is true, then all our moral judgements lack justification. This is the main thrust of the present chapter.

The argument is straightforward and I propose it in the next section. The argument shows that particularism escapes the method of coherentism (the more pure it is, the less room it leaves for coherence in our moral arguments). And there is no plausible alternative to the coherentist approach in moral epistemology.

The rest of the chapter is devoted to a rejection of various possible objections to the kind of argument that I put forward.

Particularism and coherentism

According to coherentism, foremost and most famously developed in ethics by John Rawls in his book *A Theory of Justice* and elsewhere,[6] but now, in the general form given to it in the present context, almost a commonplace, we gain justified moral opinions by testing our considered judgements about particular cases against moral principles. To use the phrase invented in a different context by Gilbert Harman, we make an 'inference to the best explanation'.[7] In pursuit of the best moral explanation (where various background theories also have weight) we search the principles that explain (morally) the truth of our particular moral judgements. We go back and forth, revising sometimes our considered judgements about particular cases, sometimes the principles intended to explain these, and even on some occasions the background theories, until we reach (asymptotically, perhaps), in Rawls's words, a state of 'reflective equilibrium'. This is a state where all our beliefs cohere, i.e., where they are closely knit together, explaining each other. If a person does reach this state, then his or her moral beliefs are justified (i.e., he or she is justified in holding them).

It is not quite clear what kind of 'justification' Rawls himself had in mind in *A Theory of Justice*, and over the years he has expressed different views about this. However, the most interesting interpretation of his view, and, furthermore, an interpretation which makes it plausible, as far as I can see, is to take the justification to be epistemic. If I find out that my beliefs are coherent (in reflective equilibrium), then while this is no guarantee of their truth and correctness, it means that I have reasons to believe that they are true or correct. This is how I am going to interpret coherentism in the present context, no matter whether this interpretation does justice to Rawls's own intentions or not.

On this interpretation, coherentism in ethics is a very widespread doctrine today. It should be observed, furthermore, that coherentism in this very general form is compatible with a kind of foundationalism in ethics, a foundationalism according to which certain moral judgements (considered ones about particular cases, say) are granted a privileged position; these statements are not incorrigible, but, according to other beliefs in the reflective equilibrium, may well have a privileged position. This is similar to how, on a coherentist view, observational statements are granted a privileged position in our web of beliefs. They owe this position to the belief that they are formed in a certain (reliable) way.[8]

If this is how we conceive of coherentism, a problem with particularism arises immediately. Particularism does not lend itself to the use of the method of coherentism. If particularism is correct, then there are no principles that explain particular cases, so there is no hope that we should be able to improve our moral thinking and reach coherence.

Of course, particularism does not exclude the possibility that there exist (accidentally) true general moral statements, of the form: 'All actions that are ϕ are wrong.' However, such accidental general moral truths do not explain particular moral truths. Nor do particular moral truths conforming to them confirm them. So our accepting them, if we do, does not enhance the coherence of our system of beliefs.

The only way for a particularist to avoid the spectre of scepticism seems to be to have recourse to an outmoded form of foundationalism of the kind once put forward by H. A. Prichard where, dogmatically, we simply trust our judgements about particular cases.[9] To be sure, in particularism we have reasons for these particular judgements, and we may even have (particular) reasons for these reasons, and so forth ('Why should I not toy with the gun?', 'Because it might go off', 'So what?', 'Because someone in the room may get hurt', 'So what?', 'Because they are all innocent human beings'), but in the final analysis we end up with reasons for which there are no further reasons ('Why not kill an innocent human being, just for the fun of it?'). And we have no reason to assume that these reasons are good ones. Our acceptance of them has no warrant.

Observe, then, that the argument is not that particularists too soon run out of reasons while generalists can go on for some time longer in their arguments. We all run out of reasons, at some point, as Wittgenstein reminded us; this is also true of generalists who want to argue in defence of one statement or other. So the difference in how soon particularists and generalists run out of reasons, if such a difference exists, is a matter of degree. However, what is not a matter of degree is the fact that, while coherentists can point to reasons why they are justified in accepting the basic premises of their argument, for the truth of which no further reasons can be adduced, foundationalists lack any corresponding reason why they are justified in holding on to their premises. The reason coherentists can point to is of course that, when they have achieved coherence, then the statements that make up their web of beliefs reinforce each other.

It might be objected to coherentism, of course, that coherence is no guarantee of truth. So why should coherentists stick to their beliefs, even if they seem to the coherentists to reinforce each other? The objection is irrelevant. We should not require from a conception of justification that it is a guarantee of truth. There are no guarantees of truth in our reasoning.

But what reason do coherentists have to stick to their favoured judgements?

Well, they have a very good reason to stick to them when they form a coherent set. After all, the coherentists believe them, i.e., believe that they are true, and, being interested in truth, the coherentists do not want to give them up. The more deeply entrenched a particular statement is in coherentists' web of beliefs, the higher the price (in terms of other statements believed to be true that must be given up) for giving it up.

To be sure, even for particularists of the foundationalist mould there is some price to be paid if they want to give up a favoured premise of a moral argument. After all, they believe it to be true. However, the price is not comparable to the corresponding price to be paid by the generalist of the coherentist mould. If the particularists are not dogmatic, they must at least suspect that their basic moral premises, for which they can give no further arguments, may be false. And it is possible for particularists to give up such a premise, without any change whatever in the rest of their beliefs.

It should be noted that the coherentists' answer to scepticism is (merely) pragmatic. Coherentists cannot prove that scepticism is incorrect. No one can prove that. Coherentists need not even know of any good reasons for the claim that scepticism is false. Perhaps there are such good reasons, perhaps there are not.[10] Be that as it may, coherentists do have a good reason to believe that scepticism is false. We have seen that, if coherentists have reached a coherent set of beliefs, and if coherentists are interested in truth, then they have good reasons to stick to these beliefs, i.e., to believe of each of them that it is true. And coherentists cannot consistently stick both to this set of beliefs and to the belief that scepticism is true. Therefore, scepticism has to yield.

The argument that particularism leads to scepticism has full bite when directed against pure forms of particularism. It has less bite, of course, when directed against less pure forms. As soon as some moral generalisations are allowed, as soon as some *prima facie* principles are admitted in the particularist's moral argument, there is some room for the application of the method of coherentism. The particularist stance is the more vulnerable to the sceptical argument, then, the more extreme it is.

But perhaps there are ways after all for the particularist to avoid scepticism? I will discuss three ideas to the effect that particularism is compatible with the existence of moral knowledge.

In the first place, it could be maintained that moral knowledge is practical. Therefore, the aforementioned argument does not stick. Moral knowledge is a matter of moral expertise, and we may assess a moral expert in roughly the same manner as we assess the expertise of a physician. This is the stance taken up by, among others, Alasdair MacIntyre,[11] Bernard Williams[12] and John McDowell.[13] It has also been adopted by some recent feminist thinkers such as Margaret Urban Walker.[14] The second idea elaborates on the former. It is the idea that casuistry, i.e., arguments from paradigmatic cases, may be a way to avoid scepticism in ethics. This is the stance taken up most famously by Albert R. Jonsen and Stephen Toulmin.[15] A third idea has been developed by Jonathan Dancy. It is that our justification of a moral judgement consists in a narrative, stressing salient features in the situation, where the persuasiveness of the justification is the persuasiveness of the narrative: an internal coherence in the account which compels assent.

I will have none of this, and in the next two sections I explain why. However, the significance of my thesis may be questioned as well. Actually, the significance of my argument can be questioned on two counts.

On the one hand, it might be argued that the kind of argument I level against particularism may, with equal force, be directed against other moral views, such as utilitarianism. This shows, then, not that there is a problem pertaining in particular to particularism but, rather, that the method of coherentism as such is in deep trouble. I reject this proposal. Utilitarianism does allow for a successful application of the method of coherentism.

On the other hand, it could be argued that moral scepticism is not such a bad thing after all. I reject this proposal too. In particular I argue that, when moral scepticism is wedded to (ontological) moral realism, i.e., the view that there are moral facts, the intellectual (and emotional) cost of it is considerable.

Particularism and practical knowledge

It might be thought that in morality we may try to achieve a kind of knowledge other than the kind we go for when using the method of coherentism. In science we try to achieve a coherent web of beliefs, but in morality we are after something else, to wit, a kind of expertise. Moral knowledge is basically practical. Morality may be considered an art – where a kind of skill (what Aristotle called *phronesis*)[16] is sought, a kind of expertise which defies theoretical formulation. To possess and exercise this skill is to be a virtuous person. If you have this skill, you get particular cases right. The kind of skill in question could never be summed up in an algorithm. The only way to learn it is through education. So, according to Jonathan Dancy, if we want to become moral experts, it is probably too late.[17]

This view was outlined in Alasdair MacIntyre's book *After Virtue* and in Bernard Williams's book *Ethics and the Limits of Philosophy*, and it is hinted at in Jonathan Dancy's *Moral Reasons*. It has also been stated by John McDowell in his 'Virtue and Reason'. In the present context I will concentrate on McDowell's argument, since he holds explicitly that particularism is compatible with moral knowledge, the very idea that I want to repudiate.

The example McDowell discusses is a person exemplifying the virtue of kindness. According to McDowell, a kind person can be relied on to behave kindly when that is what the situation requires:

A kind person has a reliable sensitivity to a certain sort of requirement that situations impose on behavior. The deliverances of a reliable sensitivity are cases of knowledge; and there are idioms according to which the sensitivity itself can appropriately be described as knowledge; a kind person knows what it is like to be confronted with a requirement of kindness. The sensitivity is, we might say, a sort of perceptual capacity.[18]

This view is combined with the claim that the deliverances of a reliable sensitivity cannot be summed up by a moral principle (explaining them). The idea that acting in the light of a specific conception of rationality must be explicable in terms of being guided by a formulable universal principle is a 'prejudice', according to McDowell.

Suppose that this is correct. Where does this leave the claim that moral knowledge is practical knowledge?

I do not deny that there may well exist practical knowledge, art, knowledge how rather than knowledge that. For example, I concede that a good physician not only possesses theoretical knowledge about medicine but also knows how to make an accurate diagnosis. The particularist could argue that, when we speak of moral 'knowledge', this should be understood in this, practical, sense. This move does not take the particularist off the sceptical hook, however. For there is a crucial difference between medicine and morality. In medicine we have access to methods of evaluation. We can assess the expertise exhibited by doctors. A physician with good judgement is a physician who, more often than less gifted ones, cures his or her patients. If we please, we may try the expertise of a doctor in a double-blind test. On particularism, a moral expert, the analogy goes, is a person who 'gets it right case by case'.[19] However, how do we tell in a particular case whether a person 'gets it right'? As a matter of fact, we do not. In morality we do not have access to anything comparable to a double-blind test. There are no moral tests whatever.

To be sure, particularists may find that a certain person often makes what they believe are right judgements. Particularists may even find that this other person seems to find moral truths more quickly than they do themselves, and they may find that this person notices relevant aspects of an action where they themselves would have missed them, had these aspects not been pointed out to them by this person. However, this kind of expertise is parasitic on the particularists' own confidence that in some circumstances they are reliable moral judges. But why should particularists believe that? Once again, they may give reasons for particular judgements, and particular reasons why these reasons are good ones (in the situation), but eventually particularists must refer to reasons for which no further reasons can be given. So these reasons have no warrant. They cannot, like the generalist's favoured principles, be tested in other situations. For in these other situations they may be no reasons whatever, or reasons to the opposite effect.

Of course, if the particularist admits that there are some (law-like) moral generalisations – if the particularist admits, for example, that some empirical characteristics tend to bring with them certain moral characteristics – he or she can obtain some structure in his or her moral reasoning, and my argument will have less bite against the position. My argument has full bite, however, when directed against extreme versions of the particularist position.

But is the situation really any better in practical medicine? Are there any double-blind medical tests valid across different medical traditions? On this objection there exist rival medical traditions, where school medicine is but one of them, each providing its own expertise. Each tradition allows of a kind of evaluation in its own terms, or, in McDowell's terms, 'from the inside out'. But no tradition, on this objection, can be evaluated 'from the outside in'.

There is some truth in this objection. There is no way to confront reality directly, since we have always to revise our beliefs in the light of other beliefs. However, at least from the point of view of a naturalised epistemology, which I here take as my point of departure, we should, when setting up our theory of knowledge, allow ourselves access to the results of the best confirmed scientific theories. This means, in the medical context, that we may take as our point of departure, when assessing the expertise of a doctor, the bulk of shared medical understanding available to us at the time of the assessment (allowing, of course, that there is much unfinished business within medicine). No parallel to this exists in morality. There exists no bulk of shared moral understanding against which we can assess the moral expertise of a person.

It might be thought that at least there are some moral truths that are not controversial among decent people sharing our own culture. This is a mistake, however. Examples cited and presumed not to be controversial concern such things as wilful cruelty to innocents or purely selfish deceit.[20] However, while most people would say that these are always wrong, a utilitarian does not. These kinds of actions and behaviour are only wrong to the extent that they produce bad consequences. In rare cases they may produce good consequences, and in those cases, on utilitarianism, they are perfectly all right. I do not say that this view is correct, but I do claim that it is decent.

I do not deny that a moral tradition similar to the Western scientific tradition may some time come to evolve, providing us with a bulk of shared moral understanding. However, if it does, I feel sure that it will do so as a result of the consistent and critical application of a generalist approach to ethics.

Today the adoption of such a generalist approach to ethics may well represent only a 'prejudice'. Or, to use a more neutral terminology, it may represent merely a methodologically and heuristically motivated 'decision'. But so does the adoption of the particularist stance. No argument seems to decide the matter, once and for all. And the choice of the generalist stance is, from the point of view of moral methodology, a wise one. We do not know beforehand that the moral order is such that we can grasp it in a generalist fashion. Nor, however, could we know beforehand that the natural order is such that we can grasp it in a generalist fashion. The grim fact seems to be that, unless the moral order is such that we can grasp it in a generalist fashion, we cannot grasp it at all. This means that the decision to apply a generalist methodology is reasonable.

McDowell is at some pains to show that a person's moral apprehension or perception may explain (fully) his or her moral action. Unless it does, the non-cognitivist may argue that the content of the apprehension or perception is not moral but factual. I find this argument superfluous, since I am no admirer of internalism in ethics. The content of the apprehension or perception may well be moral, or so I believe, even if it does not fully explain any action. However, even if moral, this does not mean that it constitutes knowledge, i.e., justified true belief. If my argument hitherto is sound, the content of a particular moral apprehension or perception may well be true, but it is not justified. McDowell does not say anything to silence this worry.

Casuistry

In their book *The Abuse of Casuistry*, Albert R. Jonsen and Stephen Toulmin protest against the 'tyranny of principles'. On their account of moral reasoning, we ought to settle hard particular moral issues in terms of cases and circumstances. Practical arguments depend for their power on how closely the present circumstances resemble those of the earlier precedent or paradigmatic cases for which the particular type of argument was originally devised. The conclusions about particular cases must remain presumptive and revisable in the light of further experience. The moral realm leaves room for honest and conscientious differences of opinion, at least in marginal or ambiguous cases. There is a bulk of shared moral understanding, however.

To understand how the authors argue, let us construct a typical case that we want to solve. Suppose that infertile couples complain that public health care does not provide sufficient help with their problems. At least in today's Sweden, only a minority get access to in vitro fertilisation (IVF) through publicly financed health care institutions. The rest have to pay for the services themselves. Some of them argue that this is unfair. To be sure, in Sweden fundamental health care is supposed to be provided by the public health system. Why do they not get the help they want? Suppose representatives of public health care institutions answer them in the following manner:

> IVF is not really health care, properly speaking. It is rather a service given to couples who want to have children to raise. It should be compared not to health care but, rather, to international adoption services. When prospective parents adopt children from foreign

countries they have to pay considerable amounts for these services. Why, then, should IVF be provided free of charge, or at only a symbolic cost?

I suppose that the casuistic way of resolving the dilemma we are now facing, if we want to judge whether the infertile couples or the medical authorities have reached the most plausible solution, would be to consider first of all the two paradigmatic cases involved in the example. Already we face a problem here for casuistry of the particularist variety. For it is not at all above controversy whether, really, health care should be supplied by society, or whether international adoption services should not be supplied by society. Suppose, however, unrealistically, that we do 'find out' that it is only fair that health care be provided by society and financed on a collective basis, while international adoption services should be financed on a private basis. These cases are paradigmatic. Where does that leave us with the vexed case we are considering?

On the model advocated by Jonsen and Toulmin, this is a matter of resemblance. It must depend on whether IVF resembles ordinary health care more than it resembles international adoption. If it does so, it should be provided gratis or at only a symbolic cost. Otherwise it should be fully paid for on an individual basis.

What are we to say about this kind of argument? Does it provide answers to particular moral questions? Does it allow of a systematic treatment of the kind required by the method of coherentism, so that we can say that the results gained by its application may be (epistemically) justified?

We must guard here against a simple misunderstanding. On the surface, the method described may seem very similar to the theoretical or generalist approach to ethics. Indeed, there exists a generalist kind of casuistry. However, when a casuist of the generalist variety confronts paradigmatic cases, this is done in the search for principles to apply. Similarities and dissimilarities are not taken at face value. An attempt is being made to stress general characteristics of the particular cases and to apply principles to them accordingly. This 'tyranny of principles' should be avoided in the method described by Jonsen and Toulmin, however. But then insurmountable problems seem to be facing us.

In the first place, Jonsen and Toulmin to the contrary notwithstanding, there are really no paradigmatic cases, beyond dispute, to depart from. I have already stated my reasons for this position.[21]

But might we not weaken their theory, in order to avoid this problem, and still retain a plausible idea of moral justification? Why not give up the idea that there exist paradigmatic cases that are beyond dispute? Why not instead say that a person, S, is justified in his or her moral belief, p, if it is supported, in the manner described by Jonsen and Toulmin, by cases that, according to S himself or herself, are paradigmatic (irrespective of how other persons judge these cases)? This, of course, means that two different people may be justified in holding opposite (contradictory) moral beliefs. However, epistemic justification is generally not taken to be a guarantee of truth, so this should not really be problematic.

Even so, even if there are cases that are paradigmatic for a person, cases for him or her to depart from in moral arguments, this does not suffice to give us a plausible idea of moral justification. The idea is much too loose, flexible and arbitrary. For it would always be possible in a controversial particular case to stick to whatever particular judgement one wants to stick to; the prospective parents may say, for example, that IVF is very much like ordinary health care, while the authorities may state that it is much more like international adoption services. How are we to resolve such a conflict? Actually, everything resembles everything else in some aspect, and is different from it in some other aspects. So long as we do not specify which aspects we are discussing, there is no telling what resembles what most. Our judgement will be completely arbitrary.

But perhaps we could handle our comparisons more or less consistently. And perhaps our enhancing consistency in our comparisons means that we increase coherence in our beliefs. For example, there could be a formal requirement of transitivity that our comparisons should meet. Suppose I hold that IVF is more like ordinary health care than international adoption, and suppose that I hold that this is even more true of tubal surgery aimed at making infertile women fertile. Then, if I accept that IVF should be provided by society, I must also accept that tubal surgery should be provided by society. If I do not, I have to give up my original judgement about the 'paradigmatic' case (which is not really allowed by Jonsen and Toulmin, but which should be allowed on a more relaxed interpretation of their idea), to wit, that ordinary health care should be provided by society, or I have to give up my judgement that tubal surgery is more similar to ordinary health care (and hence more different from international adoption) than is IVF. When all my comparisons satisfy this requirement of consistency, may we not say that they are coherent and, hence, justified?

I think not. And the reason is that this kind of consistency is too easy for a particularist to come by. The crucial notion, once again, is the notion of similarity. If we want to stick to a particular judgement about a particular case, we may always do so. We may simply revise our judgements about similarity – without having for that reason to change any other beliefs we happen to entertain. We may always find some special aspect of the case of, say, tubal surgery, which does not make it similar after all to ordinary health care. No matter what aspect we single out, there is no way that it could be shown to be inappropriate. For, on the particularist conception, it may well matter only in this case. When it is present in other situations, it may be of no importance whatever or it may carry a very different (and even opposite) weight.

It might be objected that the situation the particularistic casuist faces is not different from the situation facing the moral generalist, seeking explanatory coherence.[22] For, to be sure, when making an inference to the best (moral) explanation (of a particular moral judgement), the generalist can go in many directions. When she or he settles for one of them in particular, her or his decision must be based on an assessment of such things as simplicity, fruitfulness, generality and so forth. There is no algorithm telling which hypothesis provides the best explanation of data.

Now, this is true. However, a crucial difference remains. The notion of 'similarity' is (much) worse than the notions of simplicity, generality and fruitfulness of explanatory hypotheses. It provides for licence, where the notions of simplicity, generality and fruitfulness provide the theorist with a range of alternatives to choose from. It is no mere coincidence that science operates with the latter notions, not with the former one.

Narrative justification

According to Jonathan Dancy, moral arguments are a kind of narrative, and in our search for justified moral beliefs, we can rest satisfied with internal coherence in our moral arguments (narratives). A good argument is a narrative that 'sounds good'. I agree that moral arguments may be conceived of as narratives, but I deny that in our search for justified moral beliefs we should be satisfied with internal coherence in these narratives.

When we want to justify a moral judgement about a particular case, according to Dancy, we have to distinguish between relevant and irrelevant features. The relevant features are salient, according to Dancy. Salience is a practical notion. To see a feature as salient is to see it as making a difference to what ought to be done in the situation. A feature may be more or less salient. When we grasp what the salient features of a situation are, and when we grasp their relative weight, we grasp the shape of the situation. When we state what we have grasped, we tell a story of the situation. The story constitutes the justification of the moral judgement.

Why a 'story'? Why a 'narrative'? Why not just (simply) a description? The reason is that, according to Dancy, the order in which the salient features are mentioned is of importance:

> So the sort of description I am talking about is a form of narrative, and it can have the vices and virtues of narrative; features can be mentioned in the wrong order, and important relations without which the story does not make sense can be omitted, distorted or misplaced.[23]

I shall have little to object to this piece of moral phenomenology. I am not convinced that the order in which the salient features are mentioned is of any importance, but this is of no importance for my argument. For the sake of argument I do admit that such narratives exist and I am prepared to concur when Dancy goes on to identify them with moral justifications. But I am not satisfied with Dancy's idea about what distinguishes good justifications from bad ones of moral judgements.

Dancy does not deny that a difference between good and bad arguments exist. A good argument, a good narrative, is one which follows the shape that the situation has.[24] But how does one go about ascertaining whether a given narrative exhibits this virtue?

The generalist has an answer to this question. The generalist can consult his or her judgement about situations other than the one he or she is confronted with, and try to find out whether he or she is prepared to give the same weight to the same features in these other situations. If not, the original judgement must be revised. This move is not open to the particularist of Dancy's mould. To be sure, a particularist is capable of distinguishing persuasive from unpersuasive narratives. A story is persuasive, according to Dancy, when it 'sounds right'.[25] However, people disagree as to which narratives are persuasive and which are not so, and the same person may be in doubt about the persuasiveness of a certain narrative. More important still, even a person who is persuaded by a story may want to know whether the story is true. On the particularist view, however, there is no telling.

It is not that the distinction between true and false narratives collapses, on Dancy's view. He is a moral realist. According to him, there are true and false narratives. A narrative is true, we noted, only if it follows the shape that the situation has. However, according to Dancy, there is no way that we can tell whether a narrative is true.

An argument, Dancy claims, is persuasive if it sounds right. But a persuasive argument need not be a true (a valid or sound) argument. An argument that sounds all right (i.e., sounds sound) need not be sound.

Dancy slides over the issue by using the verb 'grasp', rather than 'forming a belief'. According to him we 'grasp' the shape of a situation. This verb has success built into it. But how do we know that we have really grasped the true shape of the situation? The beliefs we have formed about the situation need not be correct.

Dancy owes us an answer to the questions of how to distinguish good moral arguments from bad ones, and of how we distinguish a case where we have actually 'grasped' the shape of a situation from a case where we have formed a distorted opinion about it. In fact, he has even less to say about this than had Jonsen and Toulmin. In want of an answer to this question, we must tentatively conclude that particularism of Dancy's mould too leads to scepticism.

Coherentism and utilitarianism

If my argument is correct, particularism does not lend itself to a successful application of the method of coherentism. But this is true of other approaches as well, it might be argued. If so, so much the worse, perhaps, not for these various different approaches to morality, but, rather, for the method of coherentism. If generalist moral approaches like the classical utilitarian one face the same problem as particularism, to wit, that they do not lay themselves open to a successful application of the method of coherentism, then the fact that particularism is not open to a successful application of this method should not be taken to speak against it.

But does utilitarianism face the same problem with coherentism as we have seen that particularism does? I think not, but the matter is complicated.

Let us say that a particular action, a, is 'optimific' (O) if there is nothing the agent can do which would have a better outcome.[26] Then, according to utilitarianism, if an action is optimific, it is right (R). It is tempting to argue, then, that when in a particular case we observe that an action is right and optimific ($Oa\&Ra$), this may constitute evidence for utilitarianism. Indeed, $Oa\&Ra$ is evidence for utilitarianism if we find that the utilitarian formula is not only consistent with our observation in the particular case, but provides also the best (moral) explanation of it. This case constitutes evidence for utilitarianism if it is because the action in question is optimific that it is right. If, on the other hand, we face a situation where an action that is found to be optimific is not right ($Oa\&-Ra$), then this disconfirms utilitarianism. If we find an action that is optimific and also right ($Oa\&Ra$), but where we find a better explanation of its rightness (than its being optimific), then this case does not confirm utilitarianism either. If this model is to the point, utilitarianism does allow for a successful application of the method of coherentism.

Two steps in this kind of argument are controversial, however. First of all, can we really make normative observations like these in a particular case? Secondly, can we really observe whether an action is optimific or not? Is not $Oa\&Ra$ a mere fantasy?

I will not question the former possibility. We may conceive of an observation as an immediate judgement made in response to a situation without any conscious reasoning having taken place.[27] There are no good reasons to suspect that such judgements could not be of the form: 'This particular action is right (Ra).' Some authors have claimed that such judgements cannot be justified, since we need not refer to them in our best explanations of any observations. This is the position taken up by Gilbert Harman.[28] This has been disputed, most famously by Nicholas Sturgeon, who claims that we do have to refer to them in our best explanations of some observations.[29] It has also been argued, for example by Thomas Nagel, that, even if our normative observations do not live up to the empiricist criterion taken for granted in the discussion by Harman and Sturgeon, i.e., the criterion that we should only assume that something has objective existence if we have to refer to it in our best explanation of some observation, our normative observations may be justified.[30] In the present context I will not take a stand on this controversial issue.

However, even if normative observations can be justified, it seems more dubious whether we can ever be justified in our observation that a particular action is optimific. I once argued, because of this, that there cannot be any normative knowledge whatever.[31] And Folke Tersman has argued that utilitarianism in particular escapes, for this reason, a successful application of the method of coherentism.[32] The reason I adduced why we cannot observe whether a particular action is optimific was that such judgements involve complicated comparisons. We have to compare the actual outcome of the action (for very long spans of time indeed) with merely possible outcomes, had the agent acted differently. Tersman adds to this that in a successful application of the utilitarian formula complicated comparisons of happiness have to be made. These are hardly the result of observation either. And no matter how we arrive at them, he claims, we cannot be justified in making them. This is controversial. In Chapter 5 I will defend the claim that, at least in principle, we can make interpersonal comparisons of well-being. However, I do not think it controversial that we cannot be justified when making the kind of comparisons that I have stressed. We can never say with confidence about a particular action that it is, or that it is not, optimific. For all we know, in the long run, and compared to other things the agent could have done instead, any action may produce a somewhat better, or a somewhat worse, outcome.

Now, does this mean that we must give up the effort of applying the method of coherentism to utilitarian reasoning? There may exist indirect ways of applying it. Tersman mentions one such: we may test general principles in abstract thought experiments. Then we do not confront the utilitarian formula with conjunctions of the kind: $Oa\&Ra$. Rather, we confront it with a conditional: 'If this action is optimific, then it is right ($Oa\rightarrow Ra$).' Or, perhaps even with a subjunctive judgement: 'If this action were optimific, it would be right ($Oa\rightarrow Ra$).' Tersman notices, however, and I concur in his observation, that our evidence for moral principles cannot reasonably consist solely of judgements on imagined cases. And he makes a comparison with science to substantiate his point.

However, it seems to me that there exist various different, indirect methods of testing the utilitarian formula as well. That of testing principles in abstract thought experiments is only one among them. Here is another one: even if we cannot observe that a certain concrete action is optimific, it seems plausible to assume that we can sometimes be justified in our belief that a certain action is not optimific (to boil a certain child in oil for no particular reason, say). We can also be justified in our belief that, from a hedonistic point of view, the world would be better if we avoided this action (no matter how exactly we were to do this). We have good reasons to believe that, from a hedonistic point of view, this action would make the world (in one respect) worse and no reason to believe that it would make the world (in any respect) better. We can also have a firm normative belief that even if the action we were to perform, if we avoided boiling this child in oil, would be wrong, it would be 'less' wrong than the action we would perform if we did boil this child in oil. Classical hedonistic utilitarianism explains why this is so. At least it does if, as we should do, we add to the criterion of rightness an idea that what is stated in the criterion is an ideal that could be reached more or less perfectly.

Here is yet another indirect application of the method of reflective equilibrium to utilitarianism. It is based on the following argument: if utilitarianism is correct, then, at least for a person who wants to be moral, it would be rational in many cases to try to maximise expected happiness. If utilitarianism is correct, to try, in the circumstances, to maximise expected happiness would be to act 'subjectively rightly'.[33] Now, in a particular case, whether an action maximises expected happiness or not does seem to be open to inspection. We may hold a justified belief about this. If, in a particular case, we realise that a particular action does maximise expected happiness, and if, in the same situation, we form the immediate judgement, without any conscious reasoning having taken place, that, from a moral point of view, this action is responsible, and if we conclude that it is responsible because it maximises expected happiness, this may constitute evidence, directly, for the method; and, indirectly, for the utilitarian formula. That formula explains why it is responsible to maximise expected happiness (in these circumstances, for a person who wants to behave morally), i.e., why doing so would be subjectively right.

A crucial step in this argument, of course, is the claim that a belief in utilitarianism makes it responsible, in many situations, for a person who wants to be moral to try seriously to maximise expected happiness. Is this claim correct? How could it be defended? I will return to this question in the next chapter. To foreshadow that, I have only the following points to make in the present context.

It might be thought that if we try consistently to maximise expected happiness, then, in the long run, probably, we end up with better results than by consistently applying any conceivable alternative strategy. This may be so, and if 'probably' is taken in a subjective sense, it is probably true (of many utilitarians, at any rate). However, there exists no conclusive argument to the effect that, by consistently trying to maximise expected happiness, we obtain good results. Furthermore, it takes a rule–utilitarian argument to carry us from the premise that it pays in the long run to try to maximise expected happiness, if this premise could be established, to the conclusion that, in a particular case, we ought to do so. And I reject rule utilitarianism (for reasons to be spelled out in chapters to come).

When we say that it is responsible for an adherent of utilitarianism in some situations to try to maximise expected happiness, we must rest content therefore with a defence of the following sort. In the first place, the maximising method is at least in what Gilbert Harman has called 'rational equilibrium', i.e., following the procedure would not lead one to modify it.[34] This is at least true of some applications of it; I think of situations where time allows us to try to maximise expected happiness, and situations where we are not facing threats of blackmail of the kind discussed, among others, by Thomas Schelling (where it may pay to be irrational).[35] Moreover, even if, for all we know, by applying the method we may not produce better results than we would do if when taking hard decisions we were to flip a coin, at least we know that we concentrate on aspects that, according to utilitarianism, are of moral importance. And we know that we concentrate on no aspects other than these. This means that, by adopting the maximising method, we are at least doing our best.

This constitutes, for people who adhere to the utilitarian formula, the rationale behind the use of the maximising method.

To this it may be objected that hedonistic utilitarianism is not the only possible rationalisation of the use of the maximising method. The idea that an action is right if, and only if, it maximises expected happiness rationalises the use of the maximising method too – and in an even more direct manner.[36] I concede that point. However, for theoretical reasons I prefer utilitarianism (in the 'objective' formulation) to the maximising version, as a criterion of rightness. First of all, suppose I perform an action that maximises expected happiness but turns out to be a disaster. Suppose also that, in the circumstances, it was not wise of me to try to maximise expected happiness (it was a matter of mere luck that I succeeded in doing so). It would have been more responsible to abide by a certain habit instead. It seems to me awkward that, objectively speaking, we should say of this action that it was right. But according to the maximising formula it is right. This should tell in favour of hedonistic utilitarianism.

Secondly, if the maximising formula be taken to state a criterion of rightness, it becomes mysterious why we should ever go on and search for more information about a particular case, when we feel that a certain decision would be in harmony with our beliefs and values. But this is in no way mysterious.

Thirdly, we often feel that, even though our beliefs cannot be improved about a certain case, and there is no doubt what action is called for, taking our beliefs for granted, yet, for all that, we may well have gone wrong in our normative judgement. This is only comprehensible if (actual) rightness and wrongness are a matter of actual outcomes rather than (subjectively) probable ones.[37]

Finally, hedonistic utilitarianism has a more general explanatory scope than the maximising formula. Classical hedonistic utilitarianism rationalises our use of the maximising method in certain circumstances, and so does the maximising formula; but hedonistic utilitarianism also rationalises our use of other methods in other circumstances, and it is hard to see that the maximising formula accomplishes that. So hedonistic utilitarianism gives the best rationalisation of the maximising method (in the relevant kinds of context).

One further objection should be discussed. It is as follows: even if a belief in hedonistic utilitarianism gives the best rationalisation of the maximising method (in certain contexts where it seems responsible to stick to it), does this really count in favour of it? Is it really an argument for the truth of hedonistic utilitarianism that it rationalises our use of the maximising method?

It is not. But my claim is not that it is. My claim is different. It is that a belief in hedonistic utilitarianism is rendered justified by the fact that it rationalises the use of the maximising method – for a person who wants to stick to that method. And a belief in a theory which rationalises a practice that strikes us as responsible is justified, or so it seems to me, at any rate.

The intellectual cost of moral scepticism

I have argued that moral particularism must lead to moral scepticism, in a way that a generalist view such as utilitarianism does not. I have taken this to be a problem with the particularist position. In doing so, I have taken for granted that moral scepticism is an unattractive position, both intellectually and morally (or 'emotionally'). But is this really so? Why not moral scepticism?

By 'moral scepticism' I refer to the denial of moral cognitivism. Moral cognitivism is the view that there exist true and justified moral beliefs. Now, moral cognitivism can fail on two accounts: because there is no moral truth to entertain any beliefs about (ontological irrealism), or because, even though there are moral truths, we cannot gain justified belief about them. Elsewhere I have argued that moral irrealism has a price.[38] But particularism does not, as such, lead to moral irrealism. As a matter of fact, most particularists seem to be some kind of moral realist. This is true in particular of Jonathan Dancy, John McDowell, Jonsen and Toulmin, and, to some extent, Alasdair MacIntyre. It may not be true of Bernard Williams, however. Anyway, the kind of moral scepticism I have alleged follows from moral particularism does so not because, if particularism is true, there is no moral truth to gain knowledge about, but because, if moral particularism is true, we cannot gain justified beliefs about moral facts. In my argument to the effect that moral scepticism does constitute an intellectual price, therefore, I will take moral realism for granted.

Now, what kind of problem are we facing if we are, so to speak, surrounded by moral truths that we cannot grasp, or that we cannot grasp other than by accident? The problem, of course, is that, if we cannot gain justified moral belief, we cannot ever feel sure that we are doing the right thing. And even if internalism may not be a very plausible view of moral reasoning, it seems to be a psychological fact that most people, at least some of the time, want to be moral. They want to do the right thing. So moral knowledge, if such a thing is accessible, is instrumental to their goal.

To this it might be retorted that it is far from certain that moral knowledge will ever, as a matter of fact, engender right actions (where right actions would not have been forthcoming without moral knowledge). This is a bold conjecture. However, even if it could be substantiated, which I doubt, the relevance of it is even more doubtful. We would still want moral knowledge. We would like to possess moral knowledge, even if, which is not very plausible, this would not mean better odds on our ambition sometimes to be moral. We want to feel that at least we are doing our best.

Conclusion

There exists no knock-down argument that shows either that particularism is true or that generalism is true. So we have to make a choice. What stance are we to take as our point of departure in our moral reasoning? I have argued that there are good programmatic reasons for preferring generalism. Generalism does allow coherentist reasoning while a particularist approach does not.

Why do we need generalism in ethics? One obvious answer is that we need general moral principles in order to solve hard moral cases (where our common sense morality fails us) in a trustworthy manner. Why do we need a coherentist approach? The reason is that unless we achieve coherence in our web of moral beliefs, our cherished moral beliefs are not justified (for us).

If particularism is adopted, this means that, from the very start of our moral reasoning, we give up our hope of gaining justified moral beliefs. Particularism leads to scepticism. This means that particularism should only be adopted as a last resort.

The reason that particularism leads to scepticism is that it does not leave itself open to a successful application of the method of coherentism. If there are no moral principles that explain (morally) particular moral cases, then we cannot make moral inferences from our particular moral judgements to their best moral explanation. This means that there is no way that we can bring structure and coherence into our moral reasoning. And there exists no sound alternative to the method of coherentism in moral epistemology.

To this it has been retorted that moral knowledge is practical, and that moral expertise, of the same kind as, say, medical expertise, exists. Against this I have objected that there are ways to evaluate medical experts, but that there exists no way that we can assess an alleged moral expert. It has also been held that casuistry may prove a way out of the problem that, if particularism is true, we cannot gain moral knowledge. We can reach coherence in our search for solutions to moral dilemmas, because we can do so in a casuistic manner. We reach it in obtaining consistency in our arguments from paradigmatic cases. I have rejected that claim too. At least if a rather extreme version of particularism is adopted and wedded to casuistry, there is too little structure in that kind of argument to guard against arbitrary and parochial 'solutions' of hard moral cases. Finally, it has been argued by Jonathan Dancy that moral arguments are narratives, stressing salient features of a situation. A good narrative is one which follows the shape that the situation has. A persuasive narrative is one which sounds good. I have nothing to object to this. But how do we go about ascertaining that a narrative that sounds good is good? How do we tell sound moral judgements from merely persuasive ones? The generalist has an answer to this question. Dancy owes us one, however. It seems therefore that his approach too leads to scepticism.

But are there really any moral approaches that lay themselves open to the application of the method of coherentism? What of, for example, a generalist approach such as the utilitarian one? Is that really in any better state than particularism? I have claimed that, even if the argument to this effect is not quite as straightforward as one might wish, utilitarianism does lend itself to the use of the method of coherentism. And even if my argument may not convince when applied to the utilitarian view of objective rightness, it is still true of the utilitarian view of subjective rightness. This suffices to substantiate my point that moral generalism of the (broadly) utilitarian variety is not in the same predicament as particularism.

In chapters to come I will discuss what I believe is the most plausible among such generalist approaches, hedonistic utilitarianism.

Notes

1 This is a characterisation given by Jonathan Dancy in his recent book *Moral Reasons*, pp. 55–8 *et passim*.
2 Dancy, *Moral Reasons*, pp. 78–9, does accept that if two situations are exactly similar in all empirical (natural) respects they must be similar also in moral respects. He does not seem to think that this deviation from strict particularism is very important, however, since no situations, according to Dancy, are similar in all empirical (natural) respects.
3 Dancy, *Moral Reasons*, Ch. 6.
4 It is debatable whether classical hedonistic utilitarianism does provide us with a clearly empirical criterion of rightness. I discuss this problem in Ch. 5 of this book, where I argue that the utilitarian formula must be buttressed with some normative stipulations, lest it turn out, upon inspection, to be empty.
5 Cf. for example W. D. Ross, *The Right and the Good*, pp. 18–36.
6 For an instructive monograph on reflective equilibrium, see Folke Tersman's dissertation *Reflective Equilibrium*.
7 Cf. G. Harman, 'The Inference to the Best Explanation'.
8 I discuss this in my book *Moral Realism*, pp. 39–43.
9 Cf. H. A. Prichard, 'Does Moral Philosophy Rest on a Mistake?'.

10 Several thinkers have put forward the claim that coherence leads towards truth. For a recent review of their arguments, and for a defence of their claim, see Tersman, *Reflective Equilibrium*, Ch. 5.

11 Cf. for example A. MacIntyre, *After Virtue: A Study in Moral Theory*.

12 Cf. B. Williams, *Ethics and the Limits of Philosophy*.

13 Cf. J. McDowell, 'Virtue and Reason'.

14 Cf. for example M. Urban Walker, 'Moral Understandings: Alternative "Epistemology" for a Feminist Ethics'.

15 Cf. A. R. Jonsen and S. Toulmin, *The Abuse Of Casuistry: A History of Moral Reasoning*.

16 Aristotle, *Ethics*, pp. 178–80.

17 Dancy, *Moral Reasons*, p. 64. It should be noted that if this is correct, then there is little use for moral philosophers in a discipline such as medical ethics. Some of the questions raised there are general, and lack, on this conception, a solution altogether. Abortion in general is neither right nor wrong. Others are particular ('Ought this clinical trial be continued or stopped?'), and should be decided by a moral expert. However, there is little reason to believe that such an expert could be found among us moral philosophers. Our education is not special.

18 McDowell, 'Virtue and Reason', p. 88.

19 Dancy, *Moral Reasons*, p. 64.

20 These examples are given by Jonsen and Toulmin, *Abuse of Casuistry*, p. 45.

21 Drawing on one single example, a commission that both Jonsen and Toulmin worked in or with, set up to assess the protection of human subjects of biomedical and behavioural research (1974), the authors note that it was remarkable that the commission could agree on specific practical recommendations, in spite of the fact that the members of the commission did not share a common moral outlook (*Abuse of Casuistry*, p. 18). However, in many cases, this has not been a fact. To give just one example: people involved in the British Warnock Commission disagreed as to whether research on the pre-embryo should take place at all, and, if it should, for how long it should be allowed to go on. As a matter of fact, I think all sorts of disagreement come up in such commissions. Sometimes people disagree about particular recommendations because of different general moral outlooks. Sometimes people who share a common general moral outlook disagree about particular recommendations because of different factual beliefs.

22 I owe this observation to Christian Munthe.

23 Dancy, *Moral Reasons*, p. 113.

24 Dancy, *Moral Reasons*, p. 112.

25 Dancy, *Moral Reasons*, p. 113.

26 W. D. Ross coined the word 'optimific'. Cf. Ross, *The Right and the Good*, p. 34, about this.

27 Gilbert Harman, *The Nature of Morality: An Introduction to Ethics*, p. 6.

28 Harman, *Nature of Morality*.

29 Cf. for example N. Sturgeon, 'Moral Explanations'.

30 Cf. T. Nagel, *The View from Nowhere*, pp. 145–9.

31 Cf. my *Moral Realism* about this, especially Chs 3 and 4.

32 Cf. F. Tersman, 'Utilitarianism and the Idea of Reflective Equilibrium'.

33 A distinction between 'subjective' and 'objective' rightness is made by Henry
Sidgwick; cf. *The Methods of Ethics*, p. 207. The distinction as drawn by Sidgwick
is too simplistic for the present purposes, however. According to him, an action is
'subjectively' right (for a person) if it is believed (by this person) to be right.
However, on Sidgwick's own view, in particular cases we had better suspend
judgement about rightness or wrongness. But it should be possible for a rational
person to hold justified beliefs about subjective rightness. It will not do either to
identify 'subjective' rightness with (subjectively) probable rightness. For we want to
say that it is reasonable for a person to perform a subjectively right action. And it
might be too risky to perform an action that is probably right. The consequences of
it, if it turns out to be wrong after all, may be disastrous. We have therefore to take
both value and probability into account when we form a judgement as to what is
subjectively right or wrong. So subjective rightness is a matter of the proper
weighing of subjective probability and value.

34 G. Harman, *Change in View: Principles of Reasoning*, p. 112.

35 Cf. T. Schelling, *The Strategy of Conflict*.

36 Both Folke Tersman and Jack Smart have, independently of each other, made this
comment.

37 I owe this observation to Bertil Strömberg.

38 Cf. my *Moral Realism*, Ch. 5.

Chapter 3

The statement of utilitarianism

In the previous chapter I argued that it is sound moral methodology to search for a true moral principle, capable of explaining the truth of particular moral judgements. Not only are we in need of general moral principles, in order to solve hard moral cases (where our common sense morality fails us), but it seems that, unless we manage to systematise our moral reasoning with the aid of general moral principles, forming a reflective equilibrium, we are bound to end up in moral scepticism.

It is a desideratum that a moral principle (taken together with relevant factual information) imply for each action ever performed whether it is right or wrong. The principle (or theory) should also explain why each action is right or wrong. And the theory (taken together with relevant counterfactual information), should imply as well for each possible way of acting for an agent whether it would be right or wrong.

I conjecture in this chapter that hedonistic (act) utilitarianism provides us with a true moral principle, capable of explaining the truth of particular moral judgements (i.e., of those particular moral judgements that we want, upon reflection, to retain) and satisfying the desideratum stated above. In chapters to come I try to defend this conjecture.

However, it is far from clear how this theory should be stated. In the present chapter I will make this clear, at least in some respects. I will here leave out problems of value, which will be approached in the next chapter.

This is my statement of (act) utilitarianism (AU):

AU: A particular (concrete) action is right if, and only if, in the situation, there was nothing the agent could have done instead such that, had the agent done it, the world, on the whole, would have been better.

According to the same theory, an action is wrong, if, and only if, it is not right. And an action is obligatory if, and only if, had the agent acted in any way differently, the world, on the whole, would have been worse.

Notice that, according to this statement of AU, only performed, concrete actions are right or wrong.

What is an action? I will not go deep into action theory. I agree with Donald Davidson's saying[1] that actions are (concrete) events (located in space–time). Some events are actions, some are not. This is no more mysterious than the fact that while some trees are oaks, some are not.

An obvious problem with AU, of course, is how we are to understand betterness. What is it that possesses intrinsic value? In chapters to come I will defend a hedonistic answer to this question, which includes a solution (in principle) to the problem of interpersonal comparisons of well-being.

The problem of value apart, however, this is not the most usual way of stating the theory. In my statement of AU, I take concrete actions to be right or wrong and I make no reference either to alternatives of actions or to their consequences. Most statements of utilitarianism attribute rightness and wrongness to abstract entities, and they are put in terms of alternatives and consequences of actions. Both performed actions, and mere alternatives to performed actions, are supposed to be right and wrong. My statement of AU, according to which only concrete actions are right or wrong, stated without having recourse to the concept of alternatives, is not accidental, however. By focusing on concrete actions and by not introducing the notion of alternatives, I avoid some perplexities and deontic paradoxes that have sometimes been considered to put the entire utilitarian strand of thought into disrepute. For if we allow ourselves not only to say of concrete actions that they are right or wrong, but also to say so of mere alternatives to concrete actions, we soon enter into difficult problems of interpretation of the utilitarian formula, problems so intricate and recalcitrant that one may come to despair of the possibility of giving a consistent and plausible statement of utilitarianism, let alone a simple and comprehensible one. However, if we avoid these concepts, and adopt the statement of the utilitarian formula that I have suggested, we need only some reflection to realise that all these complications are really bogus ones. We are capable, for example, of sticking to the rule that, if an action is not right, it is wrong. This is a place where Berkeley's saying is in place that, 'we first raise the dust, and then complain that we cannot see.' I will try to show in the present chapter that we need not raise the dust in the first place.

Furthermore, it is also no mere accident that AU is not cast in terms of the 'consequences' of actions. The reason that it is not is that the notion of consequences is too narrow to be adequate in the present context – it must give way to the principle of counterfactual dependence, to be explained below.

However, even in my statement of AU, there are several points that must be clarified. First of all, as was just noted, in my statement of utilitarianism I use 'counterfactual' terms rather than 'causal' ones. This means that my view of the 'outcomes' of actions is very inclusive. What matters morally, according to AU, is how the world came to be when the action was performed, as compared to how it would have been had the agent done something else instead. It does not matter why this difference would have occurred. In the present chapter I will defend the claim that this makes AU as plausible as possible, and the theme will be taken up again in Chapter 10.

Secondly, in AU I consider how the world, on the whole, would have been had the action been performed, as compared to how it would have been had the agent done something else in the situation, rather than how the world would have been in the future. Does this matter?

One might find this difference between a total and a future-oriented utilitarianism of little importance in the present context. One might argue like this: since the strand of utilitarian thought I discuss is the classical, hedonistic one, this difference cannot matter. For, to be sure, I never face a situation such that, had I in this situation acted differently from the way I did act, the past would have contained a different balance of pleasure over displeasure. The only way of making the whole world better then is to make the future better.

I am not convinced by this argument and in Chapter 10 I will spell out my reasons for rejecting it. There I will argue that the past is counterfactually dependent on the present and I will discuss the moral relevance of this putative finding. However, that is a very speculative chapter and I do not expect that what I say there will meet with unanimous support. Yet, for all that, I think any one should concede that at least there is some point in speculating about how we would conceive of the matters if the past were counterfactually dependent on the present. How would we conceive of the matter if we were to find that in some situations it is true of us that, had we acted otherwise, the past would have been better? Or we can pose the question in a form that is neutral from an axiological point of view, leaving it an open question whether, for example, there might be something to G. E. Moore's idea[2] that, by inflicting displeasure (something bad) on a criminal we make the world as a whole better (because of what the criminal did in the past, she or he deserves it).

In the present chapter I will argue that, if Moore is right, we sometimes ought to make the future worse in order to make the totality better. The total view is more plausible than the future-oriented one. Furthermore, in Chapter 10 I will show that this concern for total outcomes rather than future ones, combined with a counterfactual view of outcomes, has very unexpected consequences even for hedonistic utilitarianism. In that chapter I argue that according to hedonistic utilitarianism we are morally responsible for what went on in the past.

Before entering into the problems of alternatives and outcomes of actions, however, there are some more standard distinctions that should be drawn. I am thinking of the distinctions between objective rightness and subjective rightness, and between criteria of rightness and methods of responsible decision making.

Objective rightness vs subjective rightness

My main aim is to state and defend a utilitarian criterion of objective rightness of actions. I will also have something to say about subjective rightness of actions, however. We noted in the previous chapter that a distinction between 'subjective' and 'objective' rightness is made by Henry Sidgwick.[3] I added that the distinction as drawn by Sidgwick is too simplistic for the present purposes, however. For according to Sidgwick, an action is 'subjectively' right (for a person) if it is believed (by this person) to be right. And on Sidgwick's own view, in particular cases we had better suspend judgement about rightness or wrongness. But it should be possible for a rational person sometimes to hold justified beliefs about subjective rightness. It will not do either to identify 'subjective' rightness with (subjectively) probable rightness, I added. For we want to say that, in general, it is responsible for a person to perform a subjectively right action. And it might be too risky to perform an action that is probably right. The outcome if the person performs it, if it turns out to be wrong after all, may be disastrous. We have therefore to take both value and probability into account when we form a judgement as to what is subjectively right or wrong, I concluded. Subjective rightness is a matter of the proper weighing of subjective probability and value. It represents, in a manner of speaking, the fact that the agent has done his or her best to behave responsibly.

Now, different moral theories give moral agents different goals. Since this is a treatise on hedonistic utilitarianism, let us in the following assume that a person believes that AU is true and ponder what it would mean for such a person to act subjectively rightly. Through her or his actions, she or he wants to maximise happiness. Clearly, if in a situation she or he succeeds in doing so, this is all right. Then her or his action is objectively right. But we have already noticed that it is not responsible for her or him to try to maximise happiness (since she or he does not know how to do this). Nor is it responsible for her or him to perform those actions that she or he believes are probably right. For this strategy is too risky. How is this person supposed to act, then, for us to be prepared to say of her or his actions that they were responsible (or rational)? Perhaps the following criterion (of subjective utilitarian rightness – SUR) would do:

SUR: An action (performed by a person who believes that AU is true) is subjectively right if, and only if, the person who performs it believes that it maximises expected happiness.

What does it mean to say of a concrete action, then, that it maximises expected happiness? This seems to require certain beliefs about this action by the agent. What beliefs exactly? Well, it seems that the agent must have represented to herself or himself a set of alternative ways of behaviour which seems to be open to her or him in the situation. They must exhaust all possibilities in the situation, and they must be mutually exclusive. For each among them, the agent must have formed a belief as to what would be the possible outcomes, were she or he to act in that manner. And, in relation to each among these possible outcomes, the agent must have formed an opinion as to how probable it is, provided she or he acts in the relevant way. Or, more realistically, such an opinion must be implied or indicated by the opinions held by the agent. The sum of these probabilities must be 1. Furthermore, in relation to each one among all these possible outcomes, the agent must have formed an opinion as to how good it would be (as compared to the other possible outcomes in the situation). Now, the action maximises expected happiness if, and only if, it is associated with the greatest weighed sum of values and probabilities.

Is this characterisation sufficient? Or should we also require that the probability assessments and value assessments of this person hold a certain quality? Should we require that her or his various assessments can be fitted into a 'reflective equilibrium'?

This would probably mean that the concept will be without application. Who has ever held a complicated set of opinions satisfying such rigorous requirements? But we should perhaps at least require that this person has done her or his best (in the situation) to consider relevant information, and to process it in a consistent manner. She or he should also have done her or his best to make an appropriate representation of the alternatives (whatever that may mean). I will not go into detail here, since my main objective is to state and defend criteria of objective rightness, not of subjective rightness.

Note that this is a (utilitarian) criterion of subjective rightness; it is not a method of decision making. Notice also that it is based on a controversial, general conception of rationality.

Why is it rational in a particular situation to maximise expected happiness? Why not instead adopt a maximin or a maximax principle (i.e., see to it that, if the worst comes to the worst, the outcome is as good as possible, or, if one is as lucky as one can be, then the outcome will be as good as possible, respectively)?

This is difficult to tell. There exist no knock-down arguments to either effect. I suppose I have to admit that here I am relying on an intuition that deserves, in order to be bolstered by reasons, a treatise of its own.

Criteria of rightness vs decision methods

We are now faced with two criteria, one of objective rightness and one of subjective rightness, both of a general utilitarian brand. However, these criteria should be distinguished from various suggested methods of responsible decision making. If a person believes that AU and SUR are true, how is this person supposed to go about making decisions?

What we are asking for now is a general way of behaving in practical matters.

We have not given a good answer to this (practical) question if we say that, in each situation, the agent ought to perform objectively right actions, since this is clearly not possible for any agent deliberately to do. In each situation there is something the agent can do, which is objectively right ('ought' implies 'can'), but it is never possible for the agent to ascertain whether his or her actions are objectively right or wrong, so no agent can act from a conscious goal of performing (only) right actions.

Should a person who believes in AU then try instead to perform subjectively right actions? As a method of responsible decision making, this may seem more promising.

But what does it mean more exactly to say of a person that he or she tries in a situation to maximise expected happiness? It must be understood roughly in the following manner. This person tries to represent to himself or herself all the alternative ways in which he or she can possibly act in the situation. He or she tries to make a list of such alternatives that exhausts all possibilities, and such that all the alternatives are mutually exclusive. He or she tries furthermore to form opinions about possible outcomes, were he or she to act in these possible ways, and he or she tries to form opinions about the value of these outcomes. He or she then attempts to find out which one among these possible alternatives is associated with the greatest weighed sum of values and probabilities, and tries to act in this manner.

Obviously, there are many points where this person may go wrong in his or her deliberation, even if he or she tries to do his or her best. He or she can make a too simplistic, biased and even foolish representation of the alternatives. He or she may falsely believe, for example, that he or she can perform actions that are not in his or her power to perform. He or she can leave out important possible outcomes, ignore relevant information and make unwarranted probability assessments, or go seriously wrong in his or her value assessments. He or she can, for example, make poor interpersonal comparisons of well-being, or mistaken calculations. Finally, he or she can fail when he or she attempts to perform the kind of action he or she eventually sets out to perform.

However, there is nothing in this goal that should be in principle impossible to achieve (in Chapter 5 I will argue that interpersonal comparisons of well-being are meaningful). Therefore, to try to maximise expected happiness seems to be a viable goal. We have reached it when we have done our best in forming a certain kind of opinion and when we have achieved a certain kind of consistency between our various different assessments and our actions. We have reached it even if these assessments are wide of the mark. If we succeed in reaching it we perform an action that is subjectively right. For all we know, however, this action may well be objectively wrong, even disastrous.

In some situations I think it would be appropriate for a person who believes in AU to try to perform subjectively right actions. However, for reasons already spelled out in the previous chapter, it is hard to say why he or she should do this, in the situations where this seems to be the appropriate thing to do. Furthermore, it is clear that it is not always the appropriate thing to do. I will elaborate both these points.

Let me first discuss the question of when it would not be appropriate to perform those, and only those, actions that are subjectively right, i.e., to try to maximise expected happiness. I suggest that it would not be wise to do so in the following kinds of situation.

In the first place, when there is lack of time, we should not try to perform subjectively right actions. When driving, for example, it would be ridiculous to try in all one's decisions to maximise expected happiness. In order to be a good driver, it is essential in many decisions not to deliberate. Our reactions should rather be conditioned responses to certain typical stimuli. If we attempt consciously in these situations to do our best, we will perform poorly as drivers. As a matter of fact, what distinguishes a good driver from a bad one is that the good driver is capable of not deliberating in these situations. This is not to say that, when we decide whether we should drive at all, or whether we should drive today, we should not try to maximise expected happiness. It may very well be the case that we should.

Secondly, and related to the example just discussed, there is another kind of situation where I believe it inappropriate to attempt to act subjectively rightly. I am thinking of situations where bias or wishful thinking is likely to lead us astray, such as the one where we have drunk (moderately) and contemplate whether we should drive or leave the car. If we try to maximise expected happiness it is very probable, due to wishful thinking, that we will end up with the (unwarranted) conclusion that we ought to drive. Therefore, in the situation, we should not think in terms of expected value at all. Rather, we should stick to established rules. Alcohol and driving do not go together, period.

Thirdly, there are situations of intimacy, where a calculating approach would ruin important values. When in love, and once a firm relationship is established, it is not appropriate to contemplate whether a change of the object of one's love and affection would be a change for the better. A prudent person who believes in AU, then, and who is prepared in many situations to aim at subjectively right actions, will not do so when conducting his or her most intimate life. Instead, such a person will have conditioned himself or herself to be a person who acts in his or her most intimate life out of spontaneous affection.

However, there is an appropriate limit to this. There may come a time when divorce is a viable option. A prudent person does not condition himself or herself, then, never to give up this thoughtless approach. When life has become hell, it may be time to aim once again for subjective rightness.

Fourthly, in situations of threat or blackmail it might be a good idea to be a person who is prepared irrationally to refuse to give in, since being such a person means that one is not easily exposed to threats. This is a kind of 'rational irrationality' (it is rational to adopt it and yet, for all that, irrational to act on it in an actual situation of blackmail). This theme was stated originally by Thomas Schelling, it has been developed by Derek Parfit,[4] and I have nothing to add to it.

If, in these situations, we should not try to perform subjectively right actions, what kind of conscious goal should we set ourselves? As we have seen, there exists no simple answer to this question. Instead of one method of responsible decision making, a long list of such methods appropriate in different situations surfaces, and the items on the list are only vaguely characterised. Sometimes we ought to conform to well-established idioms of action (we ought to be what Peter Railton has called 'sophisticated consequentialists'), informed by a morality spelled out on what R. M. Hare has called an 'intuitive' level.[5] Sometimes we ought not to reflect but, instead, to act out of our natural sympathy (with its bias for those who are near and dear to us). I will return to this point in Chapter 9, where I defend the claim that this possibility is open to utilitarians. And sometimes we ought stubbornly to refuse to give in to any kind of threat. The list could be added to in many ways.

Let me now return to the other point raised above. If, in some situations, we ought to try to perform (only) subjectively right actions and, if, in other situations, we ought to stick to *prima facie* moral rules, act out of our natural compassion and so forth, why should we do so? What is the rationale behind such a list of methods?

When those who believe in the truth of AU and SUR consistently adhere to the methods on the list, they do so in the hope that, by doing so, they are, in the long run, producing better outcomes than they would have done had they consistently held on to any alternative method that they can think of. This is what they hope. But can they give any reasons why their favoured list is superior to any putative competing one?

I think that such reasons can be given, but they are far from conclusive. In the first place, and negatively, we can try to ascertain that our method of decision making (our list) does not violate Gilbert Harman's 'rational equilibrium test', i.e., the list is such that following the procedures on it would not lead one to modify it.[6] Secondly, and more positively, we can try to show, in a piecemeal manner, that what is on the list deserves to be there. We can show in relation to each item that, when we have followed the kind of decision procedure described, the results, as far as we have been able to assess them, have been better than when we have followed a different procedure. The reasons we put forward, then, are of a general inductive nature.

These reasons allow for two kinds of modification. A certain method of decision making may be amended, revised or replaced by another method (in a certain kind of situation), or the scope of the method may be modified (we may give it up in some kinds of situation where we used to adhere to it, or we can add new situations to the ones where we tend to adopt it). These reasons allow us to say that, when holding on to our own favoured list of procedures of decision making, we are holding on to a list such that there exists no better alternative to it that we can think of.

Alternatives and consequences of actions

My statement of AU is not in terms of alternatives and consequences. Most contemporary statements of the utilitarian formula are. They go something like this:

> An action, *a*, is right if, and only if, there is no alternative to *a* with better consequences. An action is wrong if, and only if, it is not right. And an action is obligatory if, and only if, the consequences of it are better than the consequences of any alternative to it.

However, as was first noticed by Lars Bergström[7] this leads to paradox. Consider a simple example (mine, not Bergström's). I am in a situation where I can invite a certain friend for dinner or not invite him. Suppose the consequences of inviting him are worse than those of not doing so. I then ought not to invite him. However, since my inviting this person for dinner is an abstract entity, there may exist various different versions of it. I could call him up, for example, or I could send him a card. Suppose the consequences of my calling him up are bad but that the consequences of my sending him a card are very good (he loves receiving invitation cards). Suppose that the consequences of my calling him up are worse than those of my not inviting him at all, but that the consequences of my sending him a card are better than those of my not inviting him. It now transpires that I ought to send him an invitation card. But we have just concluded that I should not invite him. And by sending him an invitation card, I do invite him. This comes close to contradiction. At least we have arrived at incompatible prescriptions: I ought to send him an invitation card (and hence invite him) and I ought not to invite him. Different representations of the alternatives in a decision situation may yield different and incompatible prescriptions. Notice that the problem is not that, in either of the two representations of the alternatives, we have given up any structural properties that we may want such representations to respect. In both the alternatives are, for example, incompatible in pairs, we may well consider them as exhaustive of all possibilities, and so forth.

One way out of this problem may be to introduce some complication. We could try to distinguish between relevant and irrelevant representations of the alternatives. One set of alternatives may be considered to be the relevant one. This is the line taken by Bergström. Few share his exact way of delineating the concept of a relevant alternative set, but many have tried to suggest such a concept. As a matter of fact, the number of suggested alternatives to it is legion. I will not pursue this line of argument, however. It is doubtful whether it leads to the desired end, and there are several drawbacks to it. And since there exists a simple solution to the problem, there is no need to try it out in detail. The simple solution, of course, is to stick to my AU.

According to AU, concrete actions (events in the world) are right or wrong. Such concrete actions have no versions. We can give all sorts of descriptions of them, we can refer to them in various different ways, but they, the entities that satisfy or do not satisfy these descriptions, are unique.

Return to my example. Suppose I do invite the person in the example for dinner. This action of mine then is a concrete action in the actual world. Did I call him, or did I send him an invitation card? If there was no other way I could have invited him, if either of these descriptions fits my action, then the other does not. Suppose I sent him an invitation card. Then I did the right thing. At least, what I did was right provided that there was nothing else I could have done in the situation such that, had I done it, the world would have been better.

Suppose instead that I called him up. Then my action was wrong. For, in the situation, there was something I could have done instead such that, had I done it instead (sent him a card), the world (on the whole) would have been better.

This is my solution to the problem, then. I have put it forward before,[8] and it was anticipated by R. E. Bales.[9] I find it very convincing indeed, but, of course, I have encountered some objections to it. Let me comment on them.

Objections to concretism

First of all, it might be wondered, on this view, how we account for the alternatives. How do we represent the decision problem facing the person who wants to know what to do? There are probably infinitely many ways in which a person can act in a situation. If we do not make an abstract representation of them, we cannot get a grasp of what alternatives are facing us. The answer to this objection is that we do not account for the alternatives at all. Remember that what we are faced with here is a criterion of rightness and wrongness of actions, not a decision method. A decision method should include some idea of how we represent alternatives to ourselves in a comprehensive manner, but a criterion of rightness need not do that. According to my criterion, AU, we need no representation of all the alternatives facing the agent in the situation. Her or his action is right if there is nothing she or he can do instead such that, were she or he to do it, the world (on the whole) would be better. And it is wrong if there exists something she or he could have done instead such that, had she or he done it, the world (on the whole) would have been better.

We say, however, that if I had sent the person a card instead of calling him up, the world would have been better. Does 'my sending him a card' really refer to anything concrete? Lars Bergström has claimed that it does not:

When we try to solve normative problems we normally have to consider at least some actions which have not yet been done or which are never done (because they are alternatives to actions which are done), and these can hardly be concrete.[10]

This is neither relevant nor quite accurate. It is irrelevant since it conflates criteria of rightness and decision methods. What we do when we try to solve normative problems is, I suppose, to try to apply a method of decision making that we have settled for (since we believe that, in the long run, when consistently applied, it produces at least as good outcomes as any competing method that we can think of). But our criterion of rightness need not refer to explicitly formulated alternatives. AU does not.

Bergström's comment is also inaccurate. First of all, future actions are in a straightforward manner concrete. And in a way we can even conceive of alternative actions as concrete ones. We can do so if we have resort to the possible world metaphor. What I need to assume, then, is only that my reference to what I would have done in the example, had I sent my friend a card instead of calling him up, identifies a definite possible action. I find that presupposition quite plausible. The counterfactual in question should be thought of as having definite truth-conditions. We can raise questions about this action such as what kind of card I sent him, what else I did while sending him the card, and so forth, and there are true answers to all these questions.

Counterfactual act-determinism

The assumption we need is the following: when referring to merely possible actions we assume what could be called counterfactual act-determinism; i.e., that there is a unique way that, actually, I would have proceeded had I instead sent him a card. To any such description there corresponds a definite possible world. It is in fact a desideratum that a possible world semantics possess this characteristic.

But does not this mean that once again the paradoxes emerge? Suppose I do not invite the person in the example. The following three propositions then seem to hold. But do they not create a dilemma?

1. When I do not invite him I act wrongly.
2. Had I invited him I would have acted wrongly.
3. Had I invited him by sending a card I would have acted rightly.

I do not think that these propositions present us with any dilemma or with any deontic paradox. To see this, consider the following argument.

How could it be that, when I do not invite him, I act wrongly? The reason is that there was something I could have done instead such that, had I done it, the world would have been better. I could have invited him by sending him a card. How could it be that, if I had invited him, I would have acted wrongly? The reason is that, in the possible world where I invite him, I call him up (and he hates this). In this possible world (the one in which I invite him that is closest to the actual one) it is true that, in several ways, I could have acted otherwise and obtained better outcomes. I could not have invited him or I could have invited him instead by sending him a card (which he would have appreciated).

All this makes sense. And, which is of the utmost importance, in no possible world is it true of anyone (on my account) that he or she faces, for any given time interval, conflicting obligations. So the paradoxes do not emerge.

However, a problem with counterfactual act-determinism is that this principle does not get validated in standard possible world semantic systems.[11] The principle of counterfactual act-determinism is not validated in David Lewis's system as it is stated most famously in his book *Counterfactuals*. Nor is it validated by Robert Stalnaker's system as stated in 'A Theory of Counterfactuals'.

In the article 'Causation' David Lewis sums up his own and Stalnaker's position as follows:

> When my opponent says that either e would have occurred without c or e would not have occurred without c, he sounds like Robert Stalnaker. But his position is not the same, though he accepts the same disjunction of counterfactuals, and Stalnaker's defence of such disjunctions [i.e., Stalnaker's defence of counterfactual excluded middle] is of no use to him. My opponent thinks there are two relevant ways the world might be; one of them would make true one of the counterfactuals, the other would make true the other, so the disjunction is true either way. Stalnaker, like me, thinks that there is only one relevant way for the world to be, and it does not make either counterfactual determinately true. But Stalnaker, unlike me, thinks the disjoined counterfactuals are true or false relative to alternative arbitrary resolutions of a semantic indeterminacy; what makes the counter-factuals lack determinate truth[-value] is that different resolutions go different ways; but every resolution makes one or the other true, so the disjunction is determinately true despite the complementary indeterminacies of the disjuncts. A resolution of an alleged semantic determinacy is not a hidden fact about the world; and that is the difference between Stalnaker and my opponent. Stalnaker disagrees with me on a small point of semantics; my opponent, on a large point of ontology.[12]

Here I am siding with the opponent of Lewis and Stalnaker. Counterfactual act-determinism reflects a very strong semantic intuition, it seems to me. And the principle is needed not only by utilitarian moral reasoning but by all (plausible) kinds of moral reasoning (paying any attention to the consequences of actions). So it might be tempting to argue that, if a system of possible world semantics does not validate the principle, so much the worse for the system. But this conclusion is unsought and really not warranted. For it is only if we think of such possible world semantic systems as definitive (reductively) of the true meaning of counterfactuals that we end up in conflict with the semantic intuition underlying the principle of counterfactual act–determinism. If instead we conceive of possible world semantic systems not as reductive definitions of the meaning of counterfactual utterances, but as heuristic devices, helping us as far as possible to sort out the truth-conditions of such utterances, then we can hold on to our semantic (realistic) intuition and yet, for all that, make good use of these semantic systems. And this is how I believe we should proceed.

Can we perform concrete actions?

A third objection that I have encountered is that we cannot perform concrete actions. It has been put forward by Erik Carlson:

> Furthermore, there are strong reasons against adopting Tännsjö's form of concretism. The main reason is that concrete actions, as he conceives of them, are not performable in the sense relevant in normative contexts.[13]

This is strange. After all, all concrete actions are performed. But there are aspects of them, of course, that are not intentional. I suppose that this is really the thrust of Carlson's objection. 'Performing a concrete action at will seems to require superhuman precision in controlling one's body, and in measuring distances in space and time', he also writes.[14] To be sure, actions are trivially intentional. However, according to utilitarianism, intentions are of no moral importance. We are also responsible for unintentional aspects of our actions, in the sense that, if these aspects affect the outcome of the actions, they may well be what makes these acts right or wrong. Recall once again that what we are here discussing is a criterion of objective rightness of actions, not a responsible or defensible decision procedure.

To see this more clearly, consider the following example. I happen to meet an old friend on a street in a foreign country. I approach him and greet him. 'Nice to see you again, Peter Novac', I say. Intentionally, I have greeted him. I have formed the intention (a concrete event) with the abstract content (I wanted to see to it that I greeted him) and, as a result, I did greet him (in the particular manner I did). However, what I did not know was that he had become a secret agent, operating under cover. So by greeting him I also informed on him. Now, my informing on him was not intentional. However, it is true of my concrete action that it was a case of informing on this person. The action I performed satisfies both descriptions. It was a case of (intentionally) greeting my friend, but it was also a case of (unintentionally) informing on him. Clearly, from the point of view of objective rightness, the latter fact may be of the utmost importance.

Finally, the following objection has been raised to concretism. Even if concrete actions have no versions, they still have 'quasi-versions'. This means that even a concretist ends up in problems with conflicting duties. This objection has been made by Lars Bergström. The answer to it must be rather complex.

Quasi-versions of actions

An action α_1 is a *quasi-version* of an action α_2, according to Bergström, if, and only if, α_1 is different from but agent identical and not time identical with α_2, and it is logically necessary that if α_1 is performed then α_2 is also performed.[15] Let me give a simple example. Consider once again the following problem. Should I invite a certain friend for dinner or not? Suppose that, if I do, the consequences are worse than if I do not. The reason for this is that, if I invite him, I will (as a matter of fact) quarrel with him during the dinner. However, consider also the following two possibilities. Either I invite him for dinner and settle my dispute with him, or I do not invite him for dinner (and I go for a walk instead of dining with him). It would be much better if I invited him and settled my dispute with him than if I did not invite him (in spite of the fact that I went for a walk).

Suppose that, as a matter of fact, I do not invite my friend for dinner and that I do go for a walk. Am I doing the right thing or not?

My answer to this question is as follows. By not inviting him I do the right thing. In this situation (when I could invite him or not invite him) there was nothing I could do (we assume) such that, had I done it, the world would have been better. The reason is that, had I instead invited him, I would, as a matter of fact, have quarrelled with him.

The point is not that I could not help quarrelling with him. Let us assume that I could avoid this. The problem in this situation, however, where the option is whether I should invite him or not, is that there is nothing I can do which makes me not quarrel with him (later on). To be sure, if I do invite him (now) and quarrel with him (later), my quarrelling with him (later) is a moral mistake of mine. None the less, it is what would actually take place (we have assumed) were I to invite him. Therefore, it was all right of me not to invite him.

It might be thought that this is inconsistent. If I can invite him and settle my dispute with him, then it is not true that, if I were to invite him, no matter how I were to proceed when I did, I would later on quarrel with him, it might be claimed. This is a worry put forward by Holly M. Smith:

> The description of the case suggests that although the agent could perform the compound act of inviting-and-then-quarrelling, and also not-inviting-and-not-settling-the-dispute, he *could not* perform the compound act of inviting-and-then-not-quarrelling. No matter how strongly he set himself (now) to invite the friend and then not quarrel with him, in fact, when the time came, he would start quarrel.[16]

But this claim is mistaken. The description is consistent. It is true that, no matter how strongly I set myself (now) to invite the friend and then not quarrel with him, I will not do so. But this does not preclude that this is something I can do. The reason that I would quarrel with him later on, were I to invite him, is that, later on, I would make a wrong decision. There is no need to assume that I can now control my future (free) decisions.

However, it is also true that, if we consider both what happens now and what happens later on, and consider what I should have done during the entire time sequence, then it seems that what I did was plainly wrong. I did not invite him and I went for a walk in spite of the fact that there was some something else I could have done such that, had I done it, the world would have been better. The world would have been better, we have assumed, had I invited him for dinner and settled my dispute with him. This was something I had in my power to do, but I did not do it. Hence, my action during this time sequence was wrong.

In this argument I am taking for granted that in our actions, we ought to take future mistakes into account. This has been denied by, among others, Lars Bergström. According to him, past moral mistakes are relevant to the rightness of our present actions, but future mistakes are not.[17] Why, according to Bergström, is this so? He questions the conclusion that, in examples such as the one given here, I ought not to invite my putative guest. He does not say that I ought to invite him either. The alternative set in question is not the relevant one. Instead I ought to invite him and settle my dispute with him. I agree about that, of course, but why should we not say that I did the right thing when I did not invite him? According to Bergström, it would be wrong to say this because, when I decide not to invite him, it is still open to me to invite him and settle my dispute with him. Suppose, however, that the reason that I should invite him and settle my dispute with him is that, yesterday, I offended him. This was a moral mistake of mine. Yet this past mistake, according to Bergström, is relevant to my present decision. Why? Because, now, it is not open to me to change it.

I think we should resist this line. It is true that, now, I can do nothing about my past mistake. However, it is equally true that, now, I can do nothing about my future one. It is too late to do anything about the past mistake. But it is too early to do anything about my future mistake. Past and future mistakes are on an equal footing now. Therefore, we ought to treat them alike. And, obviously, we need to take our past mistakes into account. Then we should also take our future mistakes into account.

Does my answer lead to paradox? Bergström believes it does, but this is a mistake. It does not.

Both (1) that it was all right of me not to invite my putative guest for dinner and (2) that I acted wrongly when I did not invite him to dinner and went for a walk may be true if AU is true. Let us suppose that they are. It is true that I ought not to invite my friend because, if I do, then, as a matter of fact, I will not settle the dispute with him but will quarrel with him endlessly. But it was wrong of me not to invite him and settle my dispute with him. I could have done so (we have assumed), and since I did not both he and I suffer from the unresolved dispute.

The truth of (1) may be hard to accept in the light of (2). In my argument for the consistency between them I will take realism about the future for granted. This means that I take it for granted that it is true timelessly either that I will or that I will not settle my dispute with my friend. This is true, I assume, irrespective of whether we can, even in principle, find out (now) whether I will settle the dispute or not. In the example, I have assumed that, as a matter of fact, I do not invite my friend for dinner. Yet, for all that, it is true, I assume, that, had I invited him, I would have quarrelled with him.

The reason that (1) and (2) are not inconsistent may be thought to be that the 'agglomeration principle' is not valid.[18] It does not follow from the fact that I ought to do *a* and *b* that I ought to do *a* (nor does it follow from the fact that I ought to do *a* and that I ought to do *b* that I ought to do *a* and *b*). Such a reason seems somewhat superficial, however. Why does the principle not hold? We must look deeper into the matter. How do we interpret statements like (1) and (2)?

The most natural way of taking them is as follows. Normative properties (values) like rightness, wrongness and obligatoriness are *de re*, they are possessed by concrete actions. This means that (2) says something like the following. By not inviting my friend and settling my dispute with him, I performed an action that was wrong. It was wrong because there was something else I could have done, i.e., inviting him and settling the dispute (in the manner I would actually have invited him and settled the dispute, had I chosen to do so) such that, had I done it, the world (on the whole) would have been better. (2) then is not inconsistent with (1), which says of another concrete action that I perform that it is right (there was no way I could have acted otherwise during the time interval when I performed it that would actually have resulted, in the circumstances, in a better world on the whole).

This does not resolve the conflict between (1) and (2), of course. Even on AU there exist moral conflicts, i.e., situations where it is not possible for us to fulfil all our duties. In the example, not only is it true of the concrete action I perform in not inviting my friend and then going for a walk that it is wrong; it is wrong despite the fact that a (spatio-temporal) part of it is obligatory, i.e., the part consisting of my not inviting him. Is that strange? So it may seem. If (1) and (2) were read *de dicto*, if rightness, wrongness and obligatoriness were conceived of as operations on statements or properties of states of affairs, the reason the agglomeration principle is not true would be rather mysterious. Suppose that my inviting my friend and settling my dispute with him is conceived of as a conjunction of two statements or possible states of affairs, to wit, that I invite him (*p*), and that I settle my dispute with him (*q*), and suppose the conjunction of *p* and q is thought to be obligatory. It would then seem reasonable to argue that, since p and q is obligatory, so are both conjuncts; this seems to follow from a more general principle to the effect that, if p is obligatory and if q follows from p, then q is obligatory as well. If norms are read *de re*, however, the invalidity of the agglomeration principle is self-evident. One cannot agglomerate concrete things in the same way as one can agglomerate statements. No inconsistency is involved in the description of the situation. What is true of a concrete whole need not be true of each part of it. It is true of the chair I am now sitting on that it has four legs, but it is true of none of these legs that it has four legs.

Even if the statements (1) that it was all right of me not to invite my friend for dinner and (2) that I acted wrongly when I did not invite him to dinner and went for a walk are not contradictory, they may still be considered to provide little guidance to a person who wonders what to do. After all, they are in conflict. It is impossible to act on both of them. And at the beginning of the time interval, during which I can invite or not invite my friend and have dinner with him or go for a walk, they seem to 'pull in opposite directions'. This objection has been raised by Bergström[19] and by Holly M. Smith. Smith writes:

> Tännsjö defends his acceptance of this form of moral conflict by avowing a radical split between a moral principle's role as a theoretical criterion of rightness, and any role it might serve as a decisionmaking guide . . . But permitting such a radical split between these two roles of a moral principle is misguided . . . A principle's capacity to serve as a decisionmaking guide affects its acceptability as a theoretical account of rightness. Since Tännsjö's version of AU cannot be used for making decisions, it cannot be used as a criterion of rightness either.[20]

It is true that I do avow a radical split between a moral principle's role as a theoretical criterion of rightness, and any role it might serve as a decision making guide. However, this objection seems to me just irrelevant. After all, we should not expect a criterion of rightness to provide guidance in particular situations. No version of utilitarianism can guide choices in this direct manner. Who are we to say whether our actions are, on utilitarian grounds, right or wrong? What we should expect from a statement of utilitarianism is, rather, that for each concrete action, it yields (in principle) a definite answer to the question of whether it is right or wrong and an explanation of this moral fact. If we can learn anything from it at all – I discussed this problem in Chapter 2 and previously in this chapter – we can only learn it indirectly. Our choice of decision method can be informed by our adoption of a criterion of rightness.

How, then, do we go about deciding what to do in a case like the one described? Well, decisions are actions. So an answer of sorts exists to the question. We ought to behave in the situation in a manner such that there is no alternative behaviour accessible to us that would result in a better state of the world. As a matter of fact, AU provides us with a criterion of right decision.

This answer shows that a person who possesses all relevant factual information in the situation knows how to make a decision. So in a sense our criterion of rightness is relevant also to our problems of decision making. But since no one possesses all the relevant factual information in any situation, the criterion is not very informative.

How are we to argue in the example under discussion, then? This is difficult to say. In that situation, where I deliberate whether I should or whether I should not invite my putative guest, and when I speculate about what will happen if I do and if I do not, it would be responsible, I conjecture, to deliberate in a manner such that, when I consistently stick to it, it is true of me that, had I instead consistently held on to any rival manner of deliberating, the world would have been worse.

We know little about what constitutes such a manner of deliberation, I am afraid, but I have already discussed that point, so I will say no more about it in the present context.

The principle of counterfactual dependence stated

Suppose I perform a certain action, such as writing this section of this book. Suppose that there is something else I could have done instead such that, had I done it, some onerous event in the world would not have taken place. Suppose that, in that case, the world would have been much better. This is relevant to the rightness or wrongness of my action then, according to my statement of AU. In my statement of AU I am taking for granted the principle of counterfactual dependence.

Is this assumption controversial? One might be tempted to argue that, even if the world would have been better had I performed the other action, this does not matter to the moral status of my action, unless my action caused the onerous event.

I am not sure whether there is really any difference between these two positions. This depends on how we understand the concept of causality. However, if there is a difference, then I argue that the principle of counterfactual dependence is plausible, not the principle of causal dependence.

How can we think of a difference? This may be an example. Suppose I was faced with an indeterministic machine, which flipped a coin. I bet on heads and I lost. Should I have bet instead on tails? I think I should. But it is not quite clear that we should say that I caused my own loss. Still, on any plausible theory of counterfactuals we must say that, had I bet instead on tails, I would have won. This is what matters, from a broadly utilitarian perspective. A utilitarian (in contradistinction to a deontologist) does not bother with how things come about.

The total state principle stated

I can think of yet another way in which the principle of counterfactual dependence and the principle of causal dependence diverge. We hesitate to say that, through our actions, we cause events in the past. Most people seem also to believe that it is never true of us that, had we acted otherwise in a situation where that was something we could do, the past would have been different. I will reject that belief in Chapter 10, however. Now, suppose it is true of us sometimes that, if we had acted differently from the way we did, the past would have been better. Can this ever be a reason why we should have acted differently? Can an action be right, in spite of the fact that, had it not been performed, the future would have been (slightly) better, since, had it not been performed, the past would have been (much) worse?

Once again I think that, when we consider matters from a broadly utilitarian perspective, we must opt for the total state principle, rather than for the future state principle. If, contrary to what many thinkers seem to believe, the past is counterfactually dependent on our actions, in exactly the same manner as the future is, then, if we want to be true to the utilitarian spirit, we should take the past into moral account. The rationale behind utilitarianism, after all, is an intuition of impartiality. From a moral point of view, it does not matter to whom a certain pleasure or displeasure accrues, or why it occurs, or when it comes about. So, if it is true that, sometimes, had we acted differently the past would have been different, this matters to the moral status of our actions (irrespective of whether this is anything that we can find out). I will return to this point in Chapter 10, where I argue that the past is counterfactually dependent on our actions.

Act utilitarianism vs rule utilitarianism

Act utilitarianism is often contrasted to rule utilitarianism. Rule utilitarianism (RU) could be stated in the following way:

> RU: A particular action is right if, and only if, it is not proscribed by any rule or system of rules such that, if people were generally adhering to it, the world, on the whole, would be better than if they were adhering to any rule or system of rules permitting it.

There are several points in need of clarification in my statement of RU, but I will not go into these problems. I feel no inclination to defend RU. In the first place, the fact that, if everyone does not do his or her rule-utilitarian duty, my doing so may have disastrous effects seems to me to show that something has gone wrong in rule utilitarianism. A principle that prescribes that I shall refuse to obey the orders of an oppressor when no one actually joins me, and when the effect is merely that I get killed, cannot be correct. Secondly, I share the following observation made by Michael Slote:

> If optimificness makes for a morally best or most justified set of rules, why shouldn't the optimificness of *an act* (always) render it a morally best or most justified act, with the result, as against rule-utilitarianism, that it is always morally permissible to make optimising choices (act optimifically)?[21]

Moreover, in Chapter 4 I show that what has usually been considered the best argument in defence of rule utilitarianism, as compared with act utilitarianism, is not conclusive. The argument is that, in situations where cooperation is essential, every person performing his or her act-utilitarian duty does not guarantee an optimal outcome. If everyone performs his or her rule-utilitarian duty, however, an optimal outcome does get guaranteed. The situations are of the following kind. A joint venture is essential. If no one takes his or her share in the joint venture, the venture never comes about, but yet, for all that, each person may act correctly, according to act utilitarianism. For each can excuse himself or herself with a reference to the fact that the others did not take their shares either, so, in the circumstances, his or her effort would have been in vain. If everyone does his or her rule-utilitarian duty, on the other hand, the optimal outcome does come about. So the argument goes. In Chapter 4 I show, however, that if the act-utilitarian formula is applied to collective actions also, we will be able to defend the claim that if everyone (collectivities included) does his or her act-utilitarian duty, an optimal outcome is guaranteed. Hence falls the main argument in defence of rule utilitarianism. Rule utilitarianism is not exclusive in this respect.

Furthermore, in Chapter 7 I will try to show that if we wed a plausible decision method to AU, involving an idea of an 'intuitive' level of morality of the kind described by R. M. Hare, and briefly discussed in the present chapter, i.e., adopting what Peter Railton has called a 'sophisticated consequentialism', then the intuition commonly thought to provide a rationale behind RU is well taken care of.

Deontic notions

When I, being an adherent of hedonistic utilitarianism, say of an action that it is right, I imply (pragmatically) that it is optimific. I am also (strictly) implying that it is not wrong. However, this is probably not all I say.[22] It is difficult to tell just what more I am saying, though. To be sure, I am not saying that the action in question ought to be performed. This may be so, if there is no other way the agent can behave such that, if he or she were to behave in this way, the world would be equally good or better. This requirement is probably never met in practice, so there are probably no actions that are obligatory. Hence, I have little need of the notion of an obligation at all. Furthermore, and consequently, when saying of an action that it is right, I am not recommending that it be performed – it is rather that I say that the action is permissible, that it is 'all right' or 'permissible' for the agent to perform it.

When I say of an action that it is not right I do imply that it is wrong (it is a merit of AU that it satisfies this very basic requirement of deontic logic). This may be thought to imply that the agent who performs it is blameworthy. It does not, however. Actions that are blameworthy may well be right (and there may well be cases of blameless wrongdoing) – I will return to this theme in Chapter 9. Questions of blame and praise are to do not with rightness and wrongness of particular actions, but with motives and traits of characters of people who perform them.

When I accept that an action I am contemplating would be wrong, I feel some inclination not to perform it. I reject internalism, however. I believe that the connection between my belief that the action would be wrong, and my inclination not to perform it, is contingent. It varies in strength too. This is only rational, it seems to me. My concern should be stronger the more value is at stake in a certain situation. It is not important as such to perform right actions (as many as possible). The important thing is to maximise value. The true nature of this claim, however, is difficult to explain. What kind of importance is involved in this claim is hard to tell.

AU is not true by definition, then. AU makes a substantial claim. In Chapter 2 I indicated how such a claim could be put to the test. I believe that the claim is true. In this chapter and in chapters to follow I will defend the claim that it is. However, like Henry Sidgwick and G. E. Moore before me, I feel unable to explain the true nature of this claim. As a matter of fact, I share their doubt that any further explanation of the true nature of the deontic notions can be given.

This may seem problematic, but, since most people understand and handle these notions quite well without any explanation of their true nature, it is not. For the purposes of normative ethics, no explanation of the true nature of the deontic notions is required.

It should be observed too that, even if the deontic notions are indefinable, and inexplicable in terms of other, more familiar notions, it might well be the case that the deontic properties of actions will turn out to be identical with natural properties (if properties are accepted in our ontological framework). As a matter of fact, if we are prepared to quantify over properties, then my statement of AU may be understood as implying the conjecture that the property of rightness is identical to the property of being optimific (in the manner explained in this book).

In my discussion I concentrate on deontic problems, and develop and defend a theory of rightness of actions. However, I also touch upon the problem of what it means to take decisions in a 'responsible' manner. This does not mean to take them in the right manner. We cannot ascertain that we do that in general. So we have to rest satisfied with something less reassuring, i.e., if we can take our decisions in a 'responsible' manner. What does that mean?

Once again, I think we must admit that no definition, either explicit or implicit, can be given. In particular, I think that no simple reduction of the meaning of 'responsibility' in taking decisions in terms of 'rightness' and 'wrongness' of actions can be accomplished. Once again, we must rely on our capacity to use the term in question, to answer questions posed in terms of it (under what general conditions is a decision taken in a 'responsible' manner?) and so forth. My answer – as we have seen – to the question of when a decision is taken in a 'responsible' way has been informed, but it has not been fully determined, by what I believe are right-making characteristics of actions.

Finally a word about 'intrinsic value': in this chapter I have been using evaluative terminology simply as a shorthand. The utilitarian formula has been stated in terms of 'betterness' (and I speak then of betterness in itself, intrinsic value). However, my intention is to go on in chapters to come and specify what I think has intrinsic value. When this task has been completed, the utilitarian formula can be stated without any essential reference to the notion of intrinsic value. So that notion may seem then to be entirely superfluous. And yet, for all that, in Chapter 8 it will become clear that the notion of intrinsic value seems to play a crucial epistemic role in our moral arguments. So I will have to say something about the notion in that context. By way of foreshadowing this, the notion of intrinsic value seems to be beyond the reach of any explicit definition. However, it can perhaps be defined implicitly. At least there is one requirement the notion seems to satisfy: if something possesses (positive) intrinsic value, then this gives us some reason to produce it.

I return to the notion of intrinsic value in Chapter 8.

Notes

1 Cf. for example Part II of D. Davidson, *Actions and Events*.
2 Cf. G. E. Moore, *Principia Ethica*, p. 216.
3 Cf. H. Sidgwick, *The Methods of Ethics*, p. 207.
4 T. Schelling, *The Strategy of Conflict*; D. Parfit, *Reasons and Persons*, pp. 12–13.
5 Cf. R. M. Hare, *Moral Thinking*, and P. Railton, 'Alienation, Consequentialism, and the Demands of Morality'.
6 G. Harman, *Change in View: Principles of Reasoning*, p. 112.
7 L. Bergström, *The Alternatives and Consequences of Actions*.
8 In my 'The Morality of Abstract Entities' and 'Moral Conflict and Moral Realism'.
9 Cf. R. E. Bales, 'Review of Bergström's *The Alternatives and Consequences of Actions and Other Works*'.
10 L. Bergström, 'On the Formulation and Application of Utilitarianism', p. 141.
11 I owe this observation to Wlodek Rabinowicz.

12 D. K. Lewis, *Philosophical Papers*, Vol. 2, pp. 183ff.
13 E. Carlson, *Some Basic Problems of Consequentialism*, p. 154.
14 Carlson, *Some Basic Problems*, p. 155.
15 Bergström, 'On the Formulation and Application of Utilitarianism'.
16 H. M. Smith, 'Moral Realism, Moral Conflict, and Compound Acts', pp. 343–4.
17 L. Bergström, 'Utilitarianism and Future Mistakes', pp. 89–90.
18 Cf. for example Bernard Williams, 'Ethical Consistency', p. 118, for an argument along this line.
19 Bergström, 'Utilitarianism and Future Mistakes'.
20 Smith, 'Moral Realism, Moral Conflict, and Compound Acts', pp. 342–3.
21 M. Slote, *From Morality to Virtue*, p. 59.
22 I used to believe that this was all I was saying: cf. my *Moral Realism*, Ch. 4, about this, where I defend the Moorean view that deontic notions are definable in terms of value.

Chapter 4

Collective duties

Utilitarianism, the idea that an action is wrong if, and only if, there is something the agent could have done instead such that, had she or he done it the outcome would have been better (otherwise the action is right), has been said to face problems in some situations where people together cause harm (or do good). The examples of this are variations of a situation with the following traits.

A number of persons can either enter a joint project (JOIN) and, together, produce some considerable good, or individually do some small good (IN-DIVIDUATE). If, say, at least five persons cooperate in the joint effort, a lot of value is secured (on the whole). If less than five JOIN, the joint mission does not come about. If more than five persons JOIN, it does come about too, but this is a result, then, of over-determination. It suffices if five JOIN and nothing is gained if more than five JOIN. More good is produced, on the whole, if all JOIN than if, instead, each INDIVIDUATES. There is no way that these persons can communicate with each other or otherwise coordinate their actions.

Suppose there are ten persons who could JOIN. If, as a matter of fact, exactly five do, then each of them is doing her or his utilitarian duty. Had she or he acted differently, she or he would have INDIVIDUATED, we assume, and hence done some good, but the joint effort of the remaining four would then have been in vain, and the consequences, we assume, would have been worse. This is as it should be. Utilitarianism seems to give the right answer.

However, in all cases other than this (exceptional) one, utilitarianism has been accused of giving the wrong answer. Let us see how.

The wrong answer

Here is one example where utilitarianism has been thought to give the wrong answer: only four persons JOIN, and each of the remaining six INDIVIDU-ATES instead. Now, according to utilitarianism, each of these remaining six acts wrongly. She or he should have joined instead. This is as it should be. But what of the four that did JOIN? Each of them acts wrongly, according to utilitarianism. In the circumstances, where only three other persons JOINED, their

JOINING meant a waste of resources. None of them should have JOINED. Instead each should have INDIVIDUATED and produced some small good instead. This has seemed counter-intuitive. Those who JOINED only did as they should, it has been maintained.

This is another example: suppose instead that all ten JOIN. This means that, from the point of view of utilitarianism, each of them acts wrongly. By INDIVIDUATING instead of JOINING, each could have done some small good instead, and the joint mission would not have been affected (since, after all, the remaining nine JOINED). So it is true of each that she or he should have abstained from JOINING. This too has seemed counter-intuitive. For, to be sure, if each and every one had INDIVIDUATED, then the joint mission would not have come about. Then the consequences would have been worse (we have assumed).

Suppose, then, that no one JOINS (but that each INDIVIDUATES instead). Would this, according to utilitarianism, be all right? It would, for, in the circumstances, it is true of each individual that, had she or he JOINED (when no one else did), the consequences would have been worse. In the circumstances, if she or he had not JOINED, each would not have done even the little good she or he actually did, and the joint mission would still not have come about (it took five persons to make it happen). Once again this has been considered counter-intuitive for, if instead all had JOINED, then, on the whole, the consequences would have been better.

More generally, it might be objected that a moral theory cannot be correct unless it is true of it that, if everyone were to succeed in following it, this must guarantee an optimal outcome. In particular this should be true of a consequentialist theory. However, as is seen from some of the examples, this does not seem to be true of utilitarianism. If everyone INDIVIDUATES, then everyone does his or her utilitarian duty and, yet, for all that, the result is not optimal. It would have been better if all had JOINED (and even better if only five had JOINED). To be sure, utilitarianism does not necessarily steer us away from a pattern of actions with optimal results (it is all right, according to utilitarianism, if exactly five JOIN), but utilitarianism is compatible with our ending up with such a pattern (each person does the right thing when all INDIVIDUATE). And this, according to this objection, shows that there is something wrong with utilitarianism.

How should a utilitarian respond to strictures like this? I will review three possible responses. I dismiss two of them quite briefly, and I elaborate on, and defend, the third one.

Possible utilitarian responses

One way for the utilitarian to try to handle these cases would be to tinker with the counterfactuals in question. Taking the point of view of one of the persons in the example, the utilitarian could argue along the following lines: is it really true that, if I had not JOINED, when, say, as a matter of fact seven persons did, then the remaining six would have JOINED? Is it not more plausible to say that, if I had not JOINED, then neither would they? If I had INDIVIDUATED, so would they. We are not different. So it was lucky that I did JOIN. Had I not (and had the other six persons not), the consequences would have been worse.

I will not pursue this line of thought here.[1] It raises intricate problems concerning counterfactuals. In particular, it raises the problem discussed by the parties to the controversy between causal and classical (evidential) decision theory. In the final analysis, I think it fails. No implausibility is involved in the assumption that, in the situation where I act otherwise, the others stick to their action. After all, we have assumed that there is no way that I can affect what they do. Furthermore, a better way out of the problem exists for utilitarians, so there is no need for them really to tinker with the counterfactuals.

Another tack sometimes taken by thinkers of a consequentialist bent of mind has been to revise the utilitarian criterion of rightness. When I do not JOIN, and no one else does, say, then the consequences are bad. It is true of me that nothing would have been gained if instead I had JOINED, but, still, I should have done so. For I (and each of the other persons who could have joined) bear some responsibility for the bad consequences. We should, in a manner of speaking, 'distribute' the responsibility for these among us.

I will not pursue this line of thought either.[2] I think that, in the final analysis, it is at variance with the spirit of the utilitarian creed. The main problem with this line of thought is that it is difficult to stick to it, if much value is at stake when I INDIVIDUATE. If, by JOINING, when my part of the joint mission is not essential to the outcome, I forego a lot of good consequences which would have been brought about if instead I had INDIVIDUATED, we are tempted to say that, after all, I should have INDIVIDUATED. A nice illustration of this is an example given by Frank Jackson:

> X and Y jointly cause pain to Z; they act independently: had one not acted, the other still would have; and had neither acted, Z would have experienced no pain . . . had X not acted, Z's pain would have been much worse; that is, the best thing would be for neither X nor Y to act, no pain in that case; the next best thing is for both X and Y to act (as in fact happens), some pain in that case; and the worst thing would be for Y to act alone, much worse pain in that case.[3]

I think we must admit that, in the circumstances, where Y is going to act regardless of what X does, X ought to act as well. But if we do, we have to give up the idea that the responsibility for the consequences produced by the two persons together should be 'distributed' among them.

Then, finally, the most promising tack to be taken in the defence of utilitarianism in relation to the example is the following: we allow not only that individuals act rightly or wrongly, but also that collectivities do. Then we are free to say that, in the situation where no one JOINS, each person does his or her utilitarian duty, but together they act wrongly. And if all persons succeed in acting rightly (according to utilitarianism), then the result will be optimal. In the rest of this chapter I will concentrate on this idea.

This idea captures nicely the intuition that, in the examples above, something has gone wrong. When, for example, no one JOINS, there is someone who acts wrongly: all do. Together they do the wrong thing.

What should they have done instead, then? Well, there are several possibilities open, all sharing the common feature that exactly five JOIN, while exactly five INDIVIDUATE. Who JOIN and who INDIVIDUATE does not matter since, we have assumed, this does not affect the amount of good produced. If every agent, including collectivities, acts rightly (according to utilitarianism), then the outcome will be optimal.

By allowing that there are collective duties we pay due respect both to the intuition that, in the example, it was pointless for each individual to act otherwise – nothing of value would have been gained from this – and to the intuition that something did go wrong in the example (together they all acted wrongly, therefore the outcome is sub-optimal).

Collective duties

Several thinkers have suggested that, in the manner described here, a collective action may have a normative status (i.e., it could be right or wrong and, if right, even obligatory).[4] However, this suggestion has not been received with enthusiasm. Why is this so? I will consider four alleged problems with it, four problems which have brought it into (undeserved) disrepute.

I suppose the objection to the idea of collective duties that first comes to mind is that collective actions are not 'natural' entities or kinds. Unless we are able to recognise some common planning or coordination between the persons who perform the individual actions that allegedly constitute the collective action, we are not willing to acknowledge that we are in fact faced with a collective action. We need the concept of a collective action to account morally for situations where people act individually, without communication and coordination, however. So there is no application for the concept.

But I think we should resist this reluctance to speak of a collective action in the absence of collective planning or coordination. To be sure, some collective actions lacking in collective planning or coordination are not of much practical concern to us. An example is the collective action of my writing this chapter and your reading it. However, some collective actions are of much practical concern. I am thinking of collective actions where important effects are brought about (as in our abstract example above), such as general elections, traffic behaviour, and the choice of habitation or occupation. There is a point in recognising in these situations that what we are faced with are collective actions. There is a point in recognising that these collective actions have a normative status, or so I will argue. And if we acknowledge that these collective actions exist, then we may as well acknowledge that all sorts of collective action do. This is no more strange than our acknowledging the existence of scattered, strange and not very interesting objects (such as the pieces of paper upon which this chapter is printed and the planet Venus).

However, this may not seem quite convincing. Take the example of general elections. To be sure, one party in particular may be elected as a result of what the voters do, but it might be asked whether they really elect the government. If we say that they do, we seem to imply that they make a common choice. But can a collectivity make a choice?

This question has been put to me in correspondence by Earl Conee, who once toyed with the idea that there are collective duties, but who, for this reason, has now given it up. Collectivities cannot make choices, Conee now seems to believe.[5] And Holly M. Smith has argued against me, with a different example:

> Although my act of returning your lost wallet is right, and your act of thanking me is right, the compound act of my-returning-your-wallet-and-your-thanking-me cannot be right. It cannot be right because there is no single agent who could decide to do this act.[6]

However, I think this compound act can be right (or wrong). I think there is a single agent who decides to perform it, namely the collectivity in question. And this collectivity does make a common decision or choice. I think that collectivities are capable of having intentions. I have argued this elsewhere, but I will briefly restate my argument here and elaborate on it. There are further strictures on it that have to be answered.[7]

How then are we to conceive of the intention of a collectivity? Let us return to the example with the general elections. I have argued that we conceive of the intention of the voters as a conjunction of all the individual intentions behind all the individual actions that make the collective action.[8] Those who together elect the government have a common intention then. It is the intention that voter 1 votes for the party in question, that voter 2 votes for the same party, and so forth.

To be sure, this conjunction is not the content of the consciousness of any particular individual. However, we should not suppose the intention of the collectivity to be entertained by any individual. The collective action is not performed by any individual. We may say, however, that the conjunction is entertained by the collectivity. We need not say, however, if we find this mysterious, that the collectivity possesses a consciousness. We may say that the intention is held by the collectivity, but not as a part of any consciousness. This is no more mysterious than attributing a certain piece of information or instruction to a computer program. We believe that computer programs contain pieces of information and instructions, and perform various different operations, but we do not believe that computer programs possess consciousness.

But if the intention of the collectivity is a conjunction of intentions of individuals making it up, does this not mean that the intention of the collectivity may be contradictory? I think not. The intention of each individual is that he or she see to it that such and such action on his or her behalf comes about (perhaps with a hope that a joint effort will be realised). Hence, each conjunct concerns its own agent and cannot contradict the conjuncts concerned with the actions of other agents. Peter's intention is that he do so and so, Mary's intention is that she do so and so, and so forth.

Now another objection naturally arises, however. Suppose a collectivity acts, and acts wrongly. Together some people cause some unnecessary harm, we assume. They elect the wrong government, say. However, in the circumstances, the intention of the collectivity is not to cause this harm. Neither does anyone in the collectivity intend to cause this harm. Each person may hope that her or his party will win the elections, but no one can intend that it will win. At most, each can intend to give her or his vote to this party (in the hope that it will win). Does this not mean that it is implausible to say of the collectivity that it acts wrongly? If it does, it does so unintentionally.

This objection should not convince a utilitarian focusing upon objective rightness. According to the utilitarian criterion of objective rightness, the intention is of no moral importance. Of course, an action must be intentional under some description in order to be a proper object of evaluation. If not, it is simply no action. But this requirement is met when a majority votes for a certain party. Together they have an intention (the conjunction of their individual intentions). This is not to cause harm or even to have a certain government elected. But it need not be, in order for the collective action to have normative status. Even if bad consequences (rather than good ones) are caused unintentionally, this is wrong, according to utilitarianism (no matter whether the action in question is individual or collective). This is what the collectivity does, when, in this example, it acts wrongly (and elects the wrong government). It acts wrongly with no bad intention.

Then still another objection arises, however. As we have seen, it seems to be true of collectivities that even when they act rightly, i.e., act so that the outcome is optimal, they do not do this intentionally. Each individual has his or her intention with his or her individual act and the collectivity has as its intention the conjunction of such intentions, which need not be the intention that the best outcome be obtained. Does this not mean that there is no point in acknowledging that collective actions are sometimes right, sometimes wrong? Such information can never guide any actions of any collectivity.

This objection is mistaken. Let me elaborate on this point.

Can information about collective duties guide choices?

The objection is built upon a true observation, but the objection is not devastating to utilitarianism. In the first place, the utilitarian formula only states a criterion of (objective) rightness and wrongness of actions. The formula might be plausible as such, even if, when we act in a situation, the formula cannot guide our choice of action.

Secondly, our acknowledging that there are collective duties helps us in understanding the true nature of the examples discussed in this chapter. When at first we contemplated the examples at the beginning of this chapter we were inclined to say that there must be something wrong with utilitarianism, since it does not acknowledge any wrongdoing in a situation where all INDIVIDU-ATE. This could make us inclined to accept rule utilitarianism rather than act utilitarianism. When we came to recognise that there are collective duties, this objection to act utilitarianism lost its bite. Even according to act utilitarianism there is some wrongdoing involved in this case. This wrongdoing is committed by the collectivity; hence this putative argument in defence of rule utilitarianism falls. Act utilitarianism and rule utilitarianism are alike in the respect that, if everyone (including collectivities) performs his or her duty (his or her act-utilitarian and rule–utilitarian duty respectively), then the outcome is optimal.

Thirdly, and of the utmost practical importance, the information that a group of persons are together (unintentionally) doing something wrong (unintentionally they are producing a bad outcome) can guide actions. When we think it cannot, I suggest, we take too narrow a view of the situation. We concentrate too exclusively on the collectivity itself. Since it cannot do what it ought to do intentionally (produce the best outcome), it finds no guidance in information to the effect that there is one thing rather than another that it should do. However, if we also bring into consideration agents other than the collectivity itself, we see that information about what the collectivity should and should not do can guide choices.

The information that what the collectivity is about to do is wrong can be of importance for agents other than the collective agent itself. When they realise that what the collectivity is about to do is wrong, they may find good reasons to constrain the actions of the group.

Here is one simplified but possible example of this: suppose that there is a causal connection between how much alcohol is consumed in society and how many people become alcoholics. By consuming a moderate amount of alcohol each individual gains some pleasure but does no harm. However, when many people each consume a moderate amount, several people become addicted.

This is an example, then, where, individually, each who consumes a moderate amount does what it is all right to do but where all together act wrongly. Together those who drink moderately wrong those who become addicted.

This means that, even in a society where the autonomy of the individual is respected (no one is coerced only in her or his own interest; coercion is accepted only in order to stop someone from wronging someone else), society can restrain the drinking of all (by, say, tax policies). Political authorities can take legitimate measures, intended to stop all from collectively acting wrongly (by collectively harming those who become addicted).

We see, then, that even from a practical point of view it is of importance to notice that there are, besides individual obligations, collective ones. Even in situations where the collectivity cannot intentionally do its duty, other persons or collectivities, or authorities, may be in a situation where they can set the collectivity straight (once they realise that what the collectivity is about to do is wrong).

The acknowledgement of a collective duty can guide actions, then. It can guide actions of agents other than the collectivity itself.

Conclusion

The idea that collectivities can not only act, but act rightly and wrongly, has been in the air for some time now. In general it has not been taken seriously, however. This is a pity, for the idea provides the solution to some serious normative puzzles. In particular, if this idea is accepted we can show that if all agents in a situation, including collective ones, act rightly, then the outcome will be optimal.

The objections generally raised against this idea have less bite than is usually taken for granted. For example, collectivities can make choices, and the recognition that what they are about to do is wrong may be of practical importance. The information that the collectivity is about to do something seriously wrong can guide the choices of other agents, who are capable of setting the collectivity straight.

Notes

1 It was suggested to me in conversation by G. A. Cohen.
2 This line of thought is taken up most famously by Donald Regan in his book *Utilitarianism and Co-operation*, and, before him, by Jonathan Glover in 'It Makes No Difference Whether or Not I Do It'. It has been elaborated also by Derek Parfit in *Reasons and Persons*.
3 F. Jackson, 'Group Morality', p. 98.
4 I defend this view in my 'The Morality of Collective Actions'. It has been put forward earlier by Lars Bergström (in Swedish) in 'Vad är nyttomoral?' ('What is Utilitarianism?'), by B. C. Postow in 'Generalized Act Utilitarianism', and by Jackson in 'Group Morality'.

5 Cf. E. Conee, 'Review of Donald Regan's *Utilitarianism and Co-operation*', where he puts forward the view that collective actions have normative status.

6 H. M. Smith, 'Moral Realism, Moral Conflict, and Compound Acts', p. 342.

7 Cf. my 'The Morality of Collective Actions'.

8 Cf. my 'The Morality of Collective Actions' about this.

Chapter 5

Hedonism

In previous chapters I have discussed problems relating to the consequentialist aspect of utilitarianism. In the present chapter I will address some problems relating to the value aspect of it. I take my point of departure in the version of the utilitarian formula that I find personally most plausible, to wit, the classical hedonistic one, and I try to give a concise and plausible statement of it. In chapters to come I will defend my thinking that hedonistic utilitarianism is the most plausible version of utilitarianism.

Classical hedonistic utilitarianism has come into disrepute in the contemporary discussion. Few people today seem to believe that utilitarianism is a plausible doctrine at all, but those few people who do so seem almost without exception to believe in some variety of what they call 'preference utilitarianism'. I will not try to explain in this chapter why I find preference utilitarianism less satisfactory than hedonistic utilitarianism. I do that in the next chapter. Nor do I want to rebut, in this chapter, Robert Nozick's experience machine argument against hedonism. I do that in Chapter 7. My aim in this chapter is more restricted. I want to state the classical version as clearly as possible and discuss some unexpected implications and complications that it gives rise to.

In particular, I elaborate on the classical idea that what matters from a moral point of view is subjective time rather than objective time. I claim that on the most plausible version of the classical doctrine, there exist not noticeable, or 'sub-noticeable', changes of well-being.

This discussion ends up in the claim that such changes are morally relevant and in the observation that classical hedonistic utilitarianism leads to the conclusion (the ultimate in repugnance, it might seem) that there are conceivable circumstances where it would be right to torture one (otherwise perfectly happy) person in order to make sure that each of an enormous number of people, who all live very good lives indeed, experiences for a brief moment a not noticeable or sub-noticeable improvement of his or her situation. As a matter of fact, the least sub-noticeable improvement of well-being is taken as our unit, in classical hedonistic moral calculations.

Classical hedonistic utilitarians have often prided themselves on the belief that their criterion of rightness is purely empirical. It transpires from my discussion, however, that this belief is mistaken. While it is part and parcel of the spirit of classical utilitarianism that the criterion of rightness should be empirical, classical utilitarianism must be buttressed by at least some 'extra' normative stipulations, otherwise it will simply be empty. However, a rationale for at least some of these stipulations can, and will, be given.

Hedonistic utilitarianism

By 'classical' utilitarianism I refer to a moral theory according to which a particular action is right if, and only if, in the situation, there was nothing the agent could have done instead such that, had the agent done it, the world, on the whole, would have been better. According to the same theory, an action is wrong if, and only if, it is not right. Note that we are here discussing a criterion of rightness of actions, not any method of arriving at a correct moral decision (the distinction was discussed in Chapter 3).

By classical 'hedonistic' utilitarianism, I refer to a theory according to which the improvement of a situation is measured in hedonistic terms. What does that mean? I will not go deeply into moral psychology in general here. It suffices to notice that according to the theory under discussion, sentient creatures can experience or enjoy at different times various different degrees of well-being. On a rough account we distinguish between states that are pleasurable and states that are examples of displeasure. The difference between pleasure and displeasure, or the degree of well-being, is not to be identified with preferences for one state to another. The fact that a certain change would mean increased well-being (or a transition from displeasure to pleasure) may be a reason to prefer its taking place to its not taking place, but the increased well-being is not identical with this preference or with the satisfaction of it. On the contrary, on classical hedonistic utilitarianism the fact that the change means an improvement of the hedonic situation explains why it would be reasonable to want it to take place.[1] Well-being, then, is a felt quality of our experiences. In a sense, it is something 'over and above' (other) emotive, conative and cognitive aspects of the experience; however, it may well be supervenient on such aspects of it. I hold no view in particular about this.

Classical hedonistic utilitarianism presupposes that we can notice (roughly, at least) how we feel and recognise some changes in our hedonic status, and it presupposes also that possible such differences are meaningful. It does not presuppose that, actually, we can always correctly assess whether a certain proposed change would improve our hedonic status, but it does presuppose that, as a matter of fact, it would, or it would not, i.e., it does presuppose that even in such comparisons as we cannot actually make, or in such comparisons as we do make but make incorrectly, there is a fact of the matter.

Hedonistic utilitarianism presupposes furthermore that interpersonal comparisons of well-being (assessed in terms of hedonic status) are possible. We need a common unit when we measure, say, how much the situation of one person is improved when a certain change is brought about, as compared to how much the situation of another person is impoverished.

Do we also need the assumption that there is a natural zero point, a clear-cut and unique difference between positive (pleasure) and negative (displeasure) experiences?[2] I will return to these questions below. As will be seen, in simple kinds of situation we do not need this extra assumption. However, in more complicated situations we do need it.

According to the criterion of rightness, a particular (concrete) action is right if, and only if, there is no other way the agent who performed it could have acted, such that, had he or she done so, the world, on the whole, would have been better. If possible, what makes the world better or worse should be spelled out in purely empirical terms.

If only one sentient being is affected by the action, then the action is right if, and only if, there was no way the agent could have brought about a better situation for this sentient being. Whether the world is better or worse is a function of the situation of individual sentient beings.

If more than one sentient being is affected by the decision, but still a definite number of sentient beings (new sentient beings do not come into existence), then we compare the welfare differences (increments are counted as positive and decrements as negative) for each sentient being between the two states of affairs brought about by the two possible courses of action that we want to consider, and form a sum of these differences. If the agent could have acted differently in such a way that, had he or she done so, this sum of value differences would have been positive, then the action is wrong. If no such possibility exists, then the action is right.

Now, can these presuppositions be satisfied? Do our experiences exhibit any such thing as hedonic tone? And if they do, where do we find the unit which makes possible the kinds of comparison that we want to make?

I discuss these two problems in order.

Hedonic tone

It has sometimes been denied that our experiences exhibit any one phenomenal quality, a hedonic tone. Derek Parfit writes, for example:

> *Narrow Hedonists* assume, falsely, that pleasure and pain are two distinctive kinds of experience. Compare the pleasures of satisfying an intensive thirst or lust, listening to music, solving an intellectual problem, reading a tragedy, and knowing that one's child is happy. These various experiences do not contain any distinctive common quality.[3]

This is reminiscent of James Griffin, who wrote:

> The trouble with thinking of utility as *one* kind of mental state is that we cannot find any one state in all that we regard as having utility – eating, reading, working, creating, helping. What one mental state runs through them all in virtue of which we rank them as we do?[4]

It might appear from this quotation from Griffin that, according to hedonism, activities such as eating (in general), or reading (in general), or working (in general), or creating (in general), or helping (in general) have each one hedonic tone, and that it is in virtue of the tone of each activity that we rank them (in relation to each other). If this is how Griffin conceives of classical hedonism, then his conception is mistaken. From the point of view of classical hedonism, there exists no ranking of these activities. The classical hedonistic point is rather that each instance of them has a hedonic tone. Which one? Well, each instance has the hedonic tone it has. According to classical hedonism, each experience of mine has a hedonic tone; it has the hedonic tone it has. It is in virtue of this tone that we can (sometimes) say that the change from one mental state to another means an improvement, is of no importance, or is for the worse. This seems to be denied by Parfit. However, he states no argument in defence of his rejection of 'narrow hedonism'. I suppose he would claim that he is not aware of any hedonic tone. How can I convince him that the tone is there? How can I make him aware of it? How do I become aware of it?

I become aware of this tone when I realise that my hedonic situation actually changes, or might change; I realise that it changes, or might change, for the better or for the worse. I notice that earlier it had one hedonic tone, now it has another (or I notice that now it has a certain hedonic tone, later on it might come to have another).

I find it difficult to understand how this can be questioned. As a matter of fact, I feel inclined to think that what the critics of classical hedonism, such as Parfit and Griffin, have really been concerned about (or should really have been concerned about) is not the existential claim that our experiences exhibit hedonic tone, for they too must be aware of that, but rather something else. Here are some guesses at what could be the actual target of their criticism.

First of all, the target could be a much too simplistic account of the fact that our experiences have hedonic tone, attributed to classical hedonism. What the critics have wanted to protest against are the epistemological claims attributed to classical hedonists that we can always know the exact hedonic nature of each experience of ours, that we can always tell of two experiences (of our own) which one is most pleasing, and so forth. This criticism is well taken in relation to some versions of classical hedonism. As we shall see below, however, on classical hedonism in its most plausible form, the criticism is wide of the mark. According to classical hedonism in its most plausible form, we often go wrong in these kinds of judgement.

Or, secondly, these critics may really have objected to the normative claim that hedonic tone is all that matters. This claim is not only consistent with the assumption that experiences exhibit a hedonic tone, it presupposes that the hedonic tone in question exists.

Or, finally, they may have wanted to claim that sometimes people do not prefer more pleasure to less. People rank mental states on grounds other than how they feel. This seems to be the point when Griffin, after the passage just quoted, goes on to say:

> Think of the following case. At the very end of his life, Freud, ill and in pain, refused drugs except aspirin. 'I prefer', he said, 'to think in torment than not to be able to think clearly.' But can we find a single feeling or mental state present in both of Freud's options in virtue of which he ranked them as he did? The truth seems, rather, that often we just rank options, *period*.[5]

But hedonists need not deny that people sometimes rank mental states on grounds other than how they feel. Of course they do. This does not mean that hedonism is a confused or even mistaken view. It means only that not everyone is a hedonist. This should come as no surprise to a hedonist.

This being said, I turn now to the question of whether we can find the hedonistic unit we need in our intra- and interpersonal comparisons of well-being.

The least noticeable difference

The economist Edgeworth has suggested an answer to this question, well in line with the way Bentham seems to have conceived of his hedonistic theory.[6] Edgeworth is on the right track, I conjecture. However, his solution needs some refinement, in order to yield the most plausible version of classical hedonistic utilitarianism. Let me first explain his solution and then explain how it could be refined.

Edgeworth defines a unit in terms of which we can assess how much a certain change would improve or worsen the situation of a sentient being: 'Utility, as Professor Jevons says, has two dimensions: intensity and time. The unit in each dimension is the just perceivable increment.'[7]

In order to simplify, let us consider only one sentient being and one possible change. If no change is brought about, the sentient being stays in state A. If the change is brought about, the sentient being is instead in state B. Suppose that this means an improvement. How much of an improvement would the change mean? I take it that Edgeworth suggests roughly the following way of reaching an answer to this question. When assessing how much of a difference to the well-being of a certain sentient being a certain change would make, for each moment (where a 'moment' is taken to be a very short, just noticeable period of time)[8] after the change is brought about, we count the number of just noticeable possible changes existing for this sentient being between the state brought about by the change and the original state (if the change is an increase, i.e., a change for the better, the number is positive; if the change is for the worse, the number is negative; if no change is noticed, the change is, from the point of view of well-being, indifferent). If we please, we may call what we are then counting hedonistic atoms, or 'hedons'. Eventually we sum all these hedons. This sum is a measure of how much this change would better or worsen the situation of this sentient being. Or, as Edgeworth puts it, 'a mass of utility, "a lot of pleasure", is greater than another when it has more intensity–time–number units.'[9]

In the example, then, we divide the time after the change has taken place in brief moments, count the just noticeable possible changes from the original state to the one brought about by the change (the hedons) for each moment, and sum over the entire time for which any difference between the two states exists.

According to Edgeworth, all just noticeable differences are 'equitable'. This is true when we make comparisons both intrapersonally and interpersonally. Or, as Edgeworth puts it: 'Just perceivable increments of pleasure, of all pleasures for all persons, are equitable.'[10]

Two possible complications should be noted. One of them is as follows: there may exist more than one way of changing the situation from something similar to one state to something similar to another state. Various different ways of doing this may involve different numbers of just noticeable possible changes. I suggest that the relevant number is the maximum number, i.e., the number measuring the largest number of such levels possible in the situation. The argument for this suggestion will be stated below.[11]

The other possible complication is that while a certain actual time interval may be divided into, say, n moments, an alternative situation, during the same time interval, may be divided into, say, m moments, where m is different from n. The proper hedonistic utilitarian solution to this problem is, it seems to me, to concede that there may be two possible grounds for one state being better than another. One possible ground is that, in terms of well-being, the change from one state to the other would mean an improvement in intensity. The other possible ground is that while, from the point of view of intensity of well-being, there is no noticeable difference between the two states, one of them can be divided into more moments than the other (in the situation, we are more sensitive to time), which means, precisely, that it contains more hedons than the other. Felt time (subjective time), not physical time (objective time), is what matters to the utilitarian calculus. I know of no hedonistic utilitarian who has explicitly stated this consequence of the theory besides Edgeworth, who does so in passing (cf. the quotation above), but I find it congenial to the spirit of hedonistic utilitarianism and, moreover, morally quite plausible.

The idea that felt time, not physical time, is what matters morally is consistent with the possibility that some of our best experiences involve a loss of the sense of the passage of time. And it is consistent with the fact that we may find an experience seemingly endless when it is highly unpleasant. When during a brief moment of physical time we have a very rich experience, where we make fine discriminations, we may come to think of this precisely as a lack of the sense of the passage of (physical) time. Such brief moments, however, in spite of their brevity, are of high (positive or negative) value to us.

To add just one more example. The (physically) brief last moment of a drowning person, when her or his whole life opens up in a flash, may be most precious to her or him.

If many people are affected by a certain change, we make sums of hedons for all sentient beings affected by it and sum these sums of hedons. If the sum of all these sums of hedons is positive, the change would mean an improvement. If we were to act so that such an improvement was possible, then our action would be wrong. If no such improvement is possible, then our action is right.

Why ought we to conceive of well-being in terms of hedons? Why ought we to say that, when there exist more than one way of changing the situation from something similar to one state to something similar to another state, the maximum number of such changes is what matters? There exists a discussion about these questions but, in the final analysis, it seems to be the case that the hedonistic utilitarian option for hedons, rather than some other possible idea, such as the stipulation that the worst possible state, or best possible state, for each sentient being is of equal worth, rests on a normative stipulation.

In some cases, no comparisons of well-being other than these are presupposed by classical hedonistic utilitarianism. There are exceptions to this, however, and I will discuss them below.

Pleasure and displeasure

Thus far I have taken it for granted that a definite number of persons (or, rather, of sentient beings) are affected by a proposed change. This assumption is not realistic. In some cases, when deciding what we ought to do, we have to acknowledge that our various possible actions have consequences for who will live (ever, or for how long) and who will die (when). In those circumstances we cannot assess increments and decrements of well-being in the manner indicated above. In order to tell whether, for me, it would mean an improvement if, say, I dropped dead right now, we must know whether the way I feel now is better or worse than the way it feels to be dead, i.e., we need to know whether the way I feel now is better or worse than not feeling anything at all.

The hedonistic solution to this problem is to ask whether the state I am in now, on the whole, is a state of well-being (with, on balance, more pleasure than displeasure) rather than a state of ill-being (with, on balance, more displeasure than pleasure). If I am in a state of well-being which would go on for the rest of my life it would be a change for the worse to die; if I am in a state of ill-being which would go on for the rest of my life it would be a change for the better to die.

The line between pleasure and displeasure we have to draw on a phenomenalistic basis. It is assumed by classical hedonists that the line is something we can be aware of. This is how Henry Sidgwick used to argue. He claimed that 'we are led to the assumption of a hedonistic zero, or perfectly neutral feeling, as a point from which the positive quantity of pleasures may be measured', and he went on to say that 'we must therefore conceive, as at least ideally possible, a point of transition in consciousness at which we pass from the positive to the negative.'[12] From the point of view of value, he identified this transition point with the state of unconsciousness, or of not existing at all.

The identification from the point of view of value, however, of being dead, or of not existing in a conscious way, with the line between pleasure and pain must rest on a normative stipulation. It is not based on introspection. It has seemed only natural for classical hedonists to make it and, yet, for all that, it represents nothing more robust than a mere stipulation.

Hesitantly I accept this stipulation. If we accept that there is a sharp line between lives that are and lives that are not worth living, and if we accept Sidgwick's suggestion about where this line is, then we are stuck, of course, with what has been called by Derek Parfit the repugnant conclusion, i.e., the conclusion that, in some possible circumstances, we ought if possible to increase the population even up to the point where the life of each creature living is barely worth living.[13] On classical hedonistic utilitarianism, the loss of value per life lived can be compensated for by the (enormous) number of creatures living lives that are barely worth living.

This is only as it should be. After all, this conclusion was accepted by Sidgwick and it has been taken to be congenial to hedonistic utilitarianism. By many thinkers it has been considered a *reductio* of hedonistic utilitarianism. My impression is that this conclusion is perhaps not so repugnant after all, but that is something to which I will return.[14]

Sorites problems

I have claimed that Edgeworth is on the right track but that his position is in need of some refinement. This is to do with the fact that, if our units when we measure well-being are hedons, it might seem as though we should be stuck with a kind of moral conflict of a 'sorites' kind. The best way to avoid this seems to be to accept that there are not noticeable (or sub-noticeable) changes of well-being as well as noticeable ones. And, if we acknowledge that there are sub-noticeable differences of well-being, we ought to take them too into account in our moral calculations.

The reason that hedonistic utilitarianism may be thought to lead to conflicts of a sorites kind is as follows. Suppose I am allowed to decide how many people should cross a certain lawn. If one crosses the lawn this seems to be better than if no one does. No noticeable damage is done to the lawn and one person gets home faster. If well-being is measured in terms of hedons, then only noticeable differences of well-being seem to matter. Hence, it seems to be better *simpliciter* if one person crosses the lawn than if no one does. However, if I decide that (exactly) one person should cross the lawn I decide wrongly.[15] For two persons crossing the lawn (and getting home faster) is even better than one doing so, and still no noticeable damage has been done to the lawn. However, if I decide that two persons should cross the lawn I decide wrongly. For, if three persons cross the lawn this is not in any noticeable way worse than if two do. However, if I decide that three persons should cross the lawn I definitely decide wrongly. Not only must I conclude that it would be even better if four persons cross the lawn, it is also true (we assume) that if three persons cross the lawn this damages the lawn in a noticeable way, not compared to a situation where two cross it, but compared to the situation where none is allowed to do so. And, since many people enjoy the sight of the lawn (we assume), this would be much worse than if none had crossed it.

In the circumstances, then, it may seem as though, no matter what I decide, I decide wrongly. There always exists a better alternative.

Not noticeable changes of well-being

But is not my example implausible? Must we not say that, even if no one notices any change for the worse when two persons cross the lawn rather than one, there must have been a not noticeable loss of well-being involved in this step, a loss that accrues to each and every one among the persons who enjoy the sight of the lawn? And must we not pay attention also to not noticeable losses of well-being? The sum total of what the spectators lose, even if no one is capable of noticing this, is much greater than the gain the extra person makes when he or she crosses the lawn. We ought to take this accumulated, not noticeable, loss into account.

I think that this is what we ought to do, but this position may well seem at variance with what could be called the 'spirit' of Edgeworth and Bentham, and the position is not without difficulties. Apparently there are both methodological and moral reasons ready to be called forth against it. As a matter of fact, it is often taken for granted that our relevant experiential states must be known to us, since they are 'directly accessible' to us.[16] However, even if my suggestion (that we take sub-noticeable differences of well-being into account) gives rise to problems, the problems pertaining to the alternatives to it seem even worse.

Let me begin with the methodological reasons for rejecting the idea that there exist not noticeable differences of well-being. It may seem that when assessing psychic entities, such as the intensity of feelings, there is no difference between felt and actual qualities. The situation is very different with, say, experienced and real length. Here we have a genuine difference between appearances and realities. No similar distinction applies to psychic entities.

I have endorsed this point elsewhere.[17] However, I have also encountered the following objection to it: it may well be true that, in a sense, there is no difference between perceived and real displeasure or pleasure. However, even if we do have the experiences we have, we may be mistaken as to how we ought to describe or classify them. What I felt a moment ago, I did feel, and what I feel now, I do feel. However, my judgement, based on a comparison between the two, may be mistaken. Even if this is nothing I can notice, there may well exist a (not noticeable) difference between these two mental states. I suppose that this claim could be bolstered by a huge amount of evidence from cognitive psychology. After all, simple introspection seems to yield very unreliable characterisations of what goes on in our heads. It is interesting to note that David Hume seemed already (reluctantly) to have accepted the view that there is some room for mistake when we describe our mental states while entertaining them.[18]

When we bring in several states and several comparisons we may arrive at appropriate measurements of the hedonic qualities of these states. I have earlier rejected this objection but I now accept it. My main reason for rejecting it was really a moral one. I now no longer accept this moral objection.

The moral objection I have in mind is as follows: even if there exist not noticeable improvements or turns for the worse or, at least, even if we can construct such differences, they cannot be of any moral significance. A hedonistic utilitarian ought not to pay any attention to them.[19] This objection is mistaken.

Consider first a situation where one person gets his or her hedonic state worsened for a moment in a just noticeable way, but where each of several people gets his or her hedonic state improved in a not noticeable way. Could this change really be for the better? Clearly, it could mean that the sum total of well-being in the world is maximised, but could it be right to make the change? I think it could. After all, after the change has taken place, there exists more (felt) well-being than existed before it took place. To be sure, the sum total of well-being is not experienced by anyone, but this objection is a general one, often raised against hedonistic utilitarianism. By hedonistic utilitarians it is generally not taken to be decisive. The sum is after all made up of pieces of felt pleasure and displeasure, and this is what matters from a moral point of view, they claim. I concur in this claim. But the same is true of the pieces out of which the sum total in my example is made up.

Secondly, consider a situation where each of a great many people enjoy a not noticeable improvement of her or his hedonic state for a just noticeable moment, while one person gets her or his hedonic state enormously worsened for quite a while (instead of enjoying a happy life she or he experiences a life with torture and imprisonment, a life which she or he would, if possible, end, but which she or he is forced to endure). If the persons who get a not noticeable improvement are only many enough, the sum of extra well-being experienced by them may well be greater than the displeasure experienced by the person who gets her or his situation seriously worsened. Is it not morally absurd to prefer that these persons are given their 'extra', not noticeable amount of well-being, at such a cost for the one person who gets her or his life ruined?

The ultra repugnant conclusion

The conclusion that, in the circumstances, we ought to prefer that these persons are given their 'extra', not noticeable amount of well-being may seem to be the ultimate in 'repugnance', to use Parfit's word. Let me refer to it as 'the ultra repugnant conclusion'.[20]

Must we not give up hedonistic utilitarianism if it leads to the ultra repugnant conclusion? I think not.

What we are facing here are – once again – general difficulties with hedonistic utilitarianism, difficulties the utilitarian is and should be prepared to live with. One difficulty has to do, of course, with problems of distributive justice. Another has to do with the idea in general of making one person suffer for the slight benefit of anyone else. This has by critics of utilitarianism been considered unfair.[21] The special difficulty in relation to the ultra repugnant conclusion is different. It has to do primarily, I conjecture, with our lack of ability in handling in our moral imagination very large numbers. Even a very large sum does not appear very large to us. This lack of imagination on our side does not mean that large numbers do not matter. And the fact that, in the situation, each person who undergoes a certain improvement does not notice this is of no importance. The difference is, after all, a difference in his or her experience.

It should be observed that the change is not noticeable only in the situation. If we bring in additional states for comparison it transpires that the difference is there. We can notice it, indirectly, then. I will return to this point.

Of course, a utilitarian could argue that only noticeable differences matter. Even this view, however, leads to difficulties. If only noticeable differences of well-being matter, then, possibly, there may exist three possible states for a person, A, B and C. When comparing A and B the person notices no difference; when comparing B and C the person notices no difference; but when comparing A and C the person notices a difference (for the worse, let us say). If we accept that the relation of having the same value is transitive, this leads to contradiction. We may perhaps deny the transitivity of the relation of having the same value but, theoretically speaking, this seems to me (now) to be too high a price to pay.

How are we then to measure sub-noticeable differences?[22] If we stick to the interpretation where the relation of having the same value is transitive, we may use the method of introducing 'extra' states for comparison as a means of arriving at a measure of differences in well-being that are, in the situation, not noticeable (which are, that is, indirectly noticeable).

Consider again the situation with three possible states for a person, A, B and C. When comparing A and B the person notices no difference; when comparing B and C the person notices no difference; but when comparing A and C the person notices a difference: C is in a noticeable way worse (directly worse) than A. We conclude, then, that B is indirectly worse than A but indirectly better than C.

Suppose there is also another possible state, B', which satisfies the same requirements. We conclude, again, that B' is indirectly worse than A but indirectly better than C. Which is better of B and B', then? B is indirectly better than B' if, and only if, there exists a state, D, such that B is directly better than D, while B' is not directly better than D, and it is true of all states D that if B' is directly better than D, then so is B.

How many additional sub-noticeable stages, then, are we allowed to introduce? This may vary from case to case. However, my conjecture is that there exist, for each person and each just perceivable interval, a finite number of possible, intermediate, sub-noticeable stages. We stipulate that each of these stages (no matter how many they are) is of equal moral importance.

Notice that on this theory a certain difference is, or is not, noticeable depending on which comparisons we allow. If, in a situation, there exists a not noticeable difference with respect to well-being between the states A and B, we can always bring this difference to the surface by taking additional (possible) states into consideration, such as a state C, which is directly better than A, i.e., better in a noticeable way, but which is not directly better than B, i.e., better than B in any noticeable way. When C is taken into consideration we notice, indirectly, a difference between A and B. Strictly speaking, therefore, and in the present context, the commonly used terms 'not noticeable' and 'sub-noticeable' differences are misnomers. I will not try to change our habits of speaking, but, personally, I would prefer to speak of differences that are 'only indirectly noticeable'.

Sven Danielsson, who has defended the idea that there exist sub-noticeable differences of well-being and that these differences are morally important, has pointed out that the view that only (directly) noticeable differences matter morally leads to problems with the Pareto principle.[23] According to the Pareto principle, if x is better than y for some person, and there is no one for whom x is worse than y, then x is better than y. This principle, together with the classical hedonistic utilitarian doctrine, yields examples of cyclic value orderings.

To see that it does so, consider a situation where the only noticeable differences between x, y and z are that x is better than y for person A, y is better than z for person B, and z is better than x for person C. Then x is better than y, y is better than z, and z is better than x, *simpliciter*. If these are our only options, no matter which of the states we bring into existence, we act wrongly.

These are consequences we may endorse, if we give up even the idea that the relation of being 'better than' is transitive, but once again, theoretically speaking, this seems to be too high a price to pay.

Are there even smaller differences of well-being?

I have taken it for granted that, when sub-noticeable differences exist, they can in principle be brought to the surface by bringing in further comparisons, where the sub-noticeable differences become indirectly noticeable. Can we be sure that this is always possible? Or are there even finer discriminations there to be made?

Well, if there are such discriminations, we have to take them into moral account. We do not want to countenance intransitivities. However, I doubt that such finer distinctions exist. If some differences are there, it should always be possible, it seems to me, to bring them to the fore by constructing a better experience machine.[24]

Now, this is an empirical claim, so it should really be put to an empirical test. However, even though this possibility of deciding the matter through an experiment exists in principle, it will not work in practice. When the test fails, it is always possible to complain that the reason that the sub-noticeable differences of well-being do not surface as indirectly noticeable must have something to do with the experience machine used. If only a better machine were constructed, the differences would surface, one could claim.

My conjecture is that all the differences there are can in principle be brought to the fore, if only the experience machine is sufficiently finely tuned to its task. This has to remain a conjecture, however. No final proof is within reach in this area.

The unit

Sub-noticeable (or indirectly noticeable) differences of well-being are of moral importance, then. Even if our acknowledging them leads us all the way to the ultra repugnant conclusion, we should take them into account in our moral calculations. However, there is more than one way that we can do that.

One way of taking sub-noticeable differences of well-being into account would be to stick to Edgeworth's proposal that our unit is a just noticeable difference of well-being.[25] If such a unit can be divided into, say, five sub-noticeable differences of well-being, then the value of each sub-noticeable transition is one fifth (of the unit). Another way of taking sub-noticeable differences of well-being into account would be to take them as our unit.

In either case, our decision must be based on a normative assumption. I have oscillated between these two positions, but comments from both Donald Regan and Michael R. DePaul on earlier drafts of this chapter have convinced me that the latter line should be taken.

The reason that we should resist the former line is as follows. When we do pay special interest to differences that a person can notice (in the way Edgeworth does), then it would be arbitrary to limit this to the differences that the person can directly discriminate, ignoring the sub-noticeable differences we can infer on the basis of the other discriminations the person can make. As a matter of fact, this would not only be arbitrary, it would be unfair. Suppose that there are two persons, S and S#, and that both undergo a certain change for the better. To S, this change is just noticeable. However, S# notices two changes for the better. Upon closer examination it transpires that S has undergone two sub-noticeable changes of well-being in the process, while S# has undergone none. In the circumstances, would we not want to say that while S# noticed all the changes that took place S did not? Would we not like to say that both S and S# have undergone the same improvement of their situation? Would we not like to say that the fact that, in the situation, S did not (directly) notice one change should not be counted against her or him? I think we would. After all, even the change that S did not notice was a real change (to her or him).

Against both these lines it could be objected, of course, that it is unfair that those who have fine discriminatory capacities should count for more, in our moral calculations, than those with less fine ones. This has been considered a *reductio* of hedonistic utilitarianism.[26] However, this seems to be a consequence that classical hedonistic utilitarians are prepared willingly to acknowledge. An objection to this stipulation seems to be an objection to hedonistic utilitarianism as such. Furthermore, it should be noticed that, if sub-noticeable differences of well-being are taken into full account, then it is not quite true that classical hedonistic utilitarianism is biased against people with poor discriminatory capacities. It is rather biased against people with a poor sensibility. This is different and, indeed, not at all objectionable if, in the final analysis, pleasure and displeasure are what really matter.

The upshot of this, then, would be the following improvement on Edgeworth's position: the unit in our utilitarian calculus is not really the smallest just noticeable difference of well-being, but the smallest sub-noticeable difference of well-being, the one that cannot be further sub-divided.

If this stipulation be accepted, and if it be accepted that it is subjective rather than objective time that is relevant to utilitarian calculations, then it seems that considerations similar to those regarding sub-noticeable differences in well-being should lead us to suppose also that there can be sub-noticeable increments of subjective time. Such increments are relevant to utilitarian calculations in the same way as sub-noticeable increments of well-being are.

Conclusion

Edgeworth and Bentham seem not to have found interpersonal comparisons of well-being problematic. The reason, of course, is that once we have recourse to the idea of hedons these interpersonal comparisons do make sense, at least theoretically.

A complication with this measurement is that it is ambiguous. It is supposed to be a measurement in two dimensions, intensity and time. However, there are two possible ways of conceiving of time, as physical and as felt. I have argued that, in the most plausible interpretation, the classical utilitarian formula should be based on felt time rather than on physical time.

Another complication with the measurement is that it is at variance with the ambition of stating a strictly empirical criterion of rightness. The adoption of the measurement in terms of the smallest sub-noticeable differences is based on a normative assumption. There is a rationale behind this, however. If there is a real increment of well-being, we should take it fully into account in our moral calculations, irrespective of whether it is directly noticed by the person experiencing it, or only indirectly noticeable (to us, who infer its existence). Our calculations should not be biased against people who are poor judges of their own (real) mental states.

If we accept that sub-noticeable differences of well-being are morally important, and if we take the smallest sub-noticeable difference as our unit in our moral calculations (and I have argued that these are reasonable moves to make for a classical utilitarian), then we are stuck with what I have called the ultra repugnant conclusion. This is the conclusion that, under very special possible circumstances, it would be right to torture one person in order to make sure that each of an enormous number of people, who all live very good lives indeed, experiences for a brief moment a not noticeable improvement of his or her situation.

This is an unsought conclusion, but, even in the light of it, an acceptance of classical hedonistic utilitarianism for its overall plausibility can be rationally sustained.

Notes

1 My view could be called the pure (hedonistic) view. There is a less pure (hedonistic) view, which allows that pleasure and displeasure are a matter of a desire on the part of the person having the experience. If she or he wants to go on having it, she or he is having a pleasant experience; if she or he wants to get out of it, she or he is having an unpleasant experience. And the stronger the desire to go on with it, the more pleasurable is the experience. I think that, while I do hold the pure view, I could as well have stated my argument in terms of the less pure view. I owe this observation to Derek Parfit.

2 Following William P. Alston in 'Pleasure' I will use the term 'displeasure' rather than 'pain', since the latter suggests too narrow a conception, where the term stands for a bodily sensation. Probably, having bodily sensations of pain is, in most cases, for most persons, unpleasant. The displeasure then felt is, however, something over and above the mere bodily sensation.

3 D. Parfit, *Reasons and Persons*, p. 493.

4 J. Griffin, *Well-being*, p. 8.

5 Griffin, *Well-being*, p. 8.

6 According to Bentham, 'the degree of intensity possessed by that pleasure which is the faintest of any that can be distinguished to be pleasure, may be represented by unity: such a degree of intensity is in every day's experience.' Cf. J. Bentham, 'Value of a Pain or Pleasure'. According to Arrow, the idea goes back to a paper presented by Jean-Charles de Borda in 1770. I owe my historical references to Lars Bergström, 'Interpersonal Utility Comparisons'. He does not refer to Bentham, however.

7 F. Y. Edgeworth, *Mathematical Psychics*, p. 7.

8 It seems to be a psychological fact that it takes some time to notice what kind of psychological state one is in, or to notice a change in one's psychological state. The least such (physical) time, in a situation, constitutes a moment.

9 Edgeworth, *Mathematical Psychics*, p. 8.

10 Edgeworth, *Mathematical Psychics*, p. 60.

11 In order to make this idea operational, we would need to have recourse to something like the 'pleasure machine' suggested by J. J. C. Smart in Smart and B. Williams (eds), *Utilitarianism: For and Against*, p. 19.

12 Sidgwick, *The Methods of Ethics*, p. 124.

13 Sidgwick made this claim: cf. *The Methods of Ethics*, p. 415. It has been elaborated on by Derek Parfit: cf. *Reasons and Persons*. It was Parfit who invented the invective 'the repugnant conclusion'.

14 I have argued elsewhere that it is not so repugnant: see my 'Who are the Beneficiaries?'. I return to the question at the end of this chapter and, more thoroughly, in Ch. 10.

15 Cf. my 'The Morality of Collective Actions', where I mistakenly though only tentatively defend this view.

16 A recent statement of this position is given by Thomas M. Scanlon in 'The Moral Basis of Interpersonal Comparisons'. He there writes: 'If experientialism is correct, we can easily assess the quality of our own lives at a given moment, because the

presence or absence of the relevant states of consciousness is directly accessible to us' (p. 21). And R. M. Hare has written in *Moral Thinking* that 'if I am suffering to a certain degree or with a certain intensity, I must know that I am suffering to that degree and with that intensity, and vice versa' (p. 93). As I argue below, this view is mistaken.

17 Cf. my 'The Morality of Collective Actions'.

18 Cf. Book II, Part I, Section I, of D. Hume, *A Treatise of Human Nature*, where he writes: 'The raptures of poetry and music frequently rise to the greatest height; while those other impressions, properly call'd *passions*, may decay into so soft an emotion, as to become, in a manner, imperceptible' (p. 276).

19 This is the view of Lars Bergström, who writes, in 'Interpersonal Utility Comparisons', that 'the utilitarian goal is to increase the well-being of sentient creatures as much as possible. Of course, an increase will have to be noticeable to count for something. If it is not noticeable, the utilitarian would not count it as an increase at all' (p. 30).

20 Actually, this name for the conclusion was suggested to me by Derek Parfit.

21 The most elaborate defence of this claim, which I reject, is in Ragnar Ohlsson's *The Moral Import of Evil*. Ohlsson defends the principle (Ohlsson's principle) that it is never right to sacrifice one happy person (to kill or degrade or torture him or her) in order to make no matter how many already very happy persons even more happy.

22 Donald Regan has made me aware of these problems.

23 Sven Danielsson takes it for granted that the relation of 'better than' is transitive, and he can then claim that the idea that only noticeable differences matter is inconsistent with the Pareto principle. His argument is put forward in 'Hur man inte kan mäta välmåga' ('How One Cannot Measure Well-being').

24 The objection that there may exist sub-noticeable difference of well-being that are not even indirectly noticeable has been made by Folke Tersman and Jörgen Aasa, independently of each other.

25 The same line has been taken, more recently, by Yew-Kwang Ng in 'Bentham or Bergson? Finite Sensibility, Utility Functions and Social Welfare Functions'.

26 Cf. Kenneth Arrow's *Social Choice and Individual Values*, pp. 117–18, about this. A problem with Arrow's argument, which is criticised both in Ng, 'Bentham or Bergson?', and in Bergström, 'Interpersonal Utility Comparisons', is that it is cast in terms of preferences. If, instead, we cast it in terms of well-being, it is less convincing.

Chapter 6

Against preferentialism

Quite a few economists and philosophers have recently defended the view that what has intrinsic value is satisfaction of preferences – the more the better. What gives meaning to a life, what makes a life worth living, is to have one's way in affairs that matter to oneself. This is the point of departure not only for what has been called preference utilitarianism (according to which preference satisfaction is the thing that should be maximised) but also for the branch of economics called neo-classical welfare economics (defining efficiency in terms of preference satisfaction and Pareto optimality).[1]

I will not go deeply into the question of what a preference is. My own opinion is that the notion of a preference is theoretical. We impute preferences to persons on the basis of some kind of evidence, but this evidence may well under-determine the imputation as such. In particular, I do not believe that preferences are identical with (hypothetical) choices, even if information about (hypothetical) choices is the paramount kind of evidence upon which we can base our imputations of preferences to a person. And no matter how exactly we conceive of preferences, as theoretical entities or otherwise, I think we should admit that preferences can explain choices, so preferences and choices are not identical. We ought to admit also that preferences are not only distinct from (hypothetical) choices (which they can explain), they are also distinct from values. I will return to this important point below.

I will call the view that the more preference satisfaction (for a person) the better (for this person) 'preferentialism'. Preferentialism is a comparatively popular evaluative view nowadays among those thinkers who are prepared to take consequentialism seriously. But is it a plausible moral (evaluative) view? My thesis is that it is not. I will try to show first of all that preferentialism is an inherently unstable position and, secondly, that a strong argument tells against its acceptability (what I will refer to as the argument from explanatory impotence).

Welfare economy and preferentialism

Welfare economists often make ambiguous statements about preferentialism, i.e., about their value assumption. Quite a few of them try to avoid the value problem altogether. They simply deny that their theory contains any value assumption.[2] Others claim that this value assumption is so weak that it could hardly be problematic.[3] Yet others claim that the value assumption is made not by them but by the economic agents themselves. The idea behind this claim is that 'The more satisfaction of preferences the better' follows from a general and very plausible anti-paternalist view. 'Who can know better than the economic agent himself or herself what is good for him or her?' is the rhetorical question posed. The economist J. C. Harsanyi goes a step further. According to Harsanyi, the view that a person could be mistaken about what is good for him or her is confused:

> in deciding what is good and what is bad for a given individual, the ultimate criterion can only be his own wants and his own preferences. To be sure . . . a person may irrationally want something which is very 'bad for him'. But, it seems to me, the only way we can make sense of such a statement is to interpret it as a claim to the effect that, in some appropriate sense, his own preferences at some deeper level are inconsistent with what he is now trying to achieve.[4]

The question 'Who can know better than the economic agent . . .?' has often been based on a tacit assumption of moral irrealism. The argument is roughly the following: if there is no objectively correct answer to the question of what is good for an individual, what, then, is more plausible than having him or her decide this for himself or herself? I think we should resist this line of argument, however.

Consider moral irrealism first. Our belief in moral realism may well be of some consequence for other beliefs we have, it may render moral argument pointless, and so forth, but moral irrealism does not on its own imply either that paternalism or anti-paternalism is a plausible moral view. Moral irrealism is neutral between these and other moral outlooks. We cannot deduce a moral principle from a metaethical theory. I have discussed this elsewhere and will not pursue the matter any further in the present context.[5]

The accusation that the view that a person need not know what is good for him or her must be based on paternalism is false. And it is false in a demagogic fashion. A 'paternalist' is a person who is prepared to take decisions on the behalf of another person, against his or her will, in his or her own best interest. Those who share my view that people may go wrong as to what is good for them can be paternalists, but they can equally well be anti-paternalists. It is important to distinguish two questions here: on the one hand, what is good for a person and, on the other hand, who is to decide what he or she should get. A person who believes that some other person is often mistaken about his own true interests may hesitate to take decisions on his behalf. For example, she may simply suspect that the other person will dislike her interference and, for that reason, abstain from it. Yet, for all that, she may retain her own opinion about what is good for the other person. Moreover, even a person who claims that someone else may be mistaken about his own true interests may herself reject the claim that she knows this any better.

Harsanyi must be wrong, moreover, when he claims that we cannot even understand a theory according to which people can be mistaken about what is good for them. As a matter of fact, I have already, in the previous chapter, presented such a theory. I do not say that, upon critical examination, everyone must find this theory convincing. On the contrary, many people tend to find it unacceptable. But the possibility of having a discussion about this matter indicates that it is real, i.e., that the theory is at least comprehensible. Preferences and values are distinct entities.

Finally, what about the claim that it is a weak and hence not a controversial value assumption that the more satisfaction of preferences the better? Now, even if many contemporary thinkers seem to share this assumption, it is a value assumption proper. And it is an untenable value assumption, or so I will argue, at any rate. Hence preferentialism is controversial.

The value of preference satisfaction

Those who argue that the more satisfaction of preferences the better (preferentialism) rarely defend the thesis without qualifications. Mainly, two techniques have been used to qualify the thesis and to sort out those preferences that matter to a moral assessment. I will refer to these techniques or strategies as 'idealisation' and 'elimination' respectively. According to the strategy of idealisation, what should be satisfied are not our actual preferences, but the preferences we would have had if certain conditions had been fulfilled. According to the eliminative strategy, some of our actual preferences should simply be neglected; their satisfaction does not add to the welfare of a person.

Idealisation

Some idealisation is present even in descriptive economic theory. In order to be able to impute preferences to a person we must assume that her or his choices reflect preferences that are 'rational', at least in the weak sense that they are transitive, and we have to assume some stability over time in her or his preferences (reflected in her or his manner of choice). Otherwise we would be completely at a loss when it comes to deciding what her or his preferences are. But sometimes it is difficult to find a transitive pattern in the choices of a person. We solve the problem by assuming that her or his true preferences are not revealed in some of her or his choices. These choices are considered irrational.

Those who defend preferentialism often go a step further. According to J. C. Harsanyi, for example, the preferences to be satisfied are only the preferences a person would have 'if he had all the relevant factual information, always reasoned with the greatest possible care, and were in a state of mind most conducive to rational choice'.[6] And the moral philosopher Richard Brandt is even more radical in his idealisation. According to Brandt, the preferences to be satisfied are the preferences a person would hold on to after having successfully gone through 'cognitive psychotherapy'.[7]

Furthermore, some of our preferences we gladly and willingly acknowledge. But there are others that we would really like to get rid of if we could. We have preferences about our own preferences. How are these to be accounted for by the preferentialist? The most plausible solution is perhaps only to pay attention to the preferences we welcome and accept.

Most people have a certain time bias in their preferences. Most people prefer a lesser satisfaction now to a greater satisfaction tomorrow, it has been maintained. And there are other kinds of time bias. Are these irrational? If so, why? Should we perhaps pay equal respect to all preferences, present and future ones? But where does that leave our past preferences? Few are prepared to argue that the satisfaction of preferences we no longer hold increases our welfare. However, if we discount past preferences, why not discount future ones as well? But this view seems absurd. Is there a way out of this problem? I believe there is. The solution is as follows.

A person who wants his or her life to go (overall) as well as possible ought to be impartial to time. He or she ought to pay equal respect to all his or her preferences. There should be no time bias at all. However, when paying equal respect to preferences, irrespective of when they occur, the person ought only to consider such preferences as are held when they can be satisfied. R. M. Hare has introduced the terminology 'now for now' and 'then for then', when discussing this problem.[8] In his terms, if we ought to consider preferences at all (which I will argue that we should not do), we ought to consider our preferences now for now and our preferences then for then. I will call the brand of preferentialism in question the theory of simultaneous satisfaction of preferences.

There are many obvious advantages with this theory. On it, we get an explanation (a rationalisation) of the fact that we tend to discard past preferences that we no longer hold but that could in principle be satisfied now. We (reasonably) disregard them, not because they are past, but because while we held them we could not satisfy them, and when we can satisfy them we no longer hold them.

If there were a possibility open to us through our actions today to secure (through backward causation) our having our past preferences satisfied when we still held them, then, on this theory, we should take them into account. This is as it should be.

As a matter of fact, there exists a class of preferences such that, by performing an action after we have given these preferences up, we can see to it that they were satisfied when we held them. I am thinking of preferences for living in a world where, later on, one thing happens rather than something else. One example of this would be if I wish (now) to live in a world where (somewhat later on) I die young. Suppose I give up this preference later on. Does it still give me a reason for killing myself, before it is too late? On the theory of simultaneous satisfaction of preferences it does. By killing myself later on I see to it that, while I wanted to live in a world where I died young, I did. This is not to say, of course, that, necessarily, this reason cannot be outweighed by other reasons (for staying alive).[9]

The theory of simultaneous satisfaction of preferences also explains why we may disregard some future preferences. I am thinking of future preferences that we will in an even further future give up, before they can be satisfied. On the theory under consideration we need not regard them in spite of the fact that they are future. And the reason is that, when we can satisfy them, we will no longer hold them.

Is it an objection to the theory of simultaneous satisfaction of preferences that it allows us normally to disregard the last wishes of a dying person? I think this tells in favour of it.[10] And yet, for all that, there exists a kind of preference that is relevant, according to the theory of simultaneous satisfaction of preferences, even after a person's death. I am thinking of the preference of a person who wanted, while alive, to live in a world where, after she or he is dead, her or his wishes are respected.[11] But it is only as it should be, it seems to me, that such preferences, if they exist, and if preferentialism is a plausible theory (which I doubt), ought to be respected.

Another objection to the theory of simultaneous satisfaction of preferences is that it expresses a hedonistic bias. On hedonism it is natural only to be interested in satisfaction of preferences when they are actually upheld. For, on hedonism, the point in satisfying preferences is that it is pleasant to have one's preferences satisfied. And it is not pleasant to have preferences satisfied once one has given them up. However, it seems to me that the theory of simultaneous satisfaction of preferences has independent credibility. So, if hedonism makes the theory plausible, which, to some extent it does, then this is not something that should count against the theory; rather, it is something that should count in favour of hedonism.

A special problem for preferentialism in general and neo-classical welfare economics in particular is that it seems difficult to compare the strengths of preferences of separate people. Mainstream economic theory denies that interpersonal comparisons between intensities of preferences are possible or even meaningful. If such comparisons are impossible, however, it is difficult to see that comparisons between past, present and future preferences of a single person fare any better. My future self is not much more readily accessible to examination now than your present self. As a matter of fact, it seems to be less accessible to examination now. It is not much easier to tell what my preferences would be if I could get rid of some preferences that I now want to get rid of.

Elimination

Let me now turn to examples of elimination. The least controversial kind of elimination was already present in J. S. Mill. Richard Brandt and the economist and philosopher Amartya Sen have followed suit. The preferences which it is important should be satisfied for a person's welfare are only his or her self-regarding ones, i.e., his or her preferences for how his or her own life goes. In addition to these, most people also have preferences about other persons' well-being and about general states of affairs; they have moral ideals or commitments. On the view under consideration, the satisfaction of preferences of the latter kind does not add to the welfare of a person having them.

Here is a simple example: suppose that a married woman considers it her duty to wash her husband's laundry and, consequently, prefers doing this to not doing it. When she does wash her husband's laundry she probably adds to the welfare of her husband, but not to her own, according to the view under consideration. On the other hand, if she is of a masochist bent and receives pleasure from doing her husband's laundry and, because of this, prefers doing this to not doing it, then her well-being is increased when she does, on the view under consideration. Then her preference is self-regarding after all. However, I suppose Brandt would want to ask whether this masochist bent of hers could really survive 'cognitive psychotherapy'. If not, if it were to be undermined by a recognition of what has caused it, then, according to Brandt, her doing the laundry does not, after all, increase her welfare.

More controversial forms of elimination are suggested by Harsanyi. From the class of true preferences he excludes anti-social preferences, such as sadism, envy, resentment and malice.[12] And Amartya Sen goes even a step further when he questions whether we add to a person's welfare when the person has his or her way in matters that are none of his or her business. To use an example which is very much up to date as this is being written, the welfare of fundamentalist Muslims is not increased by their stopping people from reading Salman Rushdie's book *The Satanic Verses*.[13]

What has now been said in no way exhausts the literature about how to idealise or eliminate preferences in order to render it plausible to say that the more satisfaction the better (preferentialism), but enough has been said for the purposes of the present context. Two general observations about the strategies of idealisation and elimination could be made.

First of all, unless some such strategy is implemented, it seems obvious that the view that the more satisfaction of preferences the better is not tenable. At least some of these strategies meet real difficulties for preferentialism. Different thinkers would disagree about exactly which are the real difficulties, of course, but I think no one can seriously say that none is. Personally I find it clear that at least we must eliminate other-regarding preferences, if we want to hold on with any plausibility to the view that the more satisfaction of preferences the better.

Secondly, the need for, and the form of, the strategies of idealisation and elimination reveal a kind of instability inherent in preferentialism. This instability suggests that the theory, even in its most attractive version (no matter which this is), is not tenable. We can sense this instability if we confront preferentialism with plausible alternative moral (evaluative) theories and investigate how idealisation and elimination relate to these.

Which are the alternatives to preferentialism? Setting to one side evaluative idealism (the evaluative part of what G. E. Moore called 'ideal utilitarianism', which will be discussed in Chapter 8), these alternatives are, on the one hand, classical welfare theory, i.e., hedonism, and, on the other hand, perfectionism. Both these theories are alike in that (like preferentialism) they are individualistic (this is what distinguishes them from evaluative idealism, which is an impersonal view of intrinsic value), but they give competing answers to the question of what makes a life worth living (for the person living it). Both hedonism and perfectionism are inconsistent with preferentialism in a strict sense, but both doctrines represent limits which some of the most plausible strategies of idealisation and elimination, when applied to preferentialism, tend to reach (asymptotically, so to speak). In the following I will try to substantiate this claim. If it is correct, then preferentialism is an unstable position.

Let me now briefly recapitulate hedonism and state the doctrine of perfectionism.

Hedonism

Classical hedonism has been stated in Chapter 5 of this book and I have little to add to that statement in the present chapter. On hedonism, how well a person's life goes is dependent on a felt quality of the life, on how this life is experienced from the 'inside'. The better it feels, the better it is.

It is how the life actually feels that matters, not what attitude towards it the person herself or himself takes up. Even if she or he does not want to live a pleasurable life (even if she or he prefers to live a different kind of life), a life of pleasure is what is good for her or him.

In Chapter 5 we have seen that there may exist sub-noticeable differences of felt well-being. Those that actually exist are what matter to a moral (an evaluative) assessment of a person's life, not the differences she or he happens to notice.

It should be noted that, on hedonism, what has caused a certain experience is of no moral significance as such. What has caused the experience does not effect the intrinsic value of having it. The felt satisfaction torturers gain from the suffering of their victim adds to their welfare. The content of an experience coloured with hedonic tone, finally, is of no importance either. Contentment received from pushpin is no less important than contentment received from poetry, to use Bentham's own example.[14]

Perfectionism

This is the view that what matters to how well a certain life goes is to what extent the person living the life in question succeeds in fulfilling certain objectively given goals, i.e., certain goals existing independent of what the person living the life himself or herself wants and independent of how he or she feels. A person is living a good life if he or she achieves much in terms of these objectively given goals. The person reaches perfection when the goals are fulfilled.

Well-known perfectionists are Aristotle, Thomas Aquinas and Karl Marx. Their views about what makes a life worth living differ in some respects, but they all agree that a life worth living is one where certain important goals are achieved, goals such as knowledge or intellectual, artistic and physical perfection. In what sense are these goals important? These thinkers agree that the answer to this question is independent of what the person living the life in question wants or feels. The goals could be stated on an 'objective list', to use Parfit's words.[15]

According to perfectionism, a life with less pleasure may well be a better life than one with more pleasure. It is true that Aristotle tried to show that a life of perfection is also a life of felt satisfaction, but this empirical hypothesis is not very credible. Marx argued, more realistically, that in order to lead a 'good' life, in the perfectionist sense of the word, we must probably sacrifice some happiness. And Marx had only contempt for Bentham and classical hedonism.

Finally, it is not difficult to think of cases where perfection is not what a person herself or himself wants to achieve. She or he may prefer a vegetative life to one dominated by ambition. However, on perfectionism, it is only when she or he reaches perfection that her or his life goes as well as possible.

Idealisation leads to perfectionism or hedonism

Hedonism or perfectionism are limiting cases of the idealising requirement that preferences whose satisfaction matters morally should be based on relevant information and be a result of cogent reasoning. This is my first claim.

It has been retorted to the idealising requirement that it would be foolish to satisfy a person's ideal preferences if his or her actual preferences do not approximate to them. This might leave the person utterly dissatisfied. Take for example someone who likes pop music but who would have liked classical music if he or she had had his or her preferences refined: would it not be stupid to offer this person a piece of classical music now that his or her preferences are not refined? This is too simplistic, however. What the ideal version of preferentialism requires is not that this person be given classical music. What we should take into account is not this person's ideal preferences for an ideal situation, where he or she has them, but for the actual situation, where he or she is the not very refined person that he or she is.[16] The person's ideal preference for this situation is probably that he or she should receive not a piece of classical music, but a more complex piece of pop music, which could serve the purpose of educating his or her taste.

But why educate his or her taste? The ideal self, if it is not going to impose its preferences on the actual self, needs a reason for its choice for the actual situation. Some experiences must be thought by this (ideal) self to be more valuable than others. In what way more valuable, then? Answers that suggest themselves are: because they bring more happiness (hedonism), or because they mean that the person realises his or her own talents more fully (perfectionism). An answer that does not suggest itself is that this is what the ideal self, in contradistinction to the actual self, prefers. For if this answer is given, then the objection surfaces once again that to satisfy the preferences of the ideal person is to thwart the interests of the actual person.

Elimination leads to hedonism or perfectionism

The eliminative requirement that only preferences that are to do with how one's own life goes should be taken into account points towards hedonism or perfectionism in an even more obvious manner. This is my second claim.

What is the rationale behind such an eliminative requirement? Most plausibly, it seems to me, to guarantee that, whenever people have their preferences satisfied, this is something they enjoy, something producing, directly or indirectly, felt satisfaction for them; or, once again, something that means that they reach perfection of one kind or another.

Obviously, hedonism is not a limiting case of the eliminative strategy of ignoring anti-social preferences. Hedonism pays no attention to either the source or the content of our preferences. The only important thing about our preferences (from the point of view of our own welfare), according to hedonism, is whether or not we feel pleasure when we satisfy them. Perfection-ism, however, is a limiting case of the eliminative strategy of ignoring anti-social preferences. This is my third claim. Those who share Harsanyi's humanitarian conviction that anti-social preferences should not be satisfied, or Sen's liberal view that it does not add to a person's welfare when her or his preferences about things that are none of her or his business are satisfied, are on the verge of parting company with preferentialism proper. They disagree not only with classical hedonism; as it were, they are approaching a view more properly called 'perfectionism'. For, clearly, the standard they use when they judge what is good for a person may well differ from the standard the person herself or himself uses.

The argument from explanatory impotence

I will not attempt to show in this chapter that either hedonism or perfectionism is the correct moral (evaluative) view, but I will try to show that, while these are both plausible candidates in this competition (just like idealism, to be discussed in Chapter 8), preferentialism based on the view that the more satisfaction of preferences the better is not. Not only is preferentialism an unstable view, but good arguments tell against it as well.

To see why this is so we must return to the idea of a moral explanation, discussed in Chapter 2. A moral explanation is given when a particular case is subsumed under a general moral (or evaluative) principle, such as the utilitarian formula or the hedonistic hypothesis that the more pleasure the better.

A basic moral (or evaluative) principle is a universal statement of the form, 'If something is *X*, then it is intrinsically good', or 'Everything that is *X* is intrinsically good'. The same form could be used to communicate a contingent generalisation, however. What makes such a conditional or universal statement a statement of a moral (evaluative) principle, rather than a statement of a contingent generalisation, has nothing to do with logical form. Words such as 'if', 'then' and 'all' are not ambiguous. The difference lies rather in what makes the statement true. A moral (evaluative) principle, in contradistinction to a contingently true generalisation, is true, if it is true, because the property referred to in the antecedent makes things intrinsically good. The statement, together with the information that it states a moral principle, implies, moreover, that if, contrary to fact, something were *X*, it would be good. And positive instances of the formula constitute positive evidence for it. This is analogous with the way we distinguish statements of scientific laws from statements that are only contingently true.

If it is a true scientific law that all ravens are black then if, contrary to fact, this bird in the cage in front of me had been a raven, it would have been black. In a similar vein, if it is a true moral principle that all pleasurable experiences are intrinsically good, then it is true of this experience I have right now that, had it been pleasurable, it would have been intrinsically good. The fact that something is a raven or an experience of pleasure makes it black or intrinsically good respectively.

It is because scientific laws and moral (evaluative) principles support counterfactual statements that we can gain inductive support for them. As a matter of fact, inductive support and explanation go together. A positive instance of a generalisation gives inductive support to it if, and only if, the instance could be explained with reference to the generalisation. And we explain singular instances by subsuming them under general laws.[17] In Chapter 2 I showed in more detail how we do this in our moral reasoning.

Consider now the following three ideas about what makes a life worth living:

1. The satisfaction of preferences.
2. Pleasure.
3. The achievement of important goals.

Is any of these generalisations a reasonable moral (evaluative) principle? This is tantamount to asking whether any of these generalisations could play a crucial role in a moral (evaluative) explanation.

On the face of it, it is not implausible to think that (2) could do service in this respect. If we want to argue that a particular experience is intrinsically good, we could base our judgement on the observation that it is an experience of pleasure and on the generalisation that pleasure is what makes life worth living. Every pleasurable experience is good, and it is good because it is pleasurable.

In a similar vein, it does not seem too far-fetched to argue with reference to (3) that a person has had a good life (according to Aristotle, this question can only be settled in retrospect) if she or he has achieved a lot in terms of the goals on the 'objective list'. It is because of the achievements that her or his life had value.

In the present context, the first kind of generalisation seems wanting, however. Let me refer to this observation as 'the argument from explanatory impotence'. We cannot explain why something a person experiences or does is good with reference to the fact that this is what she or he wants to experience or do. This does not explain the goodness of the experience or the act.

We need only a moment's reflection to realise that such an explanation would be spurious. The explanatory relation, if any such relation is involved at all, goes in the opposite direction. A person may well desire something because it is good for her or him; indeed, for this reason the person should perhaps desire it; but her or his desiring it does not explain its goodness.

For the argument from explanatory impotence I claim no originality (other than having just given it its name). It is interesting to notice that the argument is suggested by A. Sen and B. Williams in the Introduction to the book *Utilitarianism and Beyond*, where contemporary forms of (preference) utilitarianism are examined:

> It is natural to think of choosing and valuing as related, but it is hard to avoid the suspicion that, in this presentation, the direction to the linkage has been inverted. It is not by any means unreasonable to respond to the question: 'What should I choose?', by answering, 'Whatever is most valuable.' But to respond to the question, 'What is most valuable?' or even 'What is most valuable to me?' by answering, 'Whatever I would choose', would seem to remove the content from the notion of valuing, even when qualifications are added to the supposed choice in the form of 'under ideal conditions' or 'with full

understanding'. Basing choice on valuation is cogent in a way that basing valuation on choice is not.[18]

To be sure, their argument is cast not explicitly in terms of preferences (or desires) but in terms of choices (perhaps the authors do not distinguish between the two notions in the way I have done). In order for it to be relevant to my purposes, I must rephrase their argument in terms of preferences (or desires). However, there is no difficulty in doing so (after all, when we impute preferences to a person, we have to rely on our knowledge of actual and hypothetical choices made by this person), and the force of the argument when restated remains.

This is how I want to restate their argument: to respond to the question 'What is most valuable?' or even 'What is most valuable to me?' by answering 'Whatever I prefer' would seem to remove the content from the notion of valuing, even when qualifications are added to the supposed preference in the form of 'under ideal conditions' or 'with full understanding'. Basing preference on valuation is cogent in a way that basing valuation on preference is not. But this restated argument is the argument from explanatory impotence.

Possible objections

To the argument from explanatory impotence two possible objections can be made. It could be admitted that the argument shows that the fact that a person chooses or desires something does not make it good. But perhaps preferentialism could be interpreted differently.

In the first place, it could be argued that the fact that certain things are good (and these things may be experiences, the continued existence of a certain species, or whatever anyone may come to think of), if they are, is not because people like them. These things are good (in themselves), if they are, because of certain intrinsic properties they have. The preferences, our liking of them, come in differently. Our preference for these things that are good constitute the goodness of them; they are good because we project goodness on them.

This line, which originated perhaps with John Mackie in his *Ethics: Inventing Right and Wrong*, has been taken by Wlodek Rabinowicz in conversation. The problem with it, I think, is that it gives up preferentialism altogether. What is replaced for preference satisfaction is really an 'objective list' of values *cum* a Gibbard-style[19] metaethical theory according to which these values are not part of the fabric of the world, but projected onto it by human beings. In Chapter 8 I will reject this objective list (or 'ideal') view of intrinsic value (no matter on what kind of metaethic it is based).

Another way of resisting the argument from explanatory impotence would be as follows: my liking a certain experience is not in itself enough to make it a good thing. But when I get my desire for it satisfied a preference is satisfied. And this makes my getting my preference satisfied good. For the satisfaction of preferences, in general, is something of positive intrinsic value.

I concede that the argument from explanatory impotence does not rebut this brand of preferentialism. This brand seems to me objectionable for other reasons, however. First of all, it implies that it is good for a person to have his or her will, even in cases where he or she does not, or even cannot, notice that this is so. I agree with Sidgwick's saying, using Butler's phrase, that when we 'sit down in a cool hour' we can only justify to ourselves the importance that we attach to any of these objects by considering its conducing, in one way or another, to the happiness of sentient beings.[20]

Secondly, this brand of preferentialism cannot answer the important question of what preferences we ought to have, what kinds of person we ought to be. At least, it cannot answer this question in a satisfactory way. What is suggested by this brand of preferentialism is that a person ought to have preferences that are at the same time strong and easily satisfied. However, this does not strike me, at any rate, as very plausible.

Thirdly, this brand of preferentialism is open to the following objection: suppose that I have a number of preferences and get these satisfied to a reasonable degree. This means that I lead a good life, according to this brand of preferentialism. I now go through certain experiences which lead to a situation where I find that I have doubled the number of preferences that I hold. I retain all the old ones but now I have, in addition to these, equally many new ones. The old ones are still satisfied to a reasonable degree, and so are the new ones. However, on reflection, I feel that I prefer my old, simple life to my new, more sophisticated one. Yet, for all that, in the circumstances it is quite plausible that there is more satisfaction in my new life than in my old one. On the version of preferentialism under discussion, this means that my new life may well be better than my old one. This seems utterly strange.

It might be retorted that even if, absolutely, there is more satisfaction in my new life than in my old life, there is also more dissatisfaction. For even if my new preferences are satisfied to a reasonable degree I must have, for each of them, a preference that it would go away, and these preferences are not satisfied in my new life. So, after all, there is less net satisfaction in my new life than in my old one, and, therefore, the new life is worse than the old one.

This objection is mistaken. We need not suppose that I regret that I have any one of the new preferences in particular. What I regret is the number of preferences that I now hold. This (single) preference, for fewer preferences, is not satisfied in my new life, to be sure, but it is only one preference among many. It need not be a strong one either. However, if I have it, even if it is weak, it seems strange to hold that the new sophisticated life is better than the old, simple one. So the version of preferentialism according to which it is of value as such that preferences get satisfied is not plausible.

The measurement of welfare

If hedonism is in this way superior to preferentialism, how can we explain the fact that most economists and moral theorists seem nowadays to prefer the latter to the former? The reason is methodological, I conjecture. At least if we restrict our interest to intrapersonal assessments, we can measure preferences in a systematic manner, basing our imputations of preferences on observations of hypothetical choices of rational persons. At least this is something we can do in principle (setting to one side the problem with possibly irrational preferences). The concept of pleasure is more elusive. This is why preferentialism has gained popularity in welfare economics, in decision theory, in game theory, and among recent utilitarians.

Another reason, of course, is that the notion of preference satisfaction has been fruitful within descriptive economic theory. However, when the notion has been used in normative economic welfare theory, or in normative game or decision theory, the gains in methodological terms have been bought at a high price in terms of 'validity'. That is the main thrust of the present chapter.

The methodological case, moreover, is less clear than it has often been thought to be. To be sure, if we make certain assumptions about the rationality of the economic agents, we can make fairly precise measurements of their preferences. But the utility-functions we ascribe to persons on the basis of their hypothetical choices are only unique up to positive linear transformations, as the mathematicians have it. That is, there is no natural unit and there is no manner of comparing intervals between two persons. Such comparisons are meaningless, or so many economists have argued. Interpersonal comparisons of happiness or pleasure, on the other hand, even if they are difficult to make with any precision, are meaningful, or so I have argued (in the previous chapter), at any rate.

This is a serious flaw in preferentialism, of course, for, to be sure, the most interesting assessments of welfare involve interpersonal comparisons. The Pareto criterion is insufficient in many contexts.

Admittedly, some attempts have been made to show that it is possible, after all, to compare the strength of preferences of different persons. The general idea has been to transform such comparisons into intrapersonal ones, through some method of sympathy.[21] However, even if, in some situation, I succeeded in putting myself in someone else's shoes, I would have no manner of showing that I had succeeded, or of convincing myself about this.

It could be thought that, to the extent that people are like each other in physical respects, they tend to share the same experiences in the same situations too. But how do we know that? In order to find out, we must already be able to make the relevant comparisons.[22]

The belief that, while intensities of preferences can be measured, differences of felt well-being cannot may explain the popularity of preferentialism (rather than hedonism), then. It should be noticed that the observation that this kind of methodological advantage may be merely apparent does not show that hedonism is more plausible than preferentialism. If we want to assess the plausibility of hedonism and preferentialism respectively, we ought to set aside as irrelevant these methodological questions. We have no reason to expect from reality that reality must be easy to detect, or measure. We should not accept preferentialism because (wrongly) we believe that it has a methodological advantage over hedonism. Nor should we accept hedonism because we become aware of the fact that it might have a methodological advantage over preferentialism (classical hedonism allowing in principle for interpersonal comparisons of well-being). What has intrinsic value is one thing; how we can measure and compare intrinsic value is quite another.

What about differences in perfection, then? Can we make intra- and interpersonal comparisons of perfection? Well, since perfection is probably measured in many dimensions, this seems even more difficult to do than measuring pleasure. Yet, once more, this is not evidence either for or against the truth of perfectionism.

In the next chapter, however, I will try to show that hedonism is superior not only to preferentialism, but also to perfectionism.

Conclusion

Three main hypotheses about what makes a life worth living (for the person experiencing it) are in competition: hedonism, preferentialism and perfectionism. In the present chapter I have tried to show that both hedonism and perfectionism are superior to preferentialism. In the next chapter I will indicate why I believe hedonism is more plausible, after all, than perfectionism.

Notes

1 The existing allocation of economic resources is efficient, according to mainstream welfare economics, if and only if it results in a state that is Pareto optimal. A state is Pareto optimal if and only if no possibility of reallocation exists that would improve the lot of some person, without worsening the situation of any one else (in terms of their preference satisfaction).

2 Cf. for example Peter Bohm, *Social Efficiency: A Concise Introduction to Welfare Economics*.

3 Cf. James Buchanan, 'Positive Economics, Welfare Economics, and Political Economy'.

4 J. C. Harsanyi, 'Morality and the Theory of Rational Behaviour', p. 55.

5 Cf. my *Moral Realism*, Ch. 5, about this.

6 Harsanyi, 'Morality and the Theory of Rational Behaviour', p. 55.

7 Cf. for example R. B. Brandt, 'The Explanation of Moral Language'.

8 Cf. R. M. Hare, *Moral Thinking*, p. 102.
9 Outside philosophy books we seldom come across this kind of preference; it does illustrate an important theoretical possibility, however.
10 A treatment of this problem can be found in Derek Parfit's *Reasons and Persons*, Part 2. However, Parfit does not consider the theory put forward here.
11 As noted above, I think that this kind of preference is rarely held by actual people.
12 Harsanyi, 'Morality and the Theory of Rational Behaviour', p. 56.
13 It has been pointed out to me by Bengt Brülde that, since Sen is no utilitarian, there are two possible ways that we could interpret his eliminative strategy. The thrust of his argument can be taken to be that it does not enhance the well-being of a person when this person gets her or his other-regarding preferences satisfied. This is how I have interpreted Sen, and it results in a view that is relevant to my discussion. But another way of interpreting him is to take the thrust of his argument to be that one should not satisfy these kinds of other-regarding preference, even if this means that we do not maximise preference satisfaction – we have simply no obligation to maximise preference satisfaction and in this case it would be wrong to do it. I will not try to settle the question of which interpretation is the right one.
14 This example is attributed to Bentham by J. S. Mill in 'Mill on Bentham', p. 123.
15 Cf. Parfit, *Reasons and Persons*, p. 4. On this list only personal values obtain, i.e., values that are values for an individual (a person). However, as we will see in Ch. 8, on an objective list (of intrinsic values) even impersonal values may obtain. If they do, then I will speak of an idealist view of intrinsic value or, for short, of 'idealism'.
16 I owe this important point entirely to Wlodek Rabinowicz, who made it in conversation.
17 Cf. Gilbert Harman, 'The Inference to the Best Explanation', about this.
18 A. Sen and B. Williams (eds), *Utilitarianism and Beyond*, p. 13.
19 A. Gibbard, *Wise Choices, Apt Feelings: A Theory of Normative Judgement*.
20 H. Sidgwick, *The Methods of Ethics*, p. 401.
21 Cf. for example K. J. Arrow, 'Extended Sympathy and the Possibility of Social Choice'; Hare, *Moral Thinking*, p. 128; Harsanyi, *Rational Behaviour*, p. 54.
22 This criticism of interpersonal comparisons of the intensity of preferences is put forward and discussed by Lars Bergström in 'Interpersonal Utility Comparisons'.

Chapter 7

Against perfectionism

I have argued that both hedonism and perfectionism are more plausible theories of value than preferentialism. I have also indicated that I find hedonism more plausible than perfectionism. I have not argued this point, however. This will be the object of the present chapter. My argument will be directed at what I find to be the most plausible version or aspect of perfectionism, the idea that what matters to a person is that his or her life be genuinely his or hers, that he or she be autonomous. This seems, moreover, to be a common prerequisite of various other different ideas of perfection, such as the idea that achievements are of value to us as such, or the idea that knowledge is of value to us as such, or the idea that deep personal relations or a contact with realities are of value to us as such. What these ideas share is the common assumption that, if an achievement of mine, or a piece of knowledge of mine, or a personal relation of mine is to be of value, no matter what exact content it may have, it must be my own.

The claim that autonomy has intrinsic value will be the immediate target of the argument of this chapter. The thrust of this chapter, then, is that personal autonomy is of no value as such. Personal autonomy is not a basic moral category (which does not preclude, of course, that it may often be a means to something which has value, i.e., pleasurable experiences). If this argument is sound, and if my observation that autonomy is a prerequisite of all interesting forms of perfection is correct, then, indirectly, perfectionism as such is being defeated as well.

Two contexts for autonomy

Concepts of autonomy are invoked mainly in two kinds of moral context. On the one hand, it is sometimes claimed autonomy is something which is required from us. This is the view put forward by Kant. We ought to be autonomous.[1] On the other hand, autonomy (or individuality, to use J. S. Mill's word)[2] is something we could invoke to protect ourselves against certain kinds of unjust demand: our autonomy or individuality is something which others ought to respect. We have a right to autonomy, or, our autonomy (individuality) is something which is of value to us and, therefore, of value in itself.

In this chapter I will discuss the concept of autonomy which is adequate in the latter context. Is there a tenable ideal of personal autonomy? My main thesis is that there is no such tenable ideal. It has no importance as such whether an action we perform restrains the personal autonomy of someone or not. Hence, it would not be a good argument after all against, say, manipulation of behaviour if it could be proved that it necessarily involves restrictions of personal autonomy.

The concept of autonomy

What does it mean to say of a person that she or he is 'autonomous'? In the present context the most plausible answer would be that she or he is a person who does what she or he chooses or decides to do, and who makes the choices and decisions she or he does because she or he wills it. Although this concept of autonomy is of course far from clear, I think it could still easily be made sufficiently precise for the purpose of this chapter.

In the first place, it is clear that the concept could be taken either in a straightforwardly empirical way or in some theoretical, ideal way. Are the actual will and decisions of a person what matter to her or his autonomy, or the ideal ones which she or he might have had or manifested if she or he had been, in some respect, different?

The use of ideal concepts of autonomy is very common indeed among those who follow Kant and argue that we ought to be autonomous. John Rawls, for example, writes: 'Thus acting autonomously is acting from principles that we would consent to as free and equal rational beings, and that we are to understand in this way.'[3] Philosophers who want to follow J. S. Mill tend rather to use the empirical conception of autonomy even when they depart from his terminology and use the word 'autonomy' (Mill spoke instead of individuality or self-development). Jonathan Glover, for example, writes:

> You must have the desire whose satisfaction is in question. I override your autonomy only where I take a decision on your behalf which goes against what you actually do want, not where the decision goes against what you would want if you were more knowledgeable or more intelligent.[4]

As was pointed out by J. S. Mill, both conceptions of autonomy have deep historical roots and are sometimes difficult to separate from each other.[5] I will examine both concepts, taking as my point of departure an empirical conception and postponing until later the scrutiny of various ideal ones.

It is important to notice that the actions of autonomous persons are in accordance with both their decisions and their wants. Their actions track their decisions and their decisions track their wants.

It is true that the psychology taken for granted in my definition is crude. In the final analysis, no matter how we should like to account for such things as a person's will, his or her choices or decisions and his or her actions, these are, I think, roughly the distinctions that we should like to be able to make. I am taking some unspecified causal theory of action for granted and using the word 'will' in a slightly technical sense. My will in a decision context may be at odds with several of my desires. We give greater weight to those desires that are stronger, although one strong desire may be outweighed by several other desires. What I want to do in the situation, my will in the situation, is what I believe would best fulfil all my desires. A person who 'wants', in this sense, to do one thing but who does something else is not autonomous.

In what follows I will defend the view that such weakness of the will is possible. The causal relation between what a person wants and what he or she decides to do, and between what he or she decides to do and what he or she does, must be of the 'right' or 'standard' kind, if the person's action is to be said to be autonomous. However, I cannot go into the problem here of how this is to be understood more exactly.

To begin with, let us say that persons are autonomous if they do what they decide or choose to do and do this because they actually want to do it. Their autonomy is restrained if they are hindered by some person or authority from doing what they decide or choose to do because they actually want to do it. This means that while hypnosis may present us with good examples of violations of our autonomy, it is more difficult to see that manipulation of our situation, restraints on our alternatives and so forth may equally threaten it. Autonomy is one thing, freedom another.[6] Even if only two alternatives are left open to an agent, to commit treason, for instance, or undergo torture, he or she may choose autonomously between these. It is also far from clear how blind obedience may threaten our autonomy. If I choose to obey and want to choose to obey, then I am also autonomous when acting in accord with my obedience.

The ideal of personal autonomy

Persons are autonomous if they do what they decide to do and decide to do what they decide to do because they want to do it: i.e., if their actions track their decisions, and their decisions track their wants. What, then, is the ideal of autonomy? Is it simply that people should be allowed to be autonomous? No; we ought to distinguish various aspects of autonomy. If we have a duty to be autonomous, this may be a duty always to be autonomous, but the view that we have a right to have our autonomy respected is most plausible if it is confined to what could be called personal autonomy. You could be autonomous, then, with respect to your choice of occupation, sexual partners, newspapers and so forth. The respect dearest to the adherents of the ideal of autonomy is probably such personal choices. This is also what is at the heart of Robert Nozick's idea of self-ownership in *Anarchy, State, and Utopia*. I will take the ideal of (personal) autonomy primarily to include the idea that (at least) persons should be allowed to do what they want to do, and decide to do, with themselves.

Nevertheless, is it not obviously unreasonable to maintain that people should be allowed to do what they want to do and decide to do, even with themselves? For the self-perfection (or self-destruction, for that matter) of one person may take place at the expense of some other person. It is not reasonable to hold that one person should be allowed to use the scarce resources of a society to develop her or his talent as a violin player when her or his compatriots are actually starving to death, if this would-be violinist might be an efficient farmer, as well. Yes, this is reasonable, some would say (such as Nozick), while others would say no. This is controversial, then. So in order to make the ideal as plausible as possible, I will take it to imply only that no one should be manipulated into doing what she or he does not want to do, or does not decide to do, with herself or himself, when this manipulation is in her or his own interest alone and no one else's.

The ideal of personal autonomy vaguely set forth here could be understood in at least three different ways. First of all, it could be understood as an absolute norm, one which should never have to give way to any other consideration, and which dictates that personal autonomy must never be restrained. It could also be interpreted to mean that the value of personal autonomy is infinite, or that the value of personal autonomy should be observed fully, before any other values are considered at all. To use a phrase from John Rawls: the value of personal autonomy is lexically prior to all other principles.[7]

Secondly, it could be understood to mean that it is a matter of negative intrinsic value whenever the autonomy of a person is restrained, even if in some cases it might be right to so restrain her or his autonomy (the consideration of personal autonomy is outweighed by some other consideration, say, for the happiness of this person in the long run). This is how James Griffin conceives of the ideal. According to Griffin, even 'if I constantly made a mess of my life, even if you could do better if you took charge, I would not let you do it. Autonomy has a value of its own'.[8] And yet, for all that, autonomy, 'should not be realized . . . when it sets up great anxieties in a particular person'.[9]

Thirdly, the proscription against interference with personal autonomy can be justified, not as a matter of abstract rights, or because of the intrinsic value of personal autonomy, but rather because of the overall gain in net utility obtained by universal recognition of such an absolute value (rule utilitarianism).

Is there an absolute right to personal autonomy?

Admittedly, there are many cases where the personal autonomy of someone is violated and where this is wrong. The person who gets his or her autonomy tampered with may be hurt. Or, being of a Kantian bent, he or she may feel that, when we succeed in manipulating him or her, he or she fails to live up to the standards he or she has set his or her own life. However, these examples do not show that violations of personal autonomy are wrong as such. And my thesis is that no examples that do show this can be found. We have no absolute right to personal autonomy. My present claim is that, even if personal autonomy may be of some value as such, it is at least not of infinite value.

In order to make plausible the claim that we have no absolute right to personal autonomy I need a clear example to which I can refer. What is required is a case where a person is not allowed to do what he or she wants and decides to do with himself or herself only because what he or she wants and decides to do with himself or herself is not considered to be good for him or her, and where it is nevertheless fairly obvious that it would be right not to allow him or her to do what he or she wants and decides to do with himself or herself. How could such an example be constructed? To be convincing it should be a case where the person in question has a very strong and permanent desire to do what he or she is not allowed to do. And the action he or she wants to perform must concern something he or she considers very important to his or her ego. It would not be sufficient for him or her not to attain what he or she wants and decides. He or she must be actively manipulated to do what he or she wants not to do or has not decided to do. I think the following example will serve the purpose.

Consider a man who is going to die of lung cancer. He gets little relief from the morphine he is given by his doctor, who has cut down his dose in order not to make his breathing more difficult. The doctor asks him whether he would like to have a lethal dose of the morphine. The patient refuses. To be sure, the rest of his life, consisting as it does of nothing but severe physical displeasure and discomfort until he is suffocated by his disease, will not be worth living. Although he realises this, and hopes that death will follow soon, for moral reasons he believes that it is absolutely forbidden to take a human life, or to assist when a human life is taken. That is the belief he has come to accept after having seriously considered the problem of euthanasia. To press matters, we may even assume that this person has made fidelity to religious duties and rituals the whole pattern and meaning of his life. And the causes of this religious attitude, as taken up by the patient, may be fully known to him. It is not possible, we assume, to undermine it through any kind of 'cognitive psychotherapy' of the kind mentioned in the previous chapter. Apparently, the doctor accepts his refusal. However, the doctor secretly gives the patient an overdose, thus killing him.

Let us suppose that, for one reason or another, there were just two rough options open to the doctor. She could, as she did, manipulate the patient into accepting a lethal dose, or she could give him the usual dose, but she could not, for example, force the lethal dose on the patient (which few would consider the best option in the situation, anyway). It is my considered opinion that the doctor did the right thing (let us also take it for granted that there are no bad side-effects of her action). This also seems to be the conclusion we must draw if hedonistic utilitarianism is brought to bear on this case. How could I convince those who have their doubts about this?

Perhaps most people have their doubts about it. Perhaps they would say that, in examples like the present one, the patient should not be given a lethal dose. I concede that this may be so. But I think our 'intuitions' about cases like the present one are much too biased and prejudiced to be taken at face value. We are not capable of keeping our minds clear and our heads cool when we consider cases such as this. In particular, we tend to forget that what is here being discussed is a mere thought-experiment, where there is no doubt (as there must always be in real life) that there are no bad side-effects of an act of involuntary euthanasia (not to speak of doubts concerning the value of the patient's remaining life). We should approach our intuitions more indirectly. It would probably be a good idea to take as our point of departure our intuitions about more abstract problems, such as whether we ought to avoid unnecessary displeasure or whether persons ought to be allowed to do as they please with themselves. Most people agree that we ought to avoid unnecessary pain. It is controversial, however, whether people have a right to do as they please with themselves. Since we are facing a conflict here, some intuitions will have to yield. And a certain onus rests on the person who wants to argue that, sometimes, we need not avoid avoidable pain.

If the doctor has the patient killed she assists in an act of involuntary euthanasia. By manipulating the patient into accepting the lethal dose, moreover, she restrains the personal autonomy of the patient. The patient accepts the injection only because he wrongly believes he will get his ordinary dose, but instead gets a lethal dose. Now, why should it be wrong of the doctor to do this, if it is in the interest of the patient to have the lethal dose and not in conflict with the interest of anyone else?

Peter Singer has argued, against involuntary euthanasia, that it presupposes that 'one can judge when a person's life is so bad as to be not worth living, better than the person can judge herself'.[10] Singer believes that it:

> is not clear that we are ever justified in having much confidence in our judgements about whether the life of another person is, to that person, worth living. That the other person wishes to go on living is good evidence that her life is worth living. What better evidence could there be?[11]

In relation to my example it is clear that Singer's objection fails. That the patient in my example (my thought-experiment) wants to go on living, and decides to turn the offer of euthanasia down, is not evidence at all, and certainly not good evidence, that his life is worth living. He wants to continue to live solely for moral (religious) reasons. And our judgement that his life is not worth living does not presuppose that we know this better than he does. As a matter of fact, he shares our opinion on this point. He admits that what remains of his life is not worth experiencing. He hopes that he will soon die. He, however, does not want to put an end to his own life. He feels that, if he did, it would mean that his entire life would lose its point. However, if the doctor succeeds in manipulating the patient, no harm is done to the patient (even by his own lights). To be sure, the patient kills himself, or at least accepts being killed, but the patient cannot reasonably be blamed for what he does. If anyone is to receive blame, it is the doctor. So the life of the patient retains whatever point it would have had, by his own lights, had he not been manipulated into accepting a lethal dose. Furthermore, the patient is spared unnecessary pain.

The previous example rebuts only one common argument against involuntary euthanasia. However, there also exists one consideration which could be taken into account that supports strongly the view that there is no tenable absolute ideal of personal autonomy. This consideration is the fact, and I think it is a fact, that we tend to disregard the ideal of personal autonomy when two requirements are satisfied. These requirements are, first of all, that by restraining someone's personal autonomy we can spare the person extreme pain, and, secondly, that the person concerned is someone who is dear to us, someone we really care about. There is a telling example of this in Jonathan Glover's book, *Causing Death and Saving Lives*. Although Glover argues in defence of an ideal of personal autonomy, he admits that there may be exceptional cases:

> It does not seem plausible to say that there is no *conceivable* amount of future misery that would justify killing someone against his will. If I had been a Jew in Nazi Germany, I would have considered very seriously killing myself and my family, if there was no other escape from the death camps. And, if someone in that position felt that his family did not understand what the future would feel like and so killed them against their wishes, I at least am not sure that this decision would be wrong.[12]

I believe that most of us share Glover's feelings. However, feelings are one thing, a considered moral opinion something else. Therefore, how are we to interpret Glover's example? One interpretation would be that, in situations such as the one described, we fail to make a considered moral assessment; our passionate feelings lead us astray. No moral conclusion can validly be drawn from the example. This position is difficult to sustain consistently, however. Why should we assume that our feelings have led us astray? To be sure, the example is construed so as to guarantee that we are maximally involved. And a strong emotional involvement is sometimes a sign of a bad judgement. However, our emotional involvement does not *per se* distort our judgement. An emotional involvement may prepare the ground for rash assessments when it carries a bias. In the example under discussion, however, we, who conduct the thought-experiment, should not be involved in any way that is essentially partial. The main effect of our involvement is different. Because we are so emotionally involved, we fail to detach ourselves from the problem. Had strangers been involved we might have felt that, even if we allow them to choose options that are extremely painful for them, we are still not really responsible for their suffering. In relation to strangers, because of our lack of empathy, we succeed in sticking to the abstract ideal of personal autonomy and we allow them to inflict displeasure on themselves. This attitude is certainly much easier to take up if strangers are involved. But are we any less responsible for their displeasure than we would be if those who suffered were near and dear to us? I would say that we are not. We feel this if we are deeply involved in the case. And I would say that our involved (but impartial) judgement should be given more weight than our detached one. It is a fact, or so I believe, that for almost each and any one of us, there is some amount of suffering such that, if we could stop those who are near and dear to us from voluntarily inflicting it on themselves, we would do so. This fact could reasonably be taken to indicate that there are situations where it would be positively wrong to allow even strangers to choose such options.

If, however, it is true that sometimes we are allowed to kill people against their will, there must be all sorts of situation where, in order to save people from severe pain, it is all right to restrain their personal autonomy in less serious respects. If this conclusion is sound, it means that there is no absolute right to personal autonomy. The value of personal autonomy, if it is of value in itself, is not infinite.

Are autonomous actions of value in themselves?

There is no absolute right to personal autonomy, or so I have argued at any rate. The possibility may, nevertheless, remain that there is some value in having one's personal autonomy respected, even if this value must sometimes yield to other values.

I am not quite sure how the view that personal autonomy possesses value in itself can be presented as plausibly as possible. The point cannot really be that there is some positive intrinsic value in each autonomous action. It would be strange if we could make the world better by performing as many actions as possible. Instead, there may be some negative value involved in each case where we are manipulated or otherwise made to perform an action which is not autonomous. On the other hand, the argument may be that it is good in itself to be an autonomous person, no matter how often the autonomy is exercised, i.e., a person who is capable of performing autonomous actions. According to the latter argument, if our autonomy is taken away from us (or if it is voluntarily given up by us or just, say, because of bad luck, lost), then something of value in our lives is lost. I should like to examine both possibilities.

Consider first a person who has retired from his occupation as a carpenter. He leads a quiet life in a small town which he never leaves. He is enjoying the last few years of his life doing some gardening and reading some philosophy. As far as he is concerned, his life lacks only one thing. While he would like to see his two children twice a year, each of them only visits him once a year. There is the possibility that he could visit them sometimes. They would make him feel welcome and he would enjoy staying with them for a while. He dares not make the journey, however, for fear of getting killed in some kind of accident. As a matter of fact, he never travels by car, train or aeroplane. His problem is not that he has an unrealistic view of the probability of getting killed. He knows that the chance of getting killed if he travelled once a year is in fact very small. He has none the less come to entertain the idea that nothing could be so good that it could provide a reasonable motive for him to increase the risk of getting killed in an accident by however small an amount. After all, the improvement in his life would be marginal if he saw his children twice a year instead of just once. He feels, therefore, no inclination to take the risk of going to see them.

One day a friend of this man, a retired doctor, comes to see him and offers him a new medicine. 'Take it', she says. 'It will make you react as people normally do to the risk of getting killed in an accident. The medicine will not change your view of the probabilities, but it will make you react to them in a more relaxed way. The medicine is in itself quite harmless.'

The man's answer is that he does not want to take the medicine. 'I dare not take it', he says. 'It would obviously make me a person who is prepared to gamble to some extent with life. The expected value of my life would be slightly better if I took it. I could then see my children twice a year, which is better than once a year, and it is highly improbable that I should get killed in an accident. But if I take the medicine I will go and see my children and this means that the risk that I get killed in an accident will increase somewhat. And I am not willing to do anything which increases in any way the risk of getting killed.'

The doctor, knowing how stubborn her friend is, says nothing more, but makes a birthday cake for her friend, puts the medicine into the cake and gives it to him. It does not take long before the man realises what has happened. He eats the cake and all of a sudden views the prospect of going to visit his children without horror. Then he goes to his friend, the doctor, and thanks her. 'But does it not disturb you', the doctor asks, 'that I have changed your personality against your will?' 'Not in the least', the man answers. 'I, speaking as the person you have turned me into, have no objections. Now I am capable of living a life which is slightly better than the one I, the person that used to be me, used to live.'

In the face of this example it is possible for me to assert without hesitation that the doctor did the right thing. It does not matter how little the increase in value of the life of the man was, as long as there was some improvement (and no bad side-effects). This being so, the doctor did the right thing. This conclusion, if correct, would prove that there is no value in itself in having one's will with regard to one's life respected. Is it, however, correct? Here some of the possible objections to my conclusion should be examined.

It could perhaps be suggested that there is inevitably some negative value in having one's wants frustrated. It does not feel good not to get what one wants. This argument is based on an equivocation, however. The word 'frustration' is ambiguous. It can be used either to refer to an experience (which is, more often than not, unpleasant) or to refer to an abstract relation (which cannot be felt or experienced at all). In my example above the 'frustration', if there is any, is of the abstract kind. It consists of a lack of correspondence between what is at one time wanted and what is later the case. Nothing in the example indicates, however, that the realisation of this discrepancy is followed by any unpleasant feelings on the part of the person who took the medicine. On the contrary, he says after he has taken the medicine that he is glad his (former) will was not respected. And the 'former person', who would have complained if he had 'survived' the taking of the medicine, does not exist any longer, so he cannot complain and he cannot suffer from any loss. Hence, no frustration is felt in the example.

If, however, there is nothing wrong in changing a person's character, as long as the result is that she or he will not object afterwards to the change, does not this mean that it would be unobjectionable as such to exchange one person for another?

Perhaps it does. The distinction is not quite clear between a change within a person, on the one hand, and an exchange of one person for another, on the other. The concept of a person is not absolutely definite. Except in some fanciful thought-experiments, we seldom have difficulties in identifying actual persons. Each person occupies a certain place in space–time. But it is difficult to tell what it is about such an entity in space–time that makes it a person and that makes it one person. Some would stress physical continuity, others would concentrate on mental traits, such as connectedness by memory, 'projects' and the like. Most would opt for a combination. Physical continuity and mental connectedness, however, come in degrees. It is not easy, therefore, to say when one person has been changed and when one person has been exchanged for another. So, probably, if there is nothing which makes it wrong in principle to change a person against her or his will, there is probably nothing which makes it wrong in principle to exchange one person for another. If we want to defend the former claim we should be prepared to defend the latter.

Bernard Williams argues that 'it is absurd' to demand of a person that he or she give up his or her projects which he or she is most deeply and extensively identified with. Why should this be so? The reason is, according to Williams, that it is 'to alienate him in a real sense from his actions and the source of his actions in his own convictions'.[13]

Let us for the sake of argument concede that to change a person's personality in a way which threatens his or her personal autonomy is to alienate the person not only from his or her actions and their source in his or her own convictions, but from his or her self; or is, in other words, to exchange him or her in some way for some other person. One can still wonder what is absurd about this, and Bernard Williams provides no answer to the query.

Most people seem to feel uneasy about the prospect of being exchanged for some other person. The theme is very popular in science fiction and I know of no elaboration of it where the possibility of an exchange is viewed positively. Indeed, it is not difficult to imagine situations where it would not be a good thing to be exchanged for some other person. We may suspect that the person taking our place cannot really feel happiness as we do, or we may suspect that she or he will not be able to fulfil our responsibilities, complete the various tasks we have undertaken and regard as important, and so forth. We suspect that those whom we love and receive love and affection from will not love her or him as they love us. (At the same time we may, out of jealousy, fear that they will!) Suppose, however, that the person about to take our place is precisely like us, with the sole exception that she or he does everything we do a little bit better, is a little bit more happy, and makes the people we love a little bit happier than we do. It is possible that we would nevertheless protest against being exchanged for this person, just as the carpenter in the example protested against the prospect of being exchanged for the better. Could such a protest against being exchanged have any rational foundation? I think not.

If we realise that in fact no one is experiencing any loss (I assume, for the moment, that no transempirical self is lamenting over the loss of a place in time and space), if the exchange as such does not hurt, and if it involves no bad side-effects, then there is a positive obligation on our part to get ourselves exchanged. After all, that is only what takes place when new generations replace old ones. What is so terrible about that?

But whenever a person is changed, as in the example above, or exchanged for another person, there is a lack of felt connectedness, a loss of memory; this, it could be argued, should speak against such changes or exchanges. I think not, however. First of all, the loss of memory may be 'repaired'. The man who has taken the medicine and, consequently, feels no fear may not only be made not to protest against this after the change has taken place; he may also be given the (false) impression (a quasi-memory) that (contrary to fact) he wanted to take the medicine. Secondly, even if there is a lack of mental connectedness after the man has taken the medicine, he need not be worse off in this respect than he was before he took it. Why did he feel such terror of being killed in an accident before he took the medicine? The reason for this may be hidden from him; he may have forgotten what caused the terror. On the other hand, he now has some understanding of his actual and more relaxed view of the possibility of getting killed. He may come to understand the medical explanation of what happened to him, and so forth. Thirdly, it is not self-evident that it is a condition of a good life to be completely connected by memory. Would it not, on the contrary, be unbearable if we could not forget any single thing that has happened to us? There are some memories which we are only too glad to get rid of. Generally speaking, we cannot live (well) altogether disconnected from memory, and we cannot live (well) completely connected by it either.

However, when one person is exchanged for another, there might be something involved in the transaction which is problematic from an inter-personal point of view. It is often said that when we love a person, we love a unique individual, not a generic type. And the unique individual is lost in the transaction. Does this make the exchange objectionable? I think not. At least the exchange is unobjectionable if we assume, as I have done hitherto, that, in order to be reasonable, the criterion of personal identity must be stated in empirical (physical or mental) terms. Then there is no deep difference between my actual wife and the one I would get if she was exchanged for a different but similar person. When she is exchanged, my feelings need not change; I need not even notice the change. Perhaps my feelings would change, as a matter of fact, if I were told about the exchange. The change in my feelings would be irrational, however. In the situation, nothing has happened that does not happen all the time. The difference between my former and my present wife could be less than the difference between my wife five minutes ago and my wife five years ago. In the former case we may speak of an exchange, because the change is sudden. In the latter case we ought perhaps to speak of change, not of an exchange, since continuity is preserved. However, if the result of the former change (the exchange) is less upsetting than the result of the latter change (which took place over several years), why, then, bother about the way the former change was brought about?

It might be retorted that any validity the foregoing argument may possess only exists because it presupposes much too superficial a view of autonomy – and of personal identity. Admittedly, it might be held that to act autonomously a person must do what he or she decides to do, but this is in fact not sufficient. His or her will must also be autonomous; it must, in other words, be his or her own.

The autonomous will

How, then, are we to understand the view that the will of an autonomous person must be autonomous?

In the first place, it could be a view such as Kant's that, in order to be autonomous, our actions must spring from neither our empirical selves nor our actual wants, but our noumenal selves. Only a will with that kind of origin is really our own.

In the second place (setting aside the possibility that there may be, in addition to our empirical selves, noumenal selves), it could be a view to the effect that, in order to be autonomous, our actions must be caused by not our actual wants, but our actual selves; the assumption then is that, even if there are not two kinds of self, yet there are two kinds of causality, namely event causality and agent causality.

In the third place, it could be a view like the one formulated by Harry G. Frankfurt,[14] to the effect that, in order to be autonomous (or 'free', to use Frankfurt's word), our actions must be determined by wants which are in their turn determined by, or at least not at odds with, our second-order volitions, i.e., our volitions about what desires to have, leading to action. This is how Gerald Dworkin conceives of autonomy.[15]

Both the Kantian interpretation, presupposing the existence of two kinds of self, and the interpretation presupposing the existence of two kinds of causality, are problematic from the point of view of ontological economy. Richard Taylor, who used to believe in the doctrine of agent causality, no longer does, and his argument seems to me telling:

> what is this 'person' that is supposed to be an originating cause? A person – i.e., a man or woman – is not less a part of the physical world than a clock, or a cat . . . We can therefore suppose that a person is subject to the same kind of change, and exemplifies the same kind of causation, as any other physical object.[16]

Moreover, a special problem with the Kantian interpretation is that, if our noumenal self is causally independent, then it is difficult to see that it can, in any way, be threatened by anything we do to an empirical person. The claim that autonomy must be respected, then, turns out to be vacuous. Isaiah Berlin makes this point in the following way:

> Kant's free man needs no public recognition for his inner freedom. If he is treated as a means to some external purpose, that is a wrong act on the part of his exploiters, but his own 'noumenal' status is untouched, and he is fully free, and fully a man, however he may be treated.[17]

A decisive argument against both the Kantian interpretation of 'autonomy' and the interpretation presupposing agent causality is that, even if we may have an obligation to be 'autonomous' in some such rigorous sense (I do not discuss this view in the present context), it is difficult to see that it is of any value to us that we are autonomous; i.e., if we were to lose our 'autonomy', this could mean merely a relief. It must be asked in what way it would be better to have one's actual wishes and decisions controlled by one's noumenal self rather than by someone else's. In what way would it be better to have one's actual wishes and decisions controlled by any self at all, noumenal or empirical, one's own or someone else's, rather than, say, by one's own previous wishes and decisions and traits of character, with which one is, to some extent at least, connected by memory?

If the problem is, as it is in the present book, what value lies in being autonomous, rather than what kind of obligation there may exist to be autonomous, Frankfurt's (and Dworkin's) concept might seem more promising. However, this concept creates no new complications for my argument. There can be nothing special about second-order volitions. If my first-order volitions are changed, so as to make me happier, it may happen that my second-order volitions 'protest'. But they can be modified to the same extent. This may mean an exchange of persons, if a person's identity is held to be in the integration by his or her second-order personal volitions of his or her first-order volitions. I see, however, no good reason against such an exchange as such. All the reasons adduced against changing someone's second-order volitions seem to be equally good reasons against changing first-order ones. (As a matter of fact, the carpenter's volitions, in the example above, seem to be partly of the second order.) If, then, as I claim to have done, I have disposed of all of the objections against changing these volitions, I have also disposed of the possible objections against changing second-order volitions as well.

Is it good in itself to be an autonomous person?

Several philosophers have argued that, if we were to give up our autonomy, this would mean that we were giving up not only our own personal identity, but also our mature human nature. Thus J. S. Mill, who argued in 'On Liberty' that 'the free development of individuality is one of the leading essentials of well-being', and who complained that the evil is that 'individual spontaneity is hardly recognised by the common modes of thinking as having any intrinsic worth',[18] states that:

> Human nature is not a machine to be built after a model, and set to do exactly the work prescribed for it, but a tree, which requires to grow and develop itself on all sides, according to the tendency of the inward forces which make it a living thing.[19]

Robert Wolff, who argues that men 'are no better than children' if they accept the rule of others, writes as follows:

> When I place myself in the hands of another, and permit him to determine the principles by which I shall guide my behaviour, I repudiate the freedom and reason which give me dignity. I am guilty of what Kant might have called the sin of willful heteronomy.[20]

And Joel Feinberg argues along similar lines. He invites us to imagine a person who is given but one course of action in all situations. Such a person, says Feinberg, 'could take no credit or blame' for her or his actions. She or he could have no 'dignity', in her or his own eyes or in the eyes of others. There would be no point in her or his changing her or his mind or purposes. Her or his 'self-monitoring' and 'self-critical' capacities would dry up.[21]

I am not absolutely convinced that the whole of this is true if, after all, this person is always left some course of action. If she or he decides to adopt it, wants to do so and does so, then she or he may well be responsible for her or his actions. But if her or his autonomy is taken away from her or him completely, if all the actions we attribute to her or him are really performed not by herself or himself but by someone else, then she or he is without responsibility, just as Feinberg says that the unfree man is.

How could a person be deprived of his or her autonomy? One possible way of envisaging this outcome could be as follows. The man in question has been the object of brain surgery. The result of this surgery is a complete weakness of this person's will so that thereafter none of his decisions are caused in any way by his will. Instead, his decisions are monitored externally with the aid of a little apparatus implanted in his brain. Sometimes this man decides in accordance with his will, but not because he wills it. In other cases he decides against his will. Afterwards, however, he is made to like his decisions. This man never does what is bad for him except when there are good reasons for doing so, reasons relating to the welfare of others. To avoid irrelevant problems, let us suppose that this person has freely undergone this kind of therapy.

Clearly this man has given up all of his autonomy. He does not perform one autonomous action. He is not that kind of person. He is in the hands of someone controlling him. It is true that he is 'no better than a child' after he has undergone the surgery, and perhaps he is in some respects more like a machine than like a tree.

Is this bad? Is it bad for him to be no better than a child, to lack responsibility, and to be like a machine? Is it bad in itself that he is in this situation? Must we say of the person that if his gain in felt well-being is small enough he has been 'irrational', in the sense that he has chosen a lesser good (or even something evil) before some greater good? I think not.

To be in his situation may be dangerous. He is very vulnerable indeed. However, let us assume, for the sake of argument, that he is well taken care of and that no one takes advantage of his position. Then his choice may be perfectly rational.

To be sure, the patient in my example is without responsibility for his actions; he cannot reasonably be dignified, in his own eyes or in the eyes of others, at least not because of what he has done himself; he cannot change his mind himself; his self-monitoring and self-critical capacities are destroyed. But so what?

Suppose he is happy. Remember that he chose to undergo this therapy. Suppose that, as he expected, he is slightly happier than he was before the operation took place. He might be happy, Feinberg concedes. But a 'contentment with which all this might still be consistent would not be a recognisable human happiness'.[22]

This may be so. Whether this contentment is 'human' or not is a matter of stipulation. However, even if we assume that it is not human, I still cannot see that this creates any serious trouble, for the 'person' experiencing this contentment will not be a human being, either. Feinberg says that he will be like a 'robot' (and Mill used the word 'machine'). Perhaps this is so. But then, why should he complain that his contentment is not human? He most certainly would not. He would not be allowed to complain (we may assume).

However, if it is not bad for him to be in the situation in which he is, how, then, could his being in this situation be bad in itself? It could be maintained, of course, that human contentment is superior to that experienced by non-human sentient beings. 'Man is the final end of creation', wrote Kant. 'Without man the chain of mutually subordinated ends would have no ultimate point of attachment.'[23]

How could such a claim be sustained, however? I know of no good argument in defence of it. But if our preference for human happiness cannot be based on good reasons, it seems to rest on nothing but self-indulgent, gratuitous 'speciesism'. The preference is effectively undermined, it seems to me, by the insight that human nature is the result of a blind process of natural selection; it has slowly become what it is and is slowly changing. The present state of the human gene pool is not sacred.

Nozick's experience machine, described in *Anarchy, State, and Utopia*, now comes to mind. We assume that, if we plug into the machine, then neuro-psychologists stimulate our brains so that we think and feel that we are writing great novels, or making friends, or reading interesting books. All the time we are floating in a tank, with electrodes attached to our brains. If we plug in, or, even more so, if we are manipulated to plug in, we lose all our personal autonomy, I would say. According to Nozick, we do not want to plug into this kind of machine. And there is a lesson to be learnt from this fact: 'We learn that something matters to us in addition to experience by imagining an experience machine and then realizing that we would not use it.'[24] He then goes on to state what it is that matters to us: 'Perhaps what we desire is to live (an active verb) ourselves, in contact with reality.'[25]

The truth of this argument is not unquestionable. Perhaps many people would as a matter of fact opt for the experience machine. And perhaps some people, who would not, would not opt for it because of an (unreasonable) fear that those in charge of the machine would take advantage of them in some nasty way. Moreover, those who hesitate to opt for the machine may do so because they do not like the fact that the option seems to be irrevocable. This is an unnecessary defect in Nozick's argument, however. He could allow that people now and then become conscious of their present situation; once a year they could be offered the possibility of opting out of the machine. If this is how the machine works, are we to expect that people will not opt for it or that, if they do, they will opt out of it as soon as a possibility of doing so arises?

I am not so sure of this. After all, many people choose to use drugs they know are dangerous, such as alcohol, in spite of the fact that they know that it is difficult to give up the habit of using them. So why not opt for a perfect experience machine (that you can opt out from if you like) with no bad side-effects – and stay plugged into it?

More importantly, however, the argument begs the question. As a matter of fact, by stressing the putative fact that we do not want to plug in, and then using this as an argument to the effect that it would not be a good thing for us if we did, Nozick takes for granted what is highly controversial, and what was rejected in the previous chapter, to wit, that, necessarily, our choices and desires are guides to what is good for us (preferentialism). Nozick seems to be – or to have become – aware of the problem, for later, in *The Examined Life*, he makes the following comment:

> Notice that I am not saying simply that since we desire connection to actuality the experience machine is defective because it does not give us whatever we desire . . . Rather, I am saying that the connection to actuality is important whether or not we desire it – that is *why* we desire it – and the experience machine is inadequate because it doesn't give us *that*.[26]

However, if this is taken seriously, then it emerges that, after all, Nozick does not have any argument for his position. In his famous example he is simply, in a highly dogmatic way, stating it.

Perhaps a similar argument by J. S. Mill fares better, however. According to Mill, there are higher and lower pleasures. Some kinds of pleasure are more desirable and more valuable than others. For example: 'It is better to be a human being dissatisfied than a pig satisfied; better to be Socrates dissatisfied than a fool satisfied.'[27] Perhaps we could argue, in the spirit of Mill, then, that the pleasures felt when our autonomy is gone, when, for example, we are plugged into an experience machine, or live like animals rather than as people, are of less value than the pleasures we feel as autonomous, human beings.

How do we know when we are facing a pleasure of a higher quality, then? 'Of two pleasures, if there be one to which all or almost all who have experience of both give a decided preference, irrespective of any feeling of moral obligation to prefer it, that is the more desirable pleasure.'[28] Once again it seems that preferentialism has been taken for granted. But perhaps we ought to think of the 'decided preference' not as a mere preference, but as a considered value judgement. If we do then I must say that I sympathise in principle with this test. However, how are we to apply it?

In the first place, I know of no investigation where it has been systematically put to use. It is an open question, then, whether, if it could be made operational, it would yield any result at variance with hedonism. In particular, I conjecture that, if there is no feeling of moral obligation to prefer one pleasure to the other, most people will opt for whatever it is that brings them the most intensive or endurable pleasure, irrespective of whether this is pushpin or poetry, and irrespective of whether they experience it *qua* autonomous individuals or *qua* brains in a vat. They will say that this is the best experience. I conjecture that this is true even of those who prefer being autonomous persons to being brains in a vat.

In the second place, it seems difficult to make the test operational. Suppose we have two persons, having experienced two kinds of pleasure, A and B. Now, the first person claims that A is better, the other one that B is better. What are we to say of the situation? It seems to me that, when faced with a result such as this, we can always deny that these two persons were really having the same kind of experience. Some differences in their perception may account for the difference in their judgement.

The upshot of this is that, even if there is nothing wrong in principle with Mill's argument, it is not decisive one way or the other. If it could be made operational, it might come to support hedonism just as well as the position Mill himself wants to defend.

Personal autonomy and rule utilitarianism

In the present book I have said little hitherto about rule utilitarianism. But perhaps it could provide a rationale for the belief that we ought to respect people's personal autonomy.

What is rule utilitarianism, then? I have defined it in the following manner:

RU: A particular action is right if, and only if, it is not proscribed by any rule or system of rules such that, if people were generally adhering to it, the world, on the whole, would be better than if they were adhering to any rule or system of rules permitting it.

Now, I have tried to show that personal autonomy lacks intrinsic value. To many this may still seem wrong, or even morally repugnant. I have argued that, as a matter of fact, personal autonomy lacks intrinsic value, but I do not want to argue that it is not morally repugnant to say so. And I admit that the thesis is at variance with some of our moral intuitions. I have tried to show that, if these intuitions are reflected upon, however, if they are put in philosophical perspective, they have to yield. They do not fit into our 'reflective equilibrium'. This does not mean, however, that these intuitions should be given up. Perhaps they should, but I do not want to argue this point. The fact that they are not epistemologically justified does not mean that they are not morally justified. Our belief that personal autonomy has intrinsic value may have very good consequences in the long run. This means that, on strictly utilitarian grounds, we ought to retain it in our common sense thinking about morality.

I have several times touched upon this idea that our morality must be stratified into a critical and an intuitive level, put forward most famously by R. M. Hare.[29] We must adopt some kind of what Peter Railton has called a 'sophisticated consequentialism'.[30] In Chapter 9 I defend such a stance against strictures directed against it by Jonathan Dancy. If Dancy is right, these two levels cannot cogently be kept separate. If I am right, they can. In the present chapter I will simply take this for granted.

Now, no matter whether Hare is right in his belief that our common sense morality ought to contain a principle of liberty or not, this does not affect my main point that, irrespective of what we ought to believe and to teach our children, personal autonomy does not have intrinsic value.

Against this line of argument it could be retorted, however, that the two levels of moral thinking here discussed should not be kept separate, even if it is possible to do. The argument would run as follows: if a general acceptance of a principle stating that personal autonomy be respected has better consequences than the acceptance of any alternative morality, then this shows not only that such a general acceptance should be sought, but also that, in a particular case, whatever the consequences of doing so, it is right to respect personal autonomy. This is the rule–utilitarian position.

Some commentators on Mill have argued that this is Mill's position. His virtually absolute proscription against interference with personal autonomy is justified, they argue, not because of the intrinsic value of personal autonomy, but rather because of the overall gain in net utility obtained by recognition of such an absolute value.[31]

I do not find this position defensible. I reject RU. It is acceptable to teach a morality, the general acceptance of which has the best consequences, I concede;[32] and, if such teaching has been effective, perhaps, being caught in our common sense morality, we will, as a matter of fact, conform to it, even in situations where such conformity does not produce the best possible outcome; but our conformance in these situations, producing bad effects, is really something we should avoid.

The rule–utilitarian position may seem attractive as long as we do not make a distinction between two levels of moral thinking. However, when we realise that this is something we can do, that it is one thing to question what moral beliefs we ought to have (or to teach to our children), and quite another thing to question what moral beliefs are true, any rational belief in the rule–utilitarian position gets undermined. To have grasped this distinction fully, and yet to believe that one ought to cling to optimific rules even in situations where by so doing we do not maximise intrinsic value, is to be the victim of what J. J. C. Smart has famously called 'Rule Worship'.[33]

Conclusion

If the argument of the present chapter is sound, then autonomy lacks intrinsic value. But then all sorts of putative perfectionist value such as achievement, knowledge, deep personal relations, and a contact with realities seem to go overboard as well. For, to be sure, the notion of autonomy is built into these notions.

When it is claimed that achievement, knowledge, deep personal relations, and a contact with realities are of importance as such to the value of the life of an individual, it is taken for granted that these achievements, this knowledge, these deep personal relations, and this contact with realities are truly this person's own. If, from the point of view of intrinsic value, it does not matter whether we make our own achievements, gain our own knowledge, make our own friends, or get ourselves into contact with realities, or are manipulated into these relations, then the relations as such cannot really matter to us.

Perfectionism is not a tenable view.

Notes

1 Or, perhaps we should say that, according to Kant, we cannot help being autonomous. We are, at least as noumenal selves, autonomous by nature.
2 J. S. Mill, 'On Liberty', Ch. III.
3 J. Rawls, *A Theory of Justice*, p. 516.
4 J. Glover, *Causing Death and Saving Lives*, p. 77.
5 J. S. Mill, 'On Liberty', pp. 191–2.
6 Isaiah Berlin, in 'Two Concepts of Liberty', makes the famous distinction between 'positive' and 'negative' liberty. When I contrast autonomy with liberty/freedom, my concept of autonomy is close to Berlin's concept of positive liberty and my concept of liberty/freedom is close to his concept of negative liberty.
7 Rawls insists that the proper word is 'lexicographically', but finds it too cumbersome. He defines a 'lexical order' as an order 'which requires us to satisfy the first principle in the ordering before we can move on to the second, the second before we consider the third, and so on. A principle does not come in to play until those previous to it are either fully met or do not apply' (*A Theory of Justice*, p. 43).
8 J. Griffin, *Well-being*, p. 67.
9 Griffin, *Well-being*, p. 70.
10 P. Singer, *Practical Ethics*, p. 146.

11 Singer, *Practical Ethics*, p. 146.
12 Glover, *Causing Death and Saving Lives*, p. 82.
13 B. Williams, 'A Critique of Utilitarianism', p. 116.
14 Cf. H. G. Frankfurt, 'Freedom of the Will and the Concept of a Person'.
15 Cf. G. Dworkin, 'The Concept of Autonomy'.
16 R. Taylor, 'Agent and Patient', pp. 224–5.
17 Berlin, 'Two Concepts of Liberty', p. 156.
18 Mill, 'On Liberty', p. 185.
19 Mill, 'On Liberty', p. 188.
20 R. P. Wolff, *In Defense of Anarchism*, p. 72.
21 Cf. J. Feinberg, 'Interest in Liberty on the Scales'.
22 Feinberg, 'Interest in Liberty', p. 40.
23 I. Kant, *Critique of Judgement*, p. 99.
24 R. Nozick, *Anarchy, State, and Utopia*, p. 44.
25 Nozick, *Anarchy, State, and Utopia*, p. 45.
26 R. Nozick, *The Examined Life: Philosophical Meditations*, pp. 106–7. I owe this observation to Bengt Brülde.
27 J. S. Mill, *Utilitarianism*, p. 260.
28 Mill, *Utilitarianism*, p. 259.
29 Cf. R. M. Hare, *Moral Thinking*, where a theory of two 'levels' of moral thinking is developed, and see Hare, 'What is Wrong With Slavery?', where he defends the claim that our common sense morality ought to contain a 'principle of liberty'.
30 Cf. P. Railton, 'Alienation, Consequentialism, and the Demands of Morality', about this.
31 Philosophers who have famously discussed this possible interpretation of Mill are J. O. Urmson, in 'The Interpretation of the Philosophy of J. S. Mill', and J. D. Mabbott, in 'Moral Rules'.
32 As a matter of fact, the kind of morality we ought to teach, on the most plausible version of the two levels account, is not the one with the best acceptance value, let alone the one with the best conformance value. The one we ought to teach is the one with the best educational value. This is perhaps a morality that people will accept, when it is taught to them, and such that it has better consequences for people to accept it than any other morality that they would accept, if they were taught to do so. Or, it might be a morality such that, if people were taught it, they would reject it, and the consequences of their rejection would be better than their acceptance or rejection of any other morality that they could be taught.
33 J. J. C. Smart, 'An Outline of a System of Utilitarian Ethics', p. 10. Notice that, if 'Rule Worship' is indeed a vice, it is an intellectual not a moral one. It may well be the case that, if people practise rule worship, the world is better than if they do not.

Chapter 8

Against idealism

Thus far I have taken it for granted that intrinsic value is individual. I have taken it for granted that the only plausible candidates, when we search for an answer to the question of what possesses intrinsic value, are the experiences, achievements or satisfaction of preferences of individuals. I have taken it for granted that, when something good exists, it is possible to attribute this good to someone. When something good exists we can say things like: 'It is good for Sara that she is happy', 'It is good for Peter that he got his preference for a new saxophone satisfied', 'It is good for Mary to have friends and to develop her talents for athletics.' And I have argued that upon closer inspection the only genuine individual (positive and negative) values are pleasure and displeasure (hedonism).

This assumption of value individualism is controversial, however. It has been argued most famously by G. E. Moore that, besides individual values, there exist impersonal values. We could list these, and hence speak of a list of valuable things, such as beauty, equality and so forth. These are thought to be good in themselves, but not good for anyone. When this idea is wedded to utilitarianism, G. E. Moore speaks of 'Ideal Utilitarianism'. I shall focus in this chapter on the problem of intrinsic value, so I shall call the theory under scrutiny 'idealism'.[1] This idealist line of thought has been taken up by some modern 'deep ecological' thinkers as well, who argue that the preservation of a rich variety of species in the world has intrinsic value. It is not good for any one in particular that this variety exists, but it is good in itself that it does. The most articulate among them is perhaps the Norwegian philosopher Arne Naess.[2]

I have now and then toyed with this idea myself,[3] but upon critical reflection I want to give it up. In the present chapter I will state my reasons for doing so, thus making my defence of hedonism complete. I begin my argument with a methodological observation.

Moral methodology

The methodological observation I want to make is as follows: if there are individual values, we do not have to go very far to think how we come to know that these values are important. We have direct access to them. This is true in particular about pleasure. We know from our own experience what it is like to be happy, and we realise that this is a good thing, or so I have argued, at any rate. To elaborate on this point, I would say that our knowledge that pleasure is intrinsically good is based on introspection. As we have seen in Chapter 5, however, our knowledge in this field extends beyond what is (directly) introspectively given. We have to infer the existence of sub-noticeable differences of well-being and attribute moral importance to them, and we have to settle for a morally relevant unit in our assessment of pleasure. However, these theoretical moves are something we undertake against a background of firm empirical evidence. Roughly, this is how we go about it.

We see, or observe, or grasp (through introspection) that certain experiences we have are both pleasant and intrinsically valuable. We note directly, I submit, without any conscious reasoning taking place, both that such experiences are pleasant and that they are good. And we note not only that they are good for us but also that they are good in themselves. They are of a kind that must be taken some notice of in moral action.

To be sure, when we conclude not only that these experiences are both pleasant and good, but that it is their pleasantness that makes them good, then we make an inference. This inference has been defended in previous chapters as one to the best explanation. Moreover, I would say the fact that pleasure is intrinsically valuable, and the fact that some experiences are better than others, explain our judgements to this effect.

I will not go further into any defence of the latter conjecture in the present context (the conjecture that something's actually being good explains our belief that it is), since I have defended it elsewhere.[4] It suffices here to notice that, if pleasure (or, for that matter, preference satisfaction or perfection) has positive intrinsic value, the way we come to learn about this is not mysterious. We have a direct and intimate acquaintance with it.

The situation with impersonal values is very different. Even if impersonal states of affairs, organic wholes and so forth were to possess intrinsic value, it is very mysterious how we could come to know about these values. The fact that the continued existence of the human race is of value in itself, if it is, is hardly anything that we can observe. The claim that it is of value in itself is a general one. If such a thing as the continued existence of the human race, or the continued existence of a rich variety of species, is of value in itself, then this is something that can only be known because there exists a good philosophical argument to this effect. We do not personally observe or experience it.

Tentatively, I want to argue, therefore, that we ought not to be convinced that impersonal values are real unless we can be shown somehow that this assumption fits into our web of beliefs in a crucial manner. In want of arguments to the opposite effect, we must say that impersonal values are merely speculative and highly uncertain. The claim that such things as the continued existence of the human race are of value in themselves is on a par with theological speculations about the existence of God.

The same point could also be substantiated in the following way: we know what it means for something to be good for someone. We know this because we know what it means for something to be good for us. At least we can give examples of such goods. We may be uncertain as to how exactly we are to explain these examples, but we know that they are genuine. I know, for example, that it is good for me to sail far out in the archipelago of Stockholm late in the autumn. I believe that it is good for me because it fills me with contentment (hedonism). In previous chapters I have stated my reasons for this belief. I may be wrong about this explanation, of course. Perhaps it is good for me not because it fills me with contentment, but because it is self-fulfilling (perfectionism). Or perhaps it is good because it means that I get some fundamental desires satisfied (preferentialism). Be that as it may, I feel certain that this is good for me. And I feel certain that it is good in itself that I experience what I do experience.

Intrinsic value

It might be wondered exactly what more this kind of claim means; what does it mean to say of something that it has 'intrinsic value', or that it is 'good in itself'? I do not pretend to be able to give a clear definition of the notion of intrinsic value. I suppose that the meaning of the notion can be given only indirectly. If the notion can be defined at all, it can only be defined implicitly. One requirement the notion does satisfy, however, is the following: if something is good in itself, then it is worthy of some kind of consideration. To use Shelly Kagan's phrase, if something is good in itself, then anyone has a *pro tanto* reason to promote it.[5] So to the extent that other people experience the same kind of pleasure that I do, I and other persons have a *pro tanto* reason to promote these experiences.

It is a vexed question whether we need both evaluative and normative notions in our moral theory. G. E. Moore argued famously against W. F. Frankena that we need both these kinds of notion.[6] I think Moore was right. What it is that has intrinsic value is one problem, and exactly how we should relate to intrinsic values is another.

The brand of utilitarianism defended in this book could be stated without any mention of intrinsic value. As a matter of fact, this is how I have eventually stated hedonistic utilitarianism. When I first stated the utilitarian formula in Chapter 2, I did so in evaluative terms. However, in the following chapters I eliminated the notion. I spelled out in empirical terms what it was that, according to the utilitarian formula, should be maximised. So there is no room for intrinsic value in the statement of hedonistic utilitarianism. But this does not mean that there is no room for intrinsic value in our moral reasoning.

The notion of intrinsic value plays an important epistemic role. We are on firm ground when we conclude what it is that should be taken into account in our moral arguments, what it is that is worthy of our consideration. We are on more shaky ground when we claim that we should take it into account in one particular manner (maximisation, say).

I make both the claim that what possesses intrinsic value is pleasure and displeasure and nothing else, and the claim that we ought to maximise the net balance of pleasure over displeasure. I feel more certain that I am right in the former claim than in the latter, however. The reason why I do so should be clear from what I have said in Chapter 2 (where the difficulties of finding evidence for normative theories was brought to the fore) together with what I say in this chapter (where the epistemically favoured position of personal values is being stressed).

Can we trust introspection?

My argument thus far may seem to echo a standard empiricist argument for scientific knowledge. We have reasons to have some trust in science since it is based on observational evidence. This does not make science infallible, but it places it on a more secure footing than, say, speculative theology. And I have argued that we have reasons to have some trust in the existence of personal values, since our belief in them is based on our familiarity with them. But our familiarity with them comes through introspection. So in my argument I am taking it for granted that introspection is a reliable method (on a par with observation). Is that a plausible assumption?

I admit that there are problems with introspection. Introspection is similar to observation in the sense that, in introspection too, we make immediate judgements as a response to some reality, without any conscious reasoning having taken place. However, there seems to be a crucial difference between observation on the one hand and introspection on the other. Observations can be more or less intersubjectively reliable. We tend to base scientific theory on observations that are fairly uncontroversial. Even if we can tolerate some controversy about the interpretation of what we observe, we want our scientific theories to be based on observations satisfying the following test: if several persons, suitably placed, compare their observations, they should not disagree about what they observe (under some fairly neutral description of it, at any rate). This requirement is only too easily satisfied when it comes to introspection. Since introspection is in its nature private, there is no immediate way in which we can come to question an introspective report. We can say that it sits ill with a certain theory we hold, and with certain other beliefs we hold about the person making the report, but we can in no immediate manner come to question it.

This inherently private nature of introspection has led some thinkers to reject introspection altogether in science. I do not find this strategy very plausible, however. For it seems to me that if we want to do psychology at all, we have to rely on introspective reports. Otherwise our psychological theories will tend to be barren.

This is not to say that introspective reports are infallible; they may sometimes be mistaken. And yet, for all that, this acceptance of introspection does in effect mean that we grant a certain privileged position to people themselves, when they make at least some kinds of judgement about themselves. When we admit introspection into psychology, we grant that people in general are fairly reliable, at least when they report sincerely what kinds of feeling and experience they have at the moment they report them.

But if we are prepared to base at least parts of our psychological understanding on introspective reports, then we should not hesitate also to base the evaluative part of our moral understanding on introspection.

Our understanding of personal values can be based on introspection. We introspect that we are happy (unhappy). We introspect that this is good for us (bad for us). We introspect that this is good in itself (bad in itself). And from this introspective basis we make various kinds of inference.

Our understanding of impersonal values, by contrast, cannot be based on introspection. Does that mean that we should reject the idea of impersonal values? I think it does, unless we can give a good philosophical argument to the effect that there are impersonal values. If someone claims that he or she knows that the continued existence of the human species is of value in itself, we should not take his or her claim at face value (any more than we should take the claim that someone knows that God exists at face value). And since this kind of belief cannot be given empirical support, we should ask for a good philosophical argument.

It is debatable whether there exists a good philosophical argument in defence of the claim that God exists. Is there a good philosophical argument to the effect that some impersonal values are real?

Let us consider G. E. Moore's own defence of the claim that there are impersonal values. Let us focus on what I consider his best candidate: beauty.

G. E. Moore on the intrinsic value of beauty

G. E. Moore's defence of the claim that beauty possesses positive intrinsic value is cast in the form of an attack on Henry Sidgwick's claim to the opposite effect. Sidgwick wrote that 'no one would consider it rational to aim at the production of beauty in external nature, apart from any possible contemplation of it by human beings'.[7] To this Moore retorted:

Let us imagine one world exceedingly beautiful. Imagine it as beautiful as you can; put into it whatever on this earth you most admire — mountains, rivers, the sea; trees and sunsets, stars and moon. Imagine all these combined in the most exquisite proportions, so that no one thing jars against another, but each contributes to increase the beauty of the whole. And then imagine the ugliest world you can possibly conceive. Imagine it simply one heap of filth, containing everything that is most disgusting to us, for whatever reason, and the whole, as far as may be, without one redeeming feature. Such a pair of worlds we are entitled to compare: they fall within Prof. Sidgwick's meaning, and the comparison is highly relevant to us. The only thing we are not entitled to imagine is that any human being has, or ever, by any possibility, *can*, live in either, can ever see and enjoy the beauty of the one or hate the foulness of the other. Well, even so, supposing them quite apart from any possible contemplation by human beings; still, is it irrational to hold that it is better that the beautiful world should exist, than the one which is ugly? Would it not be well, in any case, to do what we could to produce it rather than the other? Certainly I cannot help thinking that it would: and I hope that some may agree with me in this extreme instance.[8]

The restriction to 'human' beings in the quotation from Sidgwick, which is repeated by Moore, sits ill with his hedonism. Why should we not produce beautiful objects for the sake of the pleasure they would give to extra-human beings? I will consider this as a mere slip. The question, then, is whether Sidgwick or Moore is right.

It might be wondered whether either has produced any argument for his position. I think both have, but flawed ones.

Sidgwick's use of the word 'rational' might indicate that somehow he bases his moral claim on a conception of rationality. However, appearances are deceptive. When he says that it would not be rational to take up a certain aim, he only intends to say that this aim is not worthy of the attempt. What one attempts to create does not possess intrinsic value. Yet, for all that, Sidgwick does state an argument for his position. And the argument is that everyone shares his belief. Or, rather, his argument is that everyone 'would' share his belief.

How are we to understand this use of the word 'would'? Judging from his argument in other situations, I suggest the following interpretation: everyone who was to consider the matter seriously, everyone who is prepared to 'sit down in a cool hour', would concur in his judgement.

The relevance of this argument is, for obvious reasons, restricted. Furthermore, and more important still, as is pointed out by Moore, the argument is simply false. Moore, for one, does not share Sidgwick's view, not even after having seriously contemplated the matter.

But Moore's own argument fares no better. He constructs an abstract thought-experiment where we can choose between producing a beautiful and an ugly world, and he announces that he cannot help thinking that it would be well if we did what we could to produce the beautiful one. And he hopes that some may agree with him about this. Suppose that everyone does. What does this prove? It proves nothing at all, unless we take preferentialism for granted. And even if we do, we end up with the wrong kind of support for the thesis that beauty has intrinsic value. We end up, then, with the conclusion that beauty has not intrinsic value, but 'contributory' value; it is a good thing that beautiful things exist, not for its own sake, but because this is something people happen to want. Since I have argued against preferentialism in an earlier chapter, I will not now return to this topic.

Furthermore, it is clear at least that not everyone is prepared to join Moore in his judgement about his own thought-experiment. Jonathan Glover, for one, has argued very eloquently that he sides with Sidgwick:

> If, travelling in a train through the middle of a ten-mile railway tunnel, I saw a man leaning out of the window into the darkness, I might wonder what he was doing. If it turned out to be G. E. Moore spraying the walls of the tunnel with paint, because painted walls are better than unpainted ones, even if no one ever sees them, I should not be able to prove him irrational. But I should not accept his offer of the use of a second paint spray, except possibly out of politeness.[9]

As is implied in this quotation, Glover himself seems to believe that no decisive argument could be given on this issue. This may be true. As a matter of fact, I share Glover's pessimism. Impersonal values, then, are merely speculative.

The fact that no good arguments could be produced either for or against the claim that, besides individual values, impersonal values exist does not mean that we cannot take a rational stand on the issue, however. We can approach a reasonable position in the debate if we base our decision about with whom we are to side, with Sidgwick or with Moore, on something I will call the principle of the rejection of merely speculative values:

> Anything might be of value in itself, but if we know of no good reason for the claim that something in particular has intrinsic value, it is sound moral methodology to reject the claim. We have enough to bother about that we feel certain has value.

Or, if this variety of moral pragmatism may seem too strong, we may base our stand on the principle of known values taking precedence over merely speculative ones:

> We should not be prepared to sacrifice known values in the name of merely speculative, putative values, for the existence of which we possess neither observational evidence nor good theoretical reasons.

I find this latter principle very plausible. However, some may find even this one too strong. Those who do may be tempted to argue in the following manner:

would it not be rational to make a small sacrifice in terms of a known value (to cause some pain, for example) in order to safeguard an uncertain but possibly very important value (such as the survival of the human species)?

This argument is not convincing. To see why, let us consider the case more closely.

What could it mean to cause some displeasure in order to safeguard the continued existence of the human species? When we consider the case, we must think of the extinction of the human species as an event that makes no difference from a hedonistic point of view. How could this be? One explanation might be that the human species would get replaced by some other species, capable of enjoying life just as much as human beings do. Or, another explanation might be that the continued existence of the human species would, from a hedonistic point of view, be neutral. Some pleasure would be forthcoming if the species continued to exist, but this pleasure would be balanced by equal amounts of pain.

When we see the example in this perspective, I think we are prepared to hold on to the claim that we should not forego a known good in order to safeguard an uncertain and merely speculative good.

Against this it might be retorted that if we know about an uncertain value that, if it is a value at all, it is of the utmost importance, we must pay some attention to it. Its uncertainty means that it does not possess its full potential value in our calculations, but its known magnitude, if it is a value at all, must be taken into account.

I concede that point. I concede that, if we know of some value that, if it is a value at all, it is of great magnitude, then we must pay attention to it. However, I question that this is something we can ever know about. I am prepared to claim that, even if an unknown value may be great, this is something we can never know. If we are uncertain as to whether it is a value at all, then we must also be uncertain about its magnitude. After all, when we feel uncertain as to whether it is a value at all, we are open to the possibility that its magnitude may be zero. However, if we accept that it might be zero, then we must also accept that it might be close to zero. The idea of a merely speculative value that must, if it is a value at all, be of great importance is not cogent.

If this argument is correct, then the rational move is to neglect merely speculative values in our moral calculations, at least as soon as they conflict with other values. And typically, impersonal values conflict with personal values, at least to some extent. So, for all practical purposes, we could give them up altogether.

As a matter of fact, this is consistent with the way Moore himself argues about beauty. He insists that beauty has some value, but, upon closer inspection it appears that he is not prepared to sacrifice any amount of pleasure, or to create any amount of pain, however small, in order to realise beauty for beauty's sake.[10]

This seems to me rational. However, Moore's position then seems to me futile. Why not simply reject a value so completely without practical importance? Why not simply give it up, on the ground that is too speculative and uncertain?

Furthermore, when it comes to other values, Moore does seem prepared to accept that displeasure be inflicted on people for the sake of some 'organic whole' being as good as possible. For example, he does accept that a criminal be punished, even if the punishment does not deter further crimes. He accepts the sacrifice of individual value simply for the sake of the speculative value of the 'organic whole':

> It follows that, quite apart from *consequences* or any value which an evil may have as a mere means, it may, *supposing* one evil already exists, be worthwhile to create another, since, by the mere creation of this second, there may be constituted a whole less bad than if the original evil had been left to exist by itself.[11]

Accepting the principle of known values taking precedence over merely speculative ones, I reject this attitude as irrational. Having said that, I feel that I must add that I find this attitude exhibited by Moore not only irrational, but cruel.

Can we observe beauty?

The following rejoinder to my argument could be made: it might be true that we come to know personal values in a more reliable manner than we can ever hope to come to know impersonal ones, such as the value of the continued existence of the human race. However, there is one impersonal value that we seem to get to know in a manner that is even *more* reliable than that in which we get to know about personal values. This value is beauty. For, or so the argument goes, beauty, and the intrinsic value of beauty, we observe.

This is obviously not Moore's view about how we come to learn that beauty is intrinsically valuable. He seems to presuppose that somehow we simply grasp the general truth that beauty is a good-making characteristic. However, I have actually come across the following argument: when a person listens to a piece of music, then this person may well come to observe both that certain musical qualities are present in the music, and that the music is beautiful. Moreover, the same person observes that the music is (aesthetically) good. He or she then infers that it is the beauty that makes the music good.[12]

Is this a plausible view? If it is, I concede that we have come across a kind of impersonal value that, epistemologically speaking, has an even firmer footing than personal values. However, I doubt that this kind of observation is genuine.

First of all, it seems far from clear that, in normal circumstances, the claim that a piece of music is beautiful is really a claim about the piece of music as such. When I make that kind of claim, which I often do, I suspect that what I mean to say is that the music in question pleases me (or, if this is not something I say, I express my contentment with the music in question). Or, if I realise that it takes a lot of skill to produce the kind of music, what I express may (partly) be my admiration for the composer.

Secondly, even if there are some people who seriously believe that when they say that a piece of music is beautiful, they attribute a quality to this piece of music, we need not take their belief at face value. The fact that opinions are so diverse and conflicting when it comes to aesthetic judgements should give us pause. It is hard not to suspect that aesthetic value judgements, to the extent that they do not express the personal likings of the persons who make them, reflect different educational experiences. Those who make the conflicting judgements have been taught that their favourite kind of music is intrinsically good; however, different persons have been taught that different sorts of music are intrinsically good. It is far-fetched to claim that while one of two conflicting judgements may be correct in the sense that it tracks reality (the judgement that the piece of music is good is made because the piece of music is good), the other is wrong (and can be explained away as a mere result of upbringing, personal likings and so forth of the person making it). It is more plausible, I submit, to suppose that all aesthetic judgements are properly so explained. If they are, we have no reason to assume that aesthetic values are real. Even if people make these judgements in the belief that they ascribe objective qualities to pieces of music (or other artefacts), this does not mean that we have to grant the claim that these objective qualities exist.

To this it might be objected that, if aesthetic values can be explained away in this way, why should this not apply also to personal values?[13]

It is really not possible to answer this stricture in any definite manner in the present context. The discussion would take a book of its own.[14] It must suffice here to note two things.

In the first place, there seems to be much less disagreement about personal values than there is about aesthetic ones. Most people agree at least that severe experiences of displeasure are bad in themselves and should be avoided. There exist no corresponding examples from the aesthetic domain to which we could point. In the aesthetic domain, everything is controversial.

Secondly, while most people are prepared to countenance with ease the fact that other people do not share their aesthetic beliefs (*de gustibus non est disputandum*), they are hard put to it to accept that other people do not share their beliefs about personal values. At least in what they find to be paradigmatic cases of personal value, most people are prepared to go to some lengths in the attempt to prove others wrong when they find that their own opinions are not shared by others.

Both of these considerations speak with some force in defence of the claim that, while personal values are real, aesthetic values are merely 'in the mind of the beholder'. And, to say the least, in view of these considerations it seems far-fetched indeed to assume that, if (somehow) aesthetic values exist, we have observational knowledge of them.

Conclusion

In the present chapter I have admitted that there are no good philosophical reasons against the assumption that, besides personal values (pleasure and pain, in particular), there exist impersonal values, such as beauty, the continued existence of the human race, and so forth. However, there seem to be no good philosophical arguments in defence of the claim that these values exist, either. Then it is good moral methodology, I have argued, to reject the claim that these impersonal values are real. At least, we should not pay any attention to them in our moral calculations. This conclusion is based on the principle of known values taking precedence over merely speculative ones.

Notes

1 My use of the word 'idealism' is more restricted than Moore's. Ideal utilitarianism for Moore is exemplified not only by theories according to which we ought to promote impersonal values, but also by theories according to which we ought to promote values other than ones experienced by an individual, such as knowledge. In this case Derek Parfit speaks, in *Reasons and Persons*, p. 4, of an 'objective list' of personal values. Parfit confines the phrase 'objective list' to personal values. However, even impersonal values can appear on an objective list. When they do we are confronted with what I have called an idealist view of intrinsic value (idealism, for short).

2 Cf. A. Naess, 'The Shallow and the Deep: Long-range Ecological Movement. A Summary', and also his book *Ökologi, Samfunn og Livsstil*.

3 Cf. in particular my book *Conservatism for Our Time*, Ch. 3.

4 Cf. my *Moral Realism*, Ch. 3.

5 Cf. Shelly Kagan, *The Limits of Morality*, pp. 16–17.

6 Cf. G. E. Moore, 'A Reply to My Critics'.

7 H. Sidgwick, *The Methods of Ethics*, p. 114.

8 G. E. Moore, *Principia Ethica*, pp. 83–4.

9 J. Glover, *What Sort of People Should There Be?*, p. 110.

10 Moore, *Principia Ethica*, p. 84.

11 Moore, *Principia Ethica*, p. 216.

12 Lars Bergström has put forward this argument in conversation.

13 This claim is made by Gilbert Harman in the opening chapter of his book *The Nature of Morality: An Introduction to Ethics*.

14 In Ch. 3 of my book *Moral Realism* I defend the claim that personal values are genuine: *pace* Harman, our judgements about what is good and bad (for us) can best be explained, in some cases, at any rate, by this actually being the case.

Chapter 9

Blameful rightdoing and blameless wrongdoing

In his recent book *Moral Reasons*, Jonathan Dancy argues that consequentialism cannot successfully account for agent-relativity, i.e., the putative moral fact that different moral agents may have different moral goals. For example, an agent may have special obligations towards those who are near and dear to him. A moral agent may feel, with some degree of rightness, that, although she can help a stranger more, she ought rather to help her own child slightly less.

In this book I have assumed that consequentialism (I am not fond of the term 'consequentialism', but in this chapter I cannot help using it) can account successfully for agent-relativity, so I had better say something about Dancy's argument.

This argument takes the form of an attack on what Derek Parfit has said about consequentialism and agent-relativity in *Reasons and Persons*. In the present chapter I argue against Dancy that, even though there are mistakes in Parfit's argument, his conclusion is correct. Consequentialism does account, in a plausible way, for the phenomenon of agent-relativity.

According to Dancy, there are two ways a consequentialist may try to handle the phenomenon of agent-relativity.[1] Dancy wants none of these.

One way is to make a distinction between what set of motives we ought to adopt, and what actions we ought to perform. Aided by this distinction, consequentialists may argue that, in paying special attention to our own kin, for example, rather than to strangers, we act on consequentially approved motives, while performing wrong actions. No blame to us, then. Dancy attributes this idea to Parfit and attacks it.

Another way, according to Dancy, for consequentialists to account for agent-relativity would be to hold that relative values are values because the world goes better if they are included in it.[2] According to Dancy, this makes consequentialism self-effacing and this, on his account, is 'highly damaging' to consequentialism.[3]

These moves go well together. I believe that both of them are sound and should be taken up by consequentialists. I will address them in order and defend them both against the criticism levelled by Dancy.

129

Blameless wrongdoing

The idea of blameless wrongdoing has been worked out by Derek Parfit. Crucial in his presentation of it is the example of Clare. Clare loves her child. When offered a choice, because she loves her child, she benefits him rather than strangers. In so doing she acts out of a set of consequentially approved aims. Consider a case where she could do more good by helping a stranger than by helping her child. She chooses to help her child. According to Parfit, her action is wrong, since it has an alternative with better consequences (to help the stranger). However, she is blameless. She acts out of the best set of motives available to her (he assumes). According to Dancy, this means that, according to consequentialism, her action must also be right. This seems to me a mistake.

In his argument, Dancy relies on something Parfit has himself written about the case of Clare; Parfit assumes that Clare defends herself in the following way:

> I could have acted differently. But this only means that I *would* have done so if my motives had been different. Given my actual motives, it is causally impossible that I act differently. And, if my motives had been different, this would have made the outcome, on the whole, worse. Since my actual motives are one of the best possible sets, in Consequentialist terms, the bad effects *are*, in the relevant sense, part of one of the best possible sets of effects.[4]

There are many controversial points in Clare's defence.

First of all, it is not plausible to say that 'I could have acted differently' means that I would have done so if my motives had been different. I doubt that an analysis of this expression can be accomplished at all. I will not go into this problem here.[5] However, even if an analysis can be given, it is not the one suggested by Parfit. The truth of 'I would have acted differently if my motives had been different' does not guarantee the truth of 'I could have acted differently'. To see this, suppose that, in a situation, I perform a particular action, A1. In the situation it is true of me that, had my motives been different, I would instead have performed A2. However, suppose that the closest world in which my motives are different enough for me to do A2 is one in which I am very different from the way I am in the actual world. Then this means that, while this world may well be a possible one, it is not a world that is accessible to me. It would then be false to say that in the actual world I could have done A2. If, in the closest world where I perform A2 rather than A1 I have motives very different from the ones I actually have, i.e., I am very different from the way actually I am, then, actually, I do not have it in my power to perform A2. I return to this point below.

Secondly, while it may well be true that, given Clare's actual motives, it is 'causally impossible' that she act differently, the relevance of this observation is doubtful. If we have free will then, possibly, we are sometimes able to do what is 'causally impossible' (although this, of course, is something we in fact never do). Otherwise it is simply not true that, in the situation, Clare has a better alternative to her helping her own child and, by default, this action of hers would be morally permissible (in the manner Dancy argues).

According to Dancy, Clare could now argue that, by helping her child, she is performing a morally permissible action.[6] If, in the situation, she were to help the stranger, this would mean that she would have a different (and worse) set of motives, a set such that, by consistently acting on it, she would be doing more harm than she is in fact doing. But this argument is mistaken.

To understand Dancy's argument better, let us call a 'set of motives' a character. A character may be characterised by a specification of what actions it gives rise to (in various different situations). Suppose there are exactly two characters available (accessible at some time) to Clare. Either she minds about strangers and takes no care of her own child (C1), or she takes preferential care of her child and (only) some care of strangers (C2). Let us suppose that, on the whole, it is better that she possesses the latter character, C2, than the former character, C1.

Why does Dancy believe that, had Clare helped the stranger instead of her child, this would have been worse? The argument seems to be, as remarked above, that, had she helped the stranger, she would have acted from the other character, C1. And this would have been bad.[7]

The consequentialist criterion Dancy takes as his point of departure in his argument, and which he defends as appropriate, and which I accept as appropriate (it is an instance of what I have called in Chapter 3 the principle of counterfactual dependence), is this one: 'An act is right if outcomes would be better if it was done than if any alternative were done.'[8] The best way of understanding Dancy's argument is as follows: we conceive of Clare's choice of action in the situation as a choice of character from now on. In that case, by helping her child, she avoids future suffering. I find this argument flawed. So does Derek Parfit, but for a different reason.

Another way of understanding Dancy's argument would be as follows: we conceive of Clare's choice of action in the situation as a choice of character from now on and for some time in the past. What Clare must ask herself is not only what kinds of decision she would take in the future, but also what kinds of decision she would have taken in the past, were she to act impartially in this situation. There is more to this interpretation than at first meets the eye (as we shall see in Chapter 10), but it is too fanciful to capture Dancy's intentions. Furthermore, for reasons to be spelled out below, even if we accept that through our actions we might become responsible for what went on in the past (on the criterion of counterfactual dependence suggested by Dancy we do seem to become responsible in principle for past antecedents of our actions), it is not plausible to assume that, had Clare acted otherwise, she would have had a different character, as is supposed in Dancy's argument, however conceived. So there is no need to go into the complications about our possible responsibility for past antecedents of our actions in this context.

Parfit's answer to Dancy

Derek Parfit, in his reaction to Dancy's criticism, denies the relevance of the question of what must have had been different had Clare acted differently:

> When we ask whether some act of ours was irrational, or wrong, we mean to be asking about what we actually did, given the facts as they actually were. Ought we, as we actually were, to have acted differently? And our answer may depend on the following question: If we, as we were, had acted differently, what would have happened?[9]

The important line is the last one, indicating not only that our question is about ourselves as we actually were, but that, even in the possible world where we act differently, we are exactly as we are in the actual world.

I find this move strange. Why should we not allow the relevance of the question of what would have been (or, what would have had to have been) different about Clare had she acted otherwise? Since Clare would have been different had she acted differently, the person who acts differently from the way Clare does, in Clare's situation, may therefore be a person very like her, but not identical to her. Let me elaborate.

One of Parfit's worries with counterfactuals about how Clare would have been had she acted differently in the circumstances is that they may lack definite truth-conditions. I believe they have definite truth-conditions. I will return to this point. Notice, however, that if we are compatibilists, we should not hesitate to accept the assumption that Clare could have acted differently in the situation. But if she could have acted differently, then the question of what would have had to have been different in this situation, had she acted otherwise, is meaningful. Then there must exist true and false answers to it.

Parfit's main worry is not the lack of definite truth-conditions, however, but irrelevance. He does not consider the question of in what way Clare must have been different, had she acted differently, relevant to a normative assessment of her act. But if there are true and false answers to this question, then I fail to see how we can reject taking them into moral account. At least according to AU, what is relevant to the rightness and wrongness of an action is exactly this: how the world came to be when the action was performed, as compared to how the world would have been had the agent (in the same situation) acted differently. The true answer to this question is what determines the normative status of the action.

Learning about Parfit's response to Dancy's argument, I cannot help getting the impression that Parfit is not a compatibilist after all. He does not believe that we – ever – have it in our power to act otherwise than the way we actually do. But if this is correct, once again I would say that all our actions are right (there is never anything else we can do but perform them).

Parfit, as it were, replaces the question of what Clare could have done in the circumstances with a question about what would have happened had a person exactly like Clare acted differently in Clare's circumstances. This is not relevant to the normative assessment of Clare's action, however, at least not as long as, in our assessment of it, we stick to AU.

My answer to Dancy: blameful rightdoing

In contradistinction to Parfit, I admit that the question of what would have had to have been different (even with Clare) had Clare acted differently in the situation is normatively relevant. Still, Dancy's argument is flawed. The reason that his argument is mistaken is as follows: suppose that, in a particular situation, where Clare decides whether she should give some help to her child or more help to a stranger, she decides to give some help to her child (after all, the character she possesses is C2, we have assumed). Then Dancy believes that, had she given more help to the stranger, she would have had the other character, C1 – or developed it from then on. This is not true. All possible worlds where she has C1 are far away from the actual world. It is more plausible, then, to conclude that had she, in the situation, helped the stranger instead of her child, she would have suffered, in the situation, a kind of 'weakness of will'. She would have acted against her character. This means that it would have been better if she had helped this stranger. Had she helped the stranger, however, this would have been an instance of blameful rightdoing. She would have done the right thing but she would have failed to act from her best possible set of motives (character). And since blame is a matter of enhancing a person's moral motivation – we blame a person in order to strengthen his or her moral character – she would have deserved to be blamed for her weakness of character (will).

This may be a rather unusual use of the phrase 'weakness of will'. In the situation, Clare wants to do what she recognises is wrong, but, through some kind of slip of hers, she does not manage to do this. She does the right thing instead. Usually when we speak of weakness of will we have in mind a person who knows what he or she ought to do, but who does not live up to his or her own standards. He or she succumbs to some kind of immoral temptation. Clare, on the contrary, is tempted by morality to act against her character. Yet, for all that, I find the term 'weakness of will' appropriate. Clare fails to live up to her moral character, and her rightdoing, in the circumstances, is blameful.

But is this kind of blameful rightdoing possible? If Clare possesses a character,

C2, such that whenever she decides between helping her child and helping a stranger, she helps her child, must not this mean that there exists no situation such that in it she can help the stranger rather than her child? No, it need not mean this. We need not be in this way 'in the grip' of our character. Not even if we develop a very stable character which, as a matter of fact, we never depart from, need this mean that we cannot now and then depart from it, once we have chosen to develop it. We ought not to think of our character as a straitjacket.

Not even if it is 'causally impossible' that later on we depart from the character that we have once chosen (in the sense that it follows from true laws of nature – including psychological laws relevant to our behaviour – and a true statement of initial conditions that we will perform actions in accordance with our character) need this mean that we cannot now and then depart from it. On the contrary, it is more plausible in many cases, I suggest, to think of our character as a pattern in our decisions, as a kind of consistency in our (free) choices (correctly summed up, perhaps, in psychological laws). We are not in general (and should not be) enslaved by our characters. The point of developing a character is that it allows us to forego future temptations without restricting our freedom. We do not (always) want, like Ulysses, to be prohibited from yielding to the lure of the Sirens. At least I think that we should allow that sometimes we can act against our characters.

But are we not facing an inconsistency here? If, when choosing a character, Clare had only two options, is it then possible that later on she can in a particular case depart from the character she has chosen, without acting in accordance with the alternative one?

I believe it is. However, if, contrary to fact, in a particular case, she were to depart from her character, exhibiting in the situation weakness of will, it would not have been true (earlier on) that C2 was strict. It would then have been 'gappy', allowing for one 'exception'. This dependence of the past upon the present, of course, is counterfactual but not causal.

If I am right about this, it is appropriate to speak of Clare's performing a morally forbidden action (helping her child rather than the stranger) as 'blameless'. Her choice of developing C2, rather than C1, is morally all right and, therefore, blameless. Yet, for all that, her acting on C2 in the situation, where she could have departed from it, is wrong.

When choosing what kind of character to develop, we ought to opt for the best possible character, i.e., the character that, as a matter of fact, will lead us to the best choices on the whole. We ought to do so knowing that, if we succeed in developing it, we will, as a matter of fact, sometimes make moral mistakes.

The origin of these mistakes in our good character does not mean that they are not just that – mistakes. When we perform them, we forgo alternatives open to us with better consequences. In each case, we should have acted otherwise, then. However, since we know that, if we develop another character, we will, as a matter of fact, perform even more and even more serious mistakes, we had better adopt the optimal one.

A problematic point which I have only touched upon here is the following: suppose we can develop either character C or character C'. Suppose that if we develop character C rather than C' we will, as a matter of fact, perform actions with better consequences than if we develop C'. Suppose also that if we develop C' we can perform actions with better consequences than the actions we can perform if we develop C. Which character ought we to develop?

I suggest that we develop C. What matters morally is how the world would be if we were to perform one action, as compared to how it would be if we were to perform an alternative action. We ought, then, to behave strategically in relation to our own future actions. At least, this seems to be what is contained in the spirit of consequentialism.[10]

Is consequentialism self-effacing?

Finally, according to Dancy, consequentialism is 'self-effacing'. At least, this is what we must conclude, if the consequentialist argues that agent-relative aims such as love and friendship are values because the world goes better if they are included in it. For, if we see love or friendship in that way, 'we prevent it from being the value it is supposed to be'.[11]

This is a faint echo of a much stronger but invalid criticism directed against utilitarianism by Bernard Williams. According to him:

> If utilitarianism . . . determines nothing of how thought in the world is conducted, demanding merely that the way in which it is conducted must be for the best, then I hold that utilitarianism has disappeared, and that the residual position is not worth calling utilitarianism.[12]

The criticism is not well taken since, as we have seen, our acceptance of the utilitarian criterion of rightness may inform our adoption of a certain method of decision making. Utilitarianism does not determine how thought in the world is conducted, but our acceptance of utilitarianism may well do. And this must be what Williams had in mind. But it is still an open question whether our acknowledging that, for utilitarian reasons, we ought to stick to a method of decision making allowing us to show preferential concern for those who are near and dear to us must undermine our concern for those who are near and dear to us. Dancy believes that it must. If this is correct, then we may have to follow up a line of thought sketched by Sidgwick and keep the utilitarian criterion of rightness a secret.[13] And, as we shall see, this is something both Williams and Dancy find problematic. But why does Dancy believe this? Why cannot we go on showing a preferential concern for our own kin, when we know that, *sub specie aetemitatis*, our kin is not special, it is just that we are such that we care preferentially for it? After all, it is a good thing (again, *sub specie aetemitatis*) that we are like that. According to Dancy, our special concern erodes, unless we abandon or disguise the consequentialist rationale behind it.

Now, even if this were correct, I fail to see it as a high cost for consequentialism. Why not actually say as Sidgwick did[14] that consequentialism ought, for good consequentialist reasons, be kept a secret?

Dancy holds that, if there are consequentialist reasons why consequentialism should be kept a secret, and why it should be disguised, then these facts about the theory are so obviously 'damaging' to its plausibility that it is futile for the consequentialist to try to argue otherwise. As I noted above, the same point has previously been made by Bernard Williams:

> it is reasonable to suppose that maximal total utility actually requires that few, if any, accept utilitarianism. If that is right, and utilitarianism has to vanish from making any distinctive mark in the world, being left only with the total assessment from the transcendental standpoint – then I leave it for discussion whether that shows that utilitarianism is unacceptable, or merely that no one ought to accept it.[15]

I have three comments on this line of argument. First of all, even if, for some strange reason, the utilitarian criterion of rightness should be kept a secret, I fail to see what damage this does to the plausibility of consequentialism. What guarantee do we have that the true moral theory is not such that it is dangerous to learn about it?[16]

Secondly, I see no reason why the utilitarian criterion of rightness cannot be accepted by most people, informing their adoption of a method of decision making. Why keep it a secret?

Well, according to Dancy, if we do not, our most important concerns will erode. But is this correct? I think not. And this is my final comment on Dancy's argument. I do not think that Dancy is right when he argues that the (overt) recognition that love or friendship is a good thing ultimately for consequentialist reasons must make our love or friendship erode. The recognition of the consequentialist rationale of love (in general) does give a taste of forbidden fruit to our love, that is true. When, out of love, I pay special attention to a certain woman, rather than to a stranger, I may comfort myself with the thought that it is a good thing that I am the kind of person who is capable of loving someone, but I must also recognise that if, in this particular situation, I were instead to pay more attention to the stranger, without, for that reason, turning into a person who is – otherwise – not capable of loving someone else, this would be a good thing to do. I could do it but I do not, and, therefore, I make a moral mistake (which makes my love taste somewhat bitter). But that is the way I am.

This mixture of love and bad conscience (because of my belief in the truth of consequentialism) is something I do exhibit and, from the fact that I exhibit it, it follows that this is something that can be exhibited. My love survives the knowledge of its rationale; it does not erode. Therefore, I stick – without any risk – with my belief in consequentialism.

As a matter of fact, the observation that there is an element of 'forbidden fruit' in love and friendship, according to consequentialism, is as it should be. This is something most people testify that they feel when, in a world of starvation, they watch TV and show special concern for their near and dear ones.

So it is not true that our special concern for those who are near and dear to us must erode when we realise that there is a utilitarian rationale behind it. This is not only true, it is also a very mundane truth. Note that there may well be a utilitarian rationale behind my choosing to be a person who develops special relations to individual people near and dear to me. This does not mean that there is a utilitarian rationale behind each and any one of my special relations. There is none whatever. And if there were one, this would indeed be devastating to the relations, of course. It would be devastating to my relationship to my wife, for example, if I had chosen to love her on utilitarian grounds (and if I knew this, and if she knew this, and if she knew that I knew this, and so forth). But I have not chosen her on any utilitarian grounds. I simply 'fell' in love with her. My love for her is spontaneous. And my love for her is not hurt by the knowledge that, on partly utilitarian grounds, I have developed a character which makes this kind of relation possible.

Why would my love (or her relation to me) be hurt by this kind of knowledge? Could there be a better rationale for my choice of character? I fail to see that it would have been any better if I had had different reasons for choosing my character, or no reasons at all. What can threaten the particular relation is if the character it is based on is unstable. But if the character has been chosen for good reasons, then the odds that it is stable are good.

I think I have established that a utilitarian rationale behind our choice of character is not devastating to personal relations made possible by the very character we have chosen. If this is correct, then there is nothing there to prevent us from publicly accepting the utilitarian criterion of rightness, allowing that it informs our adoption of character and a certain method of decision making. However, even if there had been some good reason to keep the utilitarian criterion of rightness a secret, then – and this is my fallback claim – this would not show that utilitarianism is not correct.

Conclusion

In the present chapter I have taken it for granted that agent-relativity is a moral fact, i.e., that different moral agents may have different moral goals in the sense that, according to the correct moral theory, they ought to set themselves different goals. I have argued that consequentialism does account in a plausible way for this putative fact. Consequentialists may argue that, in paying special attention to our own kin, for example, rather than to strangers, we act on consequentially approved motives, while performing wrong actions. No blame, or at least diminished blame, to us, then. And the consequentialist may go on to argue that relative values are values because the world goes better if they are included in it.

Pace Dancy, this is something we can acknowledge, without our values eroding for this reason. So there is no need to keep the utilitarian criterion of rightness a secret. What about the assumption of this chapter, then? Is it true that we have special moral obligations to those who are near and dear to us? I can only speculate at this point. I think this is true, to some extent. Our human nature is no different today to what it was when Sidgwick pointed out that love for our near and dear ones should be encouraged because we can, because of our natural motivation, do far more good for a near and dear one than we would be likely to do for strangers. At the same time, however, I feel pretty confident that the world would go better if we were not less inclined to take responsibility for those who are near and dear to us, but more inclined also to take responsibility for strangers.

We should beware not to conceive of the situation as a zero-sum game. More concern for strangers need not mean less concern for those who are near and dear to us. On the contrary, it seems to me: by showing respect and concern for strangers we cultivate our sensitivity, and by doing so, we become capable of also showing a deeper respect and concern for those who are near and dear to us.

Furthermore, we should observe that while common sense morality, with its insistence on special obligations, has evolved in narrow societies with strong social control and little external communication, we live today in a more complex world where we are capable of affecting the well-being of people living at a long distance from us and where, through collective action, we are capable of affecting the well-being of others to quite a significant extent, without our contribution being, for each person affected, even noticeable. This creates the need for a common sense morality which, in comparison to our actual one, is more sensitive to strangers. I return to this point in Chapter 11.

If this conjecture is true, then there is less of an asymmetry for the utilitarian to explain than has often been taken for granted in the present discussion.

Notes

1 J. Dancy, *Moral Reasons*, pp. 234ff.
2 What Dancy wants to say here, I suppose, is that the world goes better if we believe in these values.

3 Dancy, *Moral Reasons*, p. 236.
4 D. Parfit, *Reasons and Persons*, pp. 32–3. Parfit's argument is quoted by Dancy, *Moral Reasons*, p. 242.
5 In my 'Morality and Modality', pp. 139–53, I argue against all sorts of 'analysis' of the concept of free will. I suggest there that 'free will' be considered a theoretical term.
6 Dancy, *Moral Reasons*, p. 241.
7 I have simplified the example by allowing only two sets of motives available to the agent. Dancy does not restrict the options as narrowly as that, but he too seems to assume that the alternative to the actual set of Clare's motives would have been radically different. This explains the fact that Clare's possession of any alternative character would have produced a worse outcome.
8 Dancy, *Moral Reasons*, p. 243.
9 This quotation is from a preliminary draft of his answer to Dancy.
10 I argue this point elsewhere; cf. my 'Moral Conflict and Moral Realism' about this. I also touched upon it in Ch. 3 of this book.
11 Dancy, *Moral Reasons*, p. 235.
12 B. Williams, 'A Critique of Utilitarianism', p. 124.
13 H. Sidgwick, *The Methods of Ethics*, p. 466.
14 Ibid.
15 B. Williams, 'A Critique of Utilitarianism', p. 135.
16 Perhaps my failure has something to do with my acceptance of moral realism. Perhaps the idea that the criterion of rightness should be kept a secret is more difficult to digest for a moral irrealist, such as, say, an emotivist. Since I do not believe that we have any utilitarian reasons for keeping the utilitarian criterion of rightness a secret, I leave this moot question without further comment.

Chapter 10

Our responsibility for the past

In his 'consequence argument' (CA) Peter van Inwagen develops the following line of thought: if determinism is true, then our actions are the consequences of the laws of nature and events in the remote past. But it is not up to us what went on before we were born, and neither is it up to us what the laws of nature are. Therefore, the consequences of these things (including our present acts) are not up to us.[1]

The logic of CA is valid. As will be seen in the sequel, however, it is far from obvious that two of the premises used by van Inwagen in CA are true. Therefore, it is possible that determinism and free will are compatible.

Van Inwagen argues, moreover, that determinism is false. However, his main argument against determinism is based on CA, and the thrust of the argument is roughly as follows: since we have moral responsibility our will must be free. And if our will is free determinism must be false. If CA may be wrong this argument may be wrong as well.

Van Inwagen also claims that it is hard to see why anyone should think that what we know renders reasonable a belief that human behaviour is determined.[2] Van Inwagen's argument is based on the view that human organisms and behaviour are terribly complex things, an assumption that quantum physics is indeterministic, and a conjecture that individual, sub-microscopic events can 'trigger' observable events.[3] However, all these assumptions and conjectures are debatable. *Pace* van Inwagen, human behaviour might very well be determined. I.e., it is possible that J. J. C. Smart is right when he holds that, if we neglect transitory particles that are created only at high energies, and cosmological matters such as the interiors of neutron stars or of black holes, physics is essentially complete.[4] This is not to say, of course, that physics is deterministic. It means, however, that the indeterminism does not affect neurophysiology or the problem of free will much. I do not argue that Smart is right, but at least his view should be taken seriously.

What we know may well render the belief in 'soft determinism' reasonable, i.e., the belief that human behaviour is determined, that this is compatible with free will (in a sense of 'free will' relevant to morality), and that, sometimes, we can act otherwise than the way we actually do. Van Inwagen has not disproved this view. His argument does indicate, however, that soft determinism combined with very plausible moral principles has a strange moral implication which has not been acknowledged by its adherents (and which has not been taken advantage of by its critics). If soft determinism is true, then, on very plausible moral principles of responsibility, implied by hedonistic utilitarianism as conceived of in this book, we are morally responsible not only for future consequences of our actions, but also for events in the (remote) past; or so I will argue, at any rate.

An example

Consider van Inwagen's own example of a judge, J, who had only to raise his right hand at a certain time in order to prevent the execution of a sentence of death upon a certain criminal, but who did not. Could J have raised his hand? It is assumed by van Inwagen that J was unbound, uninjured, and free from any paralysis of the limbs; that he decided not to raise his hand only after a suitable period of calm, rational and relevant deliberation; that he had not been subjected to any 'pressure' to decide one way or the other; that he was not under the influence of drugs, hypnosis or anything of that sort; and, finally, that there was no element in his deliberations that would have been of any special interest to a student of abnormal psychology. However, if determinism is true then clearly there are certain conditions obtaining before J was born which are such that, from a description of them together with some laws of nature, it follows logically that J did not decide to raise his hand and, hence, did not raise it (or, if Davidson is right in his insistence on the claim that there are no psycho-physical laws and in his insistence on the claim that psychological laws are not strict, at least a true physical description of J's actual action follows, which is sufficient for my argument). This cannot reasonably be denied by adherents of soft determinism.

Does this preclude that J could have raised his hand? No, it does not, say adherents of soft determinism. This means that they have to accept either that J could have performed an action such that had he performed it, i.e., had he raised his hand, then the past, even the very remote past, would have been different from the way it actually was, or the laws of nature would not have been (exactly) the same as they actually are.

As I have claimed above, I do not think the view that J could have raised his arm should be put out of court, even if determinism is true. To be sure, what went on before J was born is not 'up to him' in the sense that he can change it, nor is it 'up to him' what the laws of nature are in the sense that he can make them up or even break them. This he need not be able to do, however, in order to be able to act otherwise than the way he does. David Lewis has shown this, and this means that van Inwagen's consequence argument is much weaker than it might at first appear.[5] From the point of view of our freedom, the important thing is only that, if we had acted otherwise, then the past, or the laws of nature, would have been different. And it is far from evident that we cannot sometimes perform some actions such that, were we to perform them, then the past or the laws of nature would not have been the same.

One might wonder whether a third possibility exists. Is it possible for us to perform an action such that, had we performed it, the laws of logic would have been different? In my argument I make the tacit concession that we can never perform any such actions. If a true physical description of my present act follows logically from the laws of nature together with a true description of the state of the universe at some earlier point, then there is nothing I can do which, so to speak, 'precludes' that inference from being valid. If Quine's view of logical truth is correct my concession may turn out to be premature and even unwarranted, however.

Because of his theory of counterfactuals, David Lewis is forced to argue that, if someone had ever acted otherwise than he or she actually did, then the laws of nature would have been different (a small miracle takes place in the possible world where the person – or, rather, his or her counterpart – acts otherwise).

I find it more reasonable to assume that sometimes we can perform actions such that, if we did perform them, then the past would have been different (while the laws of nature were the same). Possible worlds, if we allow ourselves to speak figuratively of them, in which small miracles take place are not very 'close' to the actual world. Jonathan Bennett has convinced me on this point.[6] Causally possible worlds (obeying the actual laws of nature) with a past different, perhaps very different, from the actual one, at present exactly like the actual one with the sole exception that someone acts differently from the way he or she actually does (without having a different character or being otherwise very different from the way he or she actually is), and diverging in the future from the actual one because someone acted otherwise, are close to the actual one, however. I touched upon this possibility in my discussion of the example of Clare in Chapter 9, and I take it for granted in my present argument. This view seems to be part of the received opinion, too. Bertrand Russell, for one, writes, that an

> effect being *defined* as something subsequent to its cause, obviously we can have no *effect* upon the past. But that does not mean that the past would not have been different if our present wishes had been different. Obviously, our present wishes are conditioned by the past, and therefore could not have been different unless the past had been different; therefore, if our present wishes were different, the past would be different.[7]

No matter how exactly we assess the closeness between 'possible worlds' (remember that I use the notion of possible worlds only as a manner of speaking) – in terms of 'similarity'[8] or otherwise – we must acknowledge it as a fact that nomic differences are always great differences. Now, according to Bennett, the past is closed. He seems to reject that we have a free will, then. A soft determinist could consistently and even plausibly, I would say, argue instead that sometimes we can perform actions such that, if we were to perform them, then the past would have been different from the way it actually is. The moral consequences of this argument have not been fully recognised, however.

Free will

At this point it might be asked what it means for a person to have free will or, more exactly, to have it in her or his power to act differently from the way she or he does. In order to answer this question we need a general theory about modal notions. Sometimes these are explained with reference to possible worlds. I think we should resist that line. Instead, I suggest, we should take statements about, say, possibility at face value. We do understand them and, for example, we ought to recognise that it is true that I could have read a book to my daughter the other day (when, as a matter of fact, I did not) if, and only if, I could have done so, period. I suggest that we also understand such statements not as *de dicto* (it is possible that . . .) but as *de re* (it is true of me that, in the circumstances, I could have read my daughter the book).

While rejecting the brand of modal realism famously defended by David Lewis, according to which possible worlds exist, we may embrace quite a different brand of modal realism which, as a matter of fact, better deserves the name, a modal realism according to which modal properties are real properties of existing individuals. For all we know, the properties may well be causally explicable, in the final analysis, in terms of 'natural' characteristics of these individuals. Something like this seems also to have been the position that Leibniz took in his discussion with Arnauld. 'How, e.g., could Caesar have freely crossed the Rubicon if in the actual world his crossing it was inevitable?', Arnauld asks. In response to this Leibniz claims that Caesar's acting freely is a fact about this world (in Leibnizian terms it is 'written into' the concept of the actual Caesar)[9] and it is not a fact about any other world.

But, if this form of modal realism is true, how are we to proceed in order to ascertain whether I could have read a book to my daughter the other day?

To the present author, who has defended the thesis that there is moral knowledge based on moral observations, it is very tempting to argue that whether a certain agent could have acted otherwise than he or she did is something we observe. As a matter of fact, I think that scientific realists such as Armstrong and Tooley should have little objection to this since, after all, David Armstrong, for example, is prepared to argue that we can observe, in a particular case, that a sort of state of affairs ensures that a further state of affairs of a certain sort exists, 'pressure on our own body being the most salient case'.[10] It is no more mysterious to assume that we can observe whether agents, in particular circumstances, can act otherwise than they do (how differently they can act, of course, is difficult to tell and often a matter of dispute), one might argue. Such observation can be understood as a (proper) kind of causal interaction. To be sure, we are not capable of making such observations unless we possess a web of concomitant beliefs, and, certainly, also a certain kind of skill. This kind of prerequisite, though, is necessary in order for us to be able to make any observations whatever.

However, a more plausible view might be the following: when we say of a person that he or she can act otherwise than he or she actually does, we ascribe a theoretical property to that person. There is a wide variety of possible evidence for this statement, but no item in particular is decisive, and we have to countenance the possibility that such ascriptions of capability are always under-determined by the evidence available.[11]

The problem of accidental interference

It has been objected that if we are able to perform actions such that, if we were to perform them, the past would have been different, then there would be a threat of accidental interference between free acts. I might be able to perform some action such that, if I were to perform it, some event in the past would have occurred, while you are able to perform some action such that, if you were to perform it, the same event in the past would not have occurred.

Peter Forrest, who has argued that, sometimes, we can perform actions such that, if we were to perform them, then the past would have been different, has adopted some very complicated and perhaps even counter-intuitive principles about which aspects of the past we can affect and which we cannot affect, in order to make sure that such interference cannot after all take place.[12] We need not go to such trouble, however, for in order to defend the claim that, sometimes, we can perform actions such that, if we were to perform them, the past would be different, we need assume not that interference cannot take place, only that, as a matter of fact, it does not.

The reason why I am free in a certain situation to perform a certain action may well be that you, in another situation, do not perform a certain action. And your freedom in that situation to abstain from action may be due to the contingent fact that, in some situation, I do what I actually do. Possible interference in the past is no more problematic from the point of view of free will than possible interference in the future.

Methods of responsible deliberation vs criteria of rightness

I readily admit that, in our ordinary deliberations, we rarely (or never) bother about possible pasts. I will return to the problem of why this is so. However, how we actually deliberate is one thing, and how we ought to deliberate quite another. Even more importantly, though, how we ought to deliberate is one thing, and the general criteria of rightness of actions quite another. This was stressed in Chapter 3, and it is of the utmost importance to bear this distinction in mind. My interest in this book is primarily in problems of rightness and wrongness of actions.

Perhaps it is difficult to find out in enough detail what the past would have been like, had J raised his hand, in order to be able to make a well-founded assessment of whether he should have raised it or not. These problems notwithstanding, however, if soft determinism is true there does exist a correct answer to the question what the past would have been like had he raised his hand. And my thesis is that this answer is relevant to the correct answer to the question of whether, as a matter of fact, J did the right thing. The moral rightness or wrongness of our actions depends both on what will happen in the future if we perform them, as compared to what would happen if we were to act otherwise, and on what went on before them, as compared to what would have gone on before them had we acted otherwise.

This conclusion seems difficult to avoid once we accept soft determinism and wed this view to a sound theory of counterfactuals. And this conclusion seems inescapable if we accept, as most soft determinists have done, some kind of teleological moral theory which presupposes the principle of counterfactual dependence, to the effect that what matters, morally is what would happen in the world (irrespective of how it would be caused) if we were to do one thing rather than another. Act utilitarianism, as conceived of in Chapter 3, and the classical hedonistic variety of it, defended in Chapter 5, have exactly these two features. The exact (causal) relation that holds between what we were to do and what would happen is not of any direct moral importance.

The principle of counterfactual dependence defended

In Chapter 3 I briefly defended the principle of counterfactual dependence. I now return to this principle. Philosophers objecting to a consequentialist morality have argued that, no matter what happens if we do one thing rather than another (other people get hurt, rights get violated and so forth), we may be right in doing what we do, provided only that we do not personally and actively harm others, violate any rights and so forth. To this, two answers have been given by consequentialists, both correct, in my opinion. The first one is that it is far from clear what it means to 'harm' someone actively, compared to just acting so that someone who would not have been harmed if one had acted otherwise is harmed. The second one is that, irrespective of what this means, the important thing is what would happen if you acted in this way, as compared to what would have happened if you had acted otherwise. All the difference your action makes, however remote it may be, is relevant to its rightness and wrongness.

This kind of argument is difficult to accept, however, unless one is also prepared to accept that, if soft determinism is true, then what went on before the action is also relevant to its rightness or wrongness. To be sure, we do not change the past. But neither do we change the future. The cases are similar. Had we acted differently, we would not have changed the past, but it is true that, had we acted differently, the past would have been different. Had we acted differently, we would not have changed the future, but it is true that, had we acted differently, the future would have been different.

Even if we rarely know what would have gone on before our actions if we had acted otherwise, and even if, consequently, we can rarely explain the absence of these events in terms of what we actually did, what went on before our actions, as compared to what would have gone on before them if we had acted otherwise, matters to their actual rightness or wrongness.

It could be said by way of rebuttal of this claim that, even if remote consequences are relevant to the rightness of your actions, events in the past are not. For these events in the past are not 'consequences' or 'effects' of your actions at all, even in a remote sense.

We should resist this line of argument, as I have done in my statement of act utilitarianism in Chapter 3, however. For the concepts of a cause and an effect are vague. According to some definitions of a cause there is nothing in principle that precludes that we cause things in the past to happen,[13] while according to other definitions it is true by definition that a cause must temporally precede its effect. An example of the latter kind of notion, of course, can be found in David Hume's analysis of the concept of causation, and an example of the former can be found in David Lewis's writings.[14] Because of this vagueness of the notions of cause and effect utilitarians hesitate, and should hesitate, in the final analysis, to rely on them. They (should) insist, as was done in Chapter 3 of this book, that the state of the universe if a certain action is performed, as compared to what would have been the state of the universe if the action had not been performed, is what really matters to the rightness or wrongness of the action.

This insistence is shared, as it were, by modern 'causal' decision theory. What matters, according to Lewis and Skyrms and others who adhere to causal decision theory, is precisely what happens if you do one thing as compared to what would happen if you did something else. So the name 'causal decision theory' is really a misnomer. It would be more appropriate to speak of 'counterfactual' decision theory.

However, the only 'causal' decision theorist who has taken seriously the possibility that, if you wish to make rational decisions, you ought to try to assess what would precede your various alternative actions were you to perform them, is Terrance Horgan. This insight is of importance to our understanding of what has been called Newcomb's problem.[15]

The total state principle defended

The 'state of the universe' is equivocal, however. Some interpret it in the sense of the total state of the universe, as I did in Chapter 3, while others interpret it in the sense of the total future state of the universe. Lars Bergström has stipulated that it is only the future state of the universe that matters morally.[16] I have myself agreed to this stipulation.[17] This I now consider a mistake. At least one philosopher has held the opposite view. This was C. D. Broad, who, apropos of G. E. Moore's principle of organic unities, argued that the rightness or wrongness of an action depends not only on what the future would be like if the action were to be performed, as compared to what it would be like if the action were not performed, but also on what went on before it and, in the end, on how it would contribute to the total value of the universe. Broad wrote:

> the Principle of Organic Unities precludes us from asserting that, because the state of the universe, after a moment t, is intrinsically better if I do x than if I do y, therefore its total state, before and after t, is better. For, if two wholes consist of a common part and two different parts, it does not follow that that which has the better part is as good as that which has the worse one.[18]

I am not in sympathy with Moore's principle of organic unities, of course. This is clear from my defence of hedonism in previous chapters. However, I think Broad is right in his point. It is the total state of the universe that matters morally. To think otherwise is to be the victim of a temporal prejudice. Derek Parfit has shown[19] with various different examples that we seem to have such a prejudice. He has not shown that it is rational to retain it, however. And if the reality of both past and future is acknowledged, and the reality of both past and future must be acknowledged by all determinists, then this prejudice dissolves. We can only retain it as long as we believe that there is a way that we can make a difference to the future that we are incapable of making to the past. Most people seem to believe in such a difference. But no such difference exists. Thus withers our belief in the future state principle. The total state principle is correct.

Practical deliberation

If soft determinism is true and if utilitarianism in its most plausible interpretation (hedonistic utilitarianism) is a plausible moral theory, then we seem to be responsible not only for remote consequences in the future of our actions but for what went on before our actions as well. So what? What difference does this make to our practical deliberations? We may distinguish between three possibilities:

1. In our deliberations it is (sometimes, at least) possible for us to gain and take into account relevant knowledge about possible pasts as well as relevant knowledge about possible futures. This means that, if I am right about what I say about our responsibility for the past, it is possible that we may sometimes find out what we ought to do.

2. In our deliberations it is (sometimes, at least) possible for us to gain and take into account relevant knowledge about possible futures but never about possible pasts; relevant information about the past will always fail us. This means that, if I am right about what I say about our responsibility for the past, we may never find out what we ought to do, while if I am wrong about it, we may in some cases find out what we ought to do.

3. In our deliberations it is never possible for us to gain and take into account any relevant knowledge about either the possible futures or the possible pasts. This means that, irrespective of whether I am right or wrong in what I say about our responsibility for the past, we may never find out what we ought to do.

The question of what difference our moral theory makes or should make to our practical deliberations is a moot one for utilitarians. I have commented on this in Chapter 2 and in Chapter 3. Utilitarianism is here conceived of as a theory of what it actually is that makes concrete and particular actions right or wrong. But how, in a concrete situation, can an agent know whether a certain action she or he performs is right or wrong? Even if we set aside the troubles with our responsibility for the past, the difficulties may seem insuperable.

This indicates that the third possibility is actual. Utilitarianism has no practical relevance. Even if I am right in what I say about our responsibility for the past, this makes no difference to the situation, which is, anyway, very bad. To be sure, even if this is so, this is no argument against the truth of utilitarianism. Those who find utilitarianism plausible as a criterion of rightness and wrongness of actions should not give it up on the count that they find no way of using their theory.

However, if this diagnosis is correct, I am wrong in saying that utilitarianism gives a good explanation of those moral judgements about concrete cases that we want, upon critical reflection, to retain. At most, if this view is correct, utilitarianism can explain (the truth of) our judgements about certain abstract thought-experiments that we want, upon critical reflection, to retain.

However, the utilitarian could adopt a strategy of roughly the following kind: while there is a lot we do not have any firm beliefs about concerning the future, we seem to hold such beliefs about some of the things that would happen were we to act in one way rather than in another. There are also things we know little or nothing about. However, we set aside as irrelevant to our deliberation everything that we know nothing at all about, and we concentrate on the things we think we have a hint about. We make up our minds about values and probabilities as far as we have such hints, and we then try to maximise (the expected) value.

This is roughly the strategy I described in Chapter 2. This strategy seems to lead us to conclusion (2). For, to be sure, there is little we know about necessary pasts. Or is there?

In order to defend conclusion (1) one might be tempted to argue in the following manner: there may be some practical difficulties in taking the past into account in our practical deliberations, but it is not impossible in principle to do so. We do hold beliefs about possible pasts in some circumstances. In one way the past is even more accessible to us than the future. When deliberating in a concrete situation about what to do, we surely often know more about the actual past than we know about the actual future (which has not yet happened). It might perhaps be argued, however, that while we have at least some beliefs, and some very firm beliefs, about what would happen in the future if we acted in one way rather than another, we have no such beliefs about what would have preceded our action had we acted otherwise.

But is this so? One might think not. Consider the following example.[20] I deliberate about whether to marry a certain woman or not. I decide not to. I realise that the reason that I do not marry her is that my parents were very unhappy. Under the circumstances, I may well come to believe that there is no way I could have come to marry her unless my parents had not been that unhappy. But if I conditionalise this new belief on the ones I already hold this means that I should also accept that, had I married her, then my parents would not have been that unhappy. And this in turn may well mean that I should accept that I should have married her (even if we had become, while happier than my parents actually were, somewhat unhappy). So information about the past may well underpin feelings of regret.

But could such information really guide my choices? Suppose I argue in the way I did but, because of my argument, I marry the girl and find out that my parents were still unhappy. I feel cheated. But the reason is that I have argued wrongly, of course. If this is how things turn out then it was not true, after all, that the only way that I could come to marry this girl was if my parents had not been unhappy. In a similar way I may argue wrongly about the future.

But is it not a difference that I may sometimes deliberate correctly concerning the future? Suppose that in some situation only two alternatives, A and B, are facing me. I do A rather than B because I believe that, if I were to do B, then a certain disaster would happen in the future – and no disaster happens in the future. However, concerning the past there are no examples of the kind, it might be thought.

But perhaps there are. Perhaps the cases where we can take the past into account are rare, but there are some such after all. Of course, if I know that some condition in the past is, in the circumstances, causally sufficient and necessary for my performing A rather than B, and if I know that this condition obtains, then it seems pointless for me to deliberate: I already know which alternative I will perform. In a similar way it would be pointless for me to deliberate whether to do A or B if I knew that some condition C in the future actually obtains which is such that, if I were to perform A, it would obtain, while if I were to perform B, it would not obtain: this means that I already know which alternative I will actually perform. Then no deliberation is possible. Deliberation seems to presuppose some amount of ignorance as well as some amount of knowledge. Perhaps we have the relevant mixture of knowledge and ignorance concerning the future in some cases. But there may be thought to exist cases where we have it concerning the past as well.

Suppose I know that a certain condition C in the past is, in the circumstances, necessary and sufficient for my performing A rather than B but that I am ignorant as to whether C obtains or not. Then, if it is a good thing that C obtains, I may perform A in order to see to it that it obtains. I may later come to find out that it obtains and truly and proudly assert that, had I performed not A but B instead, it would not have obtained.

Could one find an example of this? I am not certain. I was once impressed with the following example. Suppose I believe in some psychological theory according to which, when people educate their children, they repeat all the mistakes committed by their own parents. I may be ignorant as to whether my parents treated me badly in a certain way. I now deliberate whether to treat my children badly in this way. First I am inclined to do so. To do so suits my interests, and it is not that bad for my children. Then I realise that, if I treat them badly, this means that I have been treated badly by my parents. Upon reflection I therefore decide not to treat my children badly. Later on my psychoanalyst helps me to find out that my parents did not treat me badly in the relevant way. I now conclude, correctly (if the relevant psychological theory is sound), that it is a good thing I did not treat my children badly. Had I done so, then not only would they have suffered, but I myself, when I was a young child, would have suffered as well.

Because of our ignorance about the actual future we often get the impression that we change it by our actions. In the envisaged situation we may get a similar impression that we change the past. We do nothing of the kind, however. But according to soft determinism we need change neither the future nor the past in order to have, in the sense relevant to morality, a 'free' choice.

Yet, for all that, I am less impressed with this example now than I was when I first put it forward. It seems to me now that actual psychological theory never provides us with theories that are deterministic enough to underpin the kind of argument here put forward. And, obviously, in our practical deliberations we hardly ever take the past into account. This may be due to the fact that there is not enough psychological knowledge available to us to substantiate any relevant beliefs about necessary pasts. Yet, for all that, we need not end up with conclusion (2), even if we grant that we cannot get adequate knowledge about the past. For, to be sure, if there is nothing we can know about relevant pasts of our actions, then we may simply set aside the past as irrelevant to our deliberation, in the same manner as we set aside as irrelevant to our deliberation aspects of the future about which we have no knowledge at all.

Conclusion

The upshot of this is that, if soft determinism is true, then we may sometimes have a moral obligation to 'make' the future worse provided that, by doing so, we 'make' the past even better. We become responsible indeed for the past as well as for the future.

This insight, if it is an insight, may be of little practical importance, since it is open to debate whether we ever know enough about various possible 'antecedents' to our actions to be able to take this into account in our practical deliberation. In spite of the fact that it is doubtful what practical relevance it has to learn that, by performing actions, we become responsible not only for the future that follows upon them, but also for the past that went on before them, I think this insight, if it is one, deserves to receive some attention. It does disturb some of our most deeply entrenched beliefs.

Notes

1 P. van Inwagen, *An Essay on Free Will*, Foreword.
2 Van Inwagen, *Essay on Free Will*, p. 198.
3 Van Inwagen, *Essay on Free Will*, p. 191.
4 Cf. J. J. C. Smart, *Ethics, Persuasion and Truth*, p. 125. Cf. also Joel Feinberg, 'Physics and the Thales Problem', about this.
5 This is the main thrust of David Lewis, 'Are We Free to Break the Laws?'.
6 Cf. J. Bennett, 'Counterfactuals and Temporal Direction'.
7 B. Russell, 'On the Notion of Cause'.
8 In Ch. 2 I argued that no cogent moral reasoning could be cast in terms of 'similarity' between new (hard) cases and paradigmatic ones. The notion of similarity is much too loose to be of any help in our moral reasoning. The same is true, I believe, in our modal arguments. If we allow ourselves the use of the notion of possible worlds metaphorically, we must still recognise that we need criteria of 'closeness' between such worlds. We cannot rely on any undefined notion of similarity.
9 Cf. G. W. Leibniz, 'Correspondence with Arnauld, 1686–87'.
10 David Armstrong, *A Combinatorial Theory of Possibility*, p. xi.
11 This may seem to be at variance with David Armstrong's 'combinatorialism', put forward in *A Combinatorial Theory of Possibility*, but need not be so. Armstrong has confessed in correspondence that, for all he knows, it may well be that modality is primitive (in the manner that I argue in 'Morality and Modality'). If so, his fallback claim, he writes, is that combinatorialism shows us the true structure of possibility. I concede that point.

12 Cf. P. Forrest, 'Backward Causation in Defence of Free Will', about this.

13 There is a lot of feeling ready to be called forth against the view that an effect could precede its cause. The thinker who has exposed most effectively how these feelings have their basis in crude prejudices is Michael Dummett, most recently in his exchange with D. H. Mellor in B. M. Taylor (ed.), *Michael Dummett: Contributions to Philosophy*.

14 Cf. for example D. K. Lewis, 'Causation', about this.

15 Cf. T. Horgan, 'Counterfactuals and Newcomb's Problem'. The problem was introduced by a physicist named Newcomb. This is a brief statement of the problem, taken from Michael D. Resnik's book *Choices: An Introduction to Decision Theory*. Suppose a being with miraculous powers of foresight, called the Predictor, offers you the following choice: there are two shoe boxes on the table between the two of you. One is red, the other blue. The tops are off the boxes and you can see that the red box has £1,000 in it and that the blue box is empty. The Predictor tells you that you are to leave the room and return in five minutes. When you return you will be offered the choice of having the contents of the blue box or that of both boxes. The Predictor also tells you that while you are out of the room he will place £1,000,000 in the blue box if he predicts that you will take just the blue box, and he will leave it empty if he predicts that you will take both boxes. You leave the room and return after five minutes. The top is still off the red box and the £1,000 is still in it. The blue box is now closed. You have heard about the Predictor before. You know that almost everyone who has taken both boxes has received just £1,000 while almost everyone who has taken just the blue box has received £1,000,000. What is your choice?

16 Cf. L. Bergström, *The Alternatives and Consequences of Actions*, for a statement of this principle.

17 In my 'Responsibility and the Explanatory View of Consequences'.

18 C. D. Broad, 'The Doctrine of Consequences in Ethics', pp. 315–16.

19 D. Parfit, *Reasons and Persons*, Part 2.

20 The example was suggested to me in conversation by Ragnar Ohlsson.

Chapter 11

Utilitarianism and common sense morality

I have claimed that hedonistic utilitarianism gives a good explanation of those common sense moral judgements that we want, upon closer inspection, to retain. Is this claim correct? In particular, does not common sense morality provide us with a host of moral judgements in conflict with utilitarianism but each such that, even upon closer examination, we want to retain it?

It is difficult to answer this question unless we know more about what common sense morality is.

What is common sense morality?

The idea of reflective equilibrium means that we have to start our moral reasoning where we stand. The morality we tend to share with people around us we call 'common sense morality'. So it is important to establish who 'we' are, if we want to answer the question of whether utilitarianism is at variance with common sense morality. My main aim is to get clear about how I think. Where else could I start? But I believe I can generalise and speak for some others as well. How many? Is there a universal moral understanding? Are there inter- and intracultural diversities? Readers must judge for themselves. The morality I call 'common sense morality' is the morality I tend to share with people around me.

However, there is an important observation to be made. Common sense morality ought not to be taken at face value. Upon reflection, we may want to revise it in a piecemeal manner. Some parts of it we do not want to retain. There are two main kinds of change to common sense morality, as I know it, that I want to make.

One change is to do with the fact that we live in a world where through our actions we are capable of affecting people who live at a long distance from us. This is made possible both because of new means of communication, allowing people living at a long distance from each other to interact, and by new techniques allowing many persons together to cause environmental problems (because of the way they commute, the way they dispose of their garbage, the way they pollute and so forth). Problems obtaining in a prisoner's dilemma

153

situation are also of interest in this connection. When several people interact in such a situation, each person, because he or she is successfully realising his or her goals, is doing worse than he or she would do if each was not successfully realising his or her goals. Such situations can obtain whenever several persons who have different goals interact without being able to affect each other's actions, for example in the production of public goods. Common sense morality gives different goals to different people (each is supposed to show preferential concern for those who are near and dear to him or her). The anonymity of modern mass societies prepares the ground for prisoner's dilemma situations involving many persons (because of anonymity there is no way of punishing a 'free rider').

Another change to common sense morality is made necessary because of a challenge to the standard notion of 'common sense morality' that has been levelled by a recent feminist critique.

I will discuss these two kinds of reform of common sense morality when I have said something more about the subject of Chapter 2, the question of why we need theory in ethics at all. Why not just stick to (a revised version of) common sense morality?

Positive reasons for theory in ethics

An obvious feature of common sense morality is that it is loose, vague and in many ways incomplete. Another obvious feature of it is that it is 'down to earth'. The advice it gives is meant to apply in ordinary circumstances, not in abstract thought-experiments. This does not mean that it cannot be a good point of departure for our moral arguments. But it means that it is open to improvement.

In Chapter 2 I argued that, unless we make our moral reasoning theoretical, we will end up in moral scepticism. Three additional arguments for theoretical moral philosophy are as follows.

In the first place, we need moral theory to take care of cases where common sense morality, because of its vagueness and incompleteness, fails us. In particular, we are at a loss in hard moral cases if we rely solely on common sense morality.

Secondly, we need moral theory to take care of cases where common sense morality involves us in moral conflict. According to common sense morality, there are cases where, whatever we do, we act wrongly, and situations such that, in them, we are confronted with conflicting moral requirements. If we succeed in refining common sense morality into moral theory, and find support in moral theory for more definite methods of responsible decision making, and if, at the same time, we succeed in bringing our moral views into reflective equilibrium, we make a definite gain in our capacity as moral agents.

Finally, and most importantly, common sense morality may be incorrect. We may need to revise it. To be sure, if coherentism is a sound strategy, we cannot ever come to have good reasons to reject common sense morality altogether. As noted above, we have to start our moral investigation where we stand. But we may well come to find faults with parts of common sense morality. Actually, examples of this have been discussed above. And the part we find faults with may well be incorrect. So we had better try to revise common sense morality, adapting it, for example, to new demands made actual by societal change.

How should we revise common sense morality, then? We should revise it, of course, in the light of moral theory.

My conjecture is that hedonistic utilitarianism provides us with the moral theory we need. To be sure, I will not be able to prove this conjecture. However, in order to make it somewhat more plausible than it might at first appear, I will discuss some areas where utilitarianism seems or has been said to be at variance with common sense morality, and I will attempt to show that appearances are deceptive.

However, before doing so, I want, as promised, to focus on the two main points where I think we have to revise common sense morality. These points are to do with remote effects of our actions, not taken care of by common sense morality, and with a sex bias in common sense morality discovered by the feminist critique of it.

The problem with remote effects

What kinds of change to common sense morality are rendered necessary because of our ability to do harm at long distances, noticeable harm, or sub-noticeable harm, individually or together with other people? I think the direction of change to common sense morality that has to take place is rather obvious. We must become more cautious in what we do; we must become more concerned both about strangers and about remote consequences of our actions (even of consequences that are to each one affected sub-noticeable). In order to handle situations of a prisoner's dilemma kind successfully we ought furthermore to be disposed to make impartial rather than partial decisions.

It might be thought that what we ought to opt for, in prisoner's dilemma situations, is a revised form of common sense morality according to which each of us ought to give no priority to those whom she or he is specially related to, if she or he believes that at least enough others will act in the same way. This suggestion has been put forward by Derek Parfit.[1]

When are we to say that 'enough' others act in the same way? According to Parfit, the crucial number is given in the following manner:[2] there will be some smallest number k such that, if k or more do not give priority to their near and dear ones, this would be better even for their near and dear ones than it would be if all gave priority to those near and dear to them. When k or more act in the same way, then enough do, in order for the revised common sense moral principle to become operative.

This is not sufficient, however. For a general acceptance of this revised form of common sense morality is compatible with no one doing the impartial action and all therefore doing, according to this revised version of common sense morality, what they should do.

We need a deeper change of common sense morality, then, in situations of prisoner's dilemma. We need a common sense morality according to which, in such situations, we ought to act in a truly and unconditionally impartial manner. Irrespective of how others act in prisoner's dilemma situations we ought, on the revised form of common sense morality, to show equal concern for strangers. On the revised form of common sense morality, even if everyone else evades taxes in order to provide a better situation for his or her children, I ought not to do so in order to provide a better situation for mine.

Can we live up to such strong requirements? Probably not. I will return to this question in my discussion of supererogation. Yet, for all that, we ought to impose such requirements on ourselves. Even if they cannot set us straight, they can steer us somewhat closer to the appropriate behaviour. Or so I will argue below.

The feminist critique

Feminist philosophers have argued, both against mainstream moral philosophy with its idea of a common sense morality and against the received opinion among moral philosophers about human moral development, that these strands of thought express a sex (male) or gender (masculine) bias. In what follows I will concentrate on the core of this criticism. The strands of thought I concentrate on constitute a core both in the sense that they are widely (though not unanimously) shared by most feminist philosophers, and in the sense that they are gaining acceptance outside the feminist camp, simply for being on the right track. So they do not belong to the more speculative periphery of feminism.

On what premises is the core of this criticism based, then? Are they tenable?

These criticisms apply (as we will see) in an obvious manner to moral theories such as Kantianism and abstract theories of moral rights. But what about utilitarianism? Do the criticisms also apply to utilitarian moral thought?

I will discuss these questions in order. I turn first of all to the question of the tenability of the point of departure for the feminist critique.

The point of departure for the feminist moral critique has been three desiderata; these have been put forward by feminist philosophers concerning theories about our moral reasoning. The desiderata belong to the core of the feminist critique and they can be summarised in the following manner.

In the first place, moral reasoning does make sense (for example, the claim that women are systematically wronged in many societies makes sense, according to feminism), so some kind of theory about our moral reasoning is in place. This theory should not endorse moral relativism[3] (according to any 'feminism' worthy of the name, it is not only true from its perspective, but it is true absolutely, that women are systematically wronged in many societies); nor should this theory be all-out particularist[4] (some general explanation exists for why the way women are treated in many societies is wrong; as a matter of fact, feminism is very much about finding and giving this explanation).

Secondly, this theory must not be too rigid or simplistic; it should be sensitive to the particularities of each case.

Thirdly, and consequently, the theory should make room for notions such as care, special relations, responsibility and agent-relativity.

Are these desiderata plausible? I think they are.

It goes without saying that the present author shares the feminist view that moral language makes sense. It so happens that I share the feminist philosophers' rejection of moral relativism as well, though this is not a point that will be substantiated in the present context; I have discussed it at length elsewhere.[5] The theoretical stance taken up by feminists, as contrasted with a particularist stance, I find perfectly plausible too. I have defended it in Chapter 2 of this book, so I will say no more about it in the present chapter.

The idea that a moral theory ought not to be too rigid or simplistic is of course open to several very different interpretations. Some of them are quite plausible, others implausible. The one presupposed by the feminist critique belongs to the plausible ones, it seems to me. This interpretation could be indicated by the following example.

Suppose a certain women wonders whether she should carry her pregnancy to term. This woman is facing a hard moral choice. On some traditional moral theory the solution is easy to find. The woman should bring some theory of human rights, or the sanctity of life doctrine, to bear on her case. If the foetus is a (potential) person, it is wrong for the woman to have an abortion since the foetus, being a (potential) person, has a right to life. And according to the sanctity of life doctrine, it is wrong for her to have the abortion for even more simplistic reasons. It is wrong since the foetus is a living human being, and living human beings ought not to be killed, period.

Now, according to the feminist critique, such moral theories are not plausible ones. They are not at all sensitive to all the particular aspects of the situation in which this woman is placed.

This is not only a sign of the inadequacy of these theoretical approaches. According to many feminists, the idea that hard cases can be solved on such a narrow basis of information reveals a male or masculine prejudice as well. This is how the discussion connects with feminism. And to the extent that common sense morality is believed to contain this strand of thought, common sense morality too reveals a sex or male bias, so we ought to change our conception of it.

It is true that solving hard cases in this way, through the application of a simple and very general theory of rights, has by some experts on human moral development been considered a token of maturity (Freud, Piaget, Kohlberg). According to the feminist critique, however, it is rather a sign of puerility. If we take a critical (feminist) stance on common sense morality, we must admit that these methods of solving hard cases are not uncontroversially parts of the core of common sense morality. They are rather idiosyncrasies, and the intellectual price for giving them up is perhaps not high.

The idea that a plausible moral theory should give room for the notions of care, special relations, responsibility and agent-relativity strikes me too as very plausible. The feminist critique is here also in line with a standard view of common sense morality, it seems to me. Now, a moral theory should take as its point of departure aspects of our actual moral practice. And it is a fact that notions such as care, special relations, responsibility and agent-relativity do have a role to play in our actual moral practice. So it is a desideratum that our favoured moral theory explains this role, in a not eliminative manner.

We have already seen that some standard moral theories face up poorly to these desiderata. I am thinking of simplistic theories of rights, Kantianism, the sanctity of life doctrine, and so forth. Even moral particularism and virtue ethics have problems with the desiderata. It is difficult, on these views, to show why the way women are treated in most societies is wrong. The particularist can give reasons why women should not be treated like this, but these reasons do not explain the wrongness of the treatment, or so I have argued in Chapter 2, at any rate. The situation for a virtue ethicist is similar. The virtue ethicist is concerned not primarily with the wrongness of actions but with vice and virtue exhibited by people's character. The virtue ethicist can condemn (indirectly) a certain treatment of women, of course, and say that those who uphold it exhibit bad traits of character (vice). But this does not explain the wrongness of the treatment in question. For, to be sure, the treatment cannot be wrong because it is upheld by vicious persons! But what about hedonistic utilitarianism; how does it face up to the desiderata here specified?

It seems to me that hedonistic utilitarianism satisfies these desiderata in a very natural way. Let me elaborate this point.

First of all, utilitarianism is a moral theory. As stated and defended in the present book it takes as its point of departure the idea that our moral reasoning makes sense, and it avoids moral particularism and moral relativism by providing an explanation of the (absolute) truth of those particular moral judgements that we want, upon reflection, to retain; or so I have argued, at any rate.

Secondly, utilitarianism is not simplistic. The distinction used by utilitarians between a criterion of rightness and a responsible method of decision making is subtle. The criterion of rightness as stated in the present book is sensitive to the particularities of a situation. Any variation in the situation that might affect the value of the outcome of the action is morally relevant, so the utilitarian has no problem in encompassing the feminist criticism. As a matter of fact, the utilitarian must concur in Carol Gilligan's assessment that the example of Abraham, who is willing to sacrifice the life of his son in order to demonstrate the integrity and supremacy of his faith, so often referred to with admiration in traditional moral reasoning, shows 'the danger of an ethics abstracted from life'.[6]

Finally, does utilitarianism give room for the notions of care, special relations, responsibility and agent-relativity?

This might at first seem to be a problem for utilitarianism, since these notions are not part of the statement of the utilitarian criterion of rightness. However, we have seen that they play an important indirect role in our moral reasoning, according to utilitarianism. Our belief in the truth of utilitarianism informs our adoption of a responsible method of decision making. It is not very far-fetched to assume that for most persons in most situations this method has recourse to the notions of care, special relations, responsibility and agent-relativity. As a matter of fact, this is the lesson to be learnt from the case of Clare, discussed in Chapter 9. We saw that these notions are not of direct importance to a moral evaluation of an action, but they are indirectly of the utmost importance. When a two level approach is brought to bear on the moral situation of human beings, when rules of thumb are designed for use in situations of responsible moral choice, the notions of care, special relations, responsibility and agent-relativity all play crucial roles (explained at length in this book).

But if this is correct, if utilitarianism makes all these concessions to the feminist critique, and accepts its revised view of common sense morality, how is it that most present-day feminists have rejected utilitarianism?

The reason they have done so, I am afraid to say, is to do with their lack of deep familiarity with the utilitarian doctrine and also, to some extent, with their lack of familiarity with the utilitarian tradition. Present-day feminists have not seriously considered the utilitarian doctrine as a possible point of departure for their critique.

Why is this so? The explanation, I conjecture, is that utilitarianism has not been a theory in vogue in the period when the modern feminist critique was articulated. So modern feminists – like most moral philosophers during the period – rejected utilitarianism for poor and ill-considered reasons.

In the past, feminism and utilitarianism did go together.[7] Early feminists such as Mary Wollstonecraft, Harriet Taylor and John Stuart Mill were all of a utilitarian bent. This has not been the case during the seventies, eighties and early nineties of the twentieth century. My hope is that the situation might change in the future.

Utilitarianism is today, just as much as it was during the nineteenth century, a natural point of departure for a critique of all sorts of social injustice, not only sexism. I am thinking of challenges put to us by phenomena such as maltreatment of animals, global injustices between rich and poor countries, growing social and economic differences within rich countries too, and even problems of population policy and of inter-generation justice.

The last example might seem a bit rash considering a problem I have now and then touched upon in this book, to wit, the problem that utilitarianism gives rise to what Derek Parfit has called 'the repugnant conclusion'. How can this conclusion be reconciled with common sense morality?

The repugnant conclusion

Utilitarianism leads to the conclusion that, in order to maximise happiness, we ought to make each person only moderately happy (rather than very happy) if this means that, instead of only a few people living, a great many people will live. This conclusion has been thought to be repugnant to common sense. This is a mistake. There exists no answer from common sense morality to the problem posed by the repugnant conclusion. For this conclusion is the result of an advanced thought-experiment. And the typical common sense reaction to such thought-experiments is to deny their moral relevance. Common sense does not enter into these sorts of speculation! So this conclusion is irrelevant to common sense morality, which deals exclusively with more practical situations, situations more 'down to earth'.

The repugnant conclusion is of the utmost relevance, however, to theoretical ethics. I have already discussed the ultra repugnant conclusion. Here I will defend the more basic claim that the repugnant conclusion is, if not sought, yet acceptable. Reasons of consistency, intellectual economy, and fruitfulness in our attempt to enhance common sense moral reasoning push us towards accepting it.

When we try to assess how repugnant the repugnant conclusion really is we must guard against several kinds of possible misunderstanding.

First of all, we must remember that the repugnant conclusion stresses a mere logical possibility. An actual increase in the world population, or an aspect of it, may well in some situation mean a loss of welfare; I am thinking in particular of those children who are born into extreme poverty.

Secondly, we should be careful not to ask ourselves in which world we want to live: in one where a few very happy persons live, or in one where very many moderately happy persons live. It is natural to prefer to live in the world where each person is very happy. This does not answer the question which of these worlds is the better one, however. The question is clearly biased. If we should discuss the matter at all from the point of view of which world we would opt for, if we were offered a choice, we should be forced to make our choice behind a veil of ignorance. But then both a maximising strategy and a strategy of maximin seem to push us towards accepting the repugnant conclusion. As a matter of fact, the maximin strategy seems to push us even more strongly in that direction: we ought to opt for the greatest number, irrespective of how much well-being we produce, as soon as those who live have lives worth living.

Is it possible to take the decision about the number of people who will live behind a veil of ignorance? Derek Parfit has argued that this is not possible: 'We can imagine a different possible history, in which we never existed. But we cannot assume that, in the actual history of the world, it might be true that we never exist.'[8] I do not find this convincing. It is difficult to imagine what it would be like to take a decision behind a veil of ignorance in the first place – what would it be like not to know one's sex, for example. However, I see no special problem in holding it open whether, depending on my choice, I will exist or not. We need only to assume that, if I opt for a small but very happy population, there is a considerable risk that, all of a sudden, I perish. I will never get out of the original position. The risk is lower (we cannot pretend that there is any exact precision in this kind of estimation) if I opt for a more numerous population.

Thirdly, a likely misunderstanding in our apprehension of the repugnant conclusion is to do with the fact that our actual moral sense seems to be based on identification. However, our capacity to identify with others is limited. Most of us care about our own family, those who are near and dear to us. We take less interest in our fellow nationals but more interest in them than in people living far away from us. However, it is widely recognised that we ought to care about strangers. We ought to generalise our sympathy even to them. We have extra difficulties in doing so when it comes to very large numbers of people. Such numbers mean little to us. However, large numbers matter. In the same manner as we generalise our sympathy to strangers we ought (mechanically, if necessary) to generalise our sympathy to large numbers of people. If we do we may have to accept the repugnant conclusion, after all.

Fourthly, and perhaps most importantly, we may believe that, in a world where each person is only moderately happy, a world where, on balance, each person lives a life barely worth living is a world where everyone is much worse off than are at least the happiest people in our world. Is this view correct? I think not.

The view I am prepared to defend is somewhat pessimistic but still, I am afraid, realistic. My impression is that if only our basic needs are satisfied, then most of us are capable of living lives that, on balance, are worth experiencing. However, no matter how 'lucky' we are, how many 'gadgets' we happen to possess, we rarely reach beyond this level. If sometimes we do, this has little to do with material affluence; rather, bliss, when it does occur, seems to be the ephemeral result of such things as requited love, successful creative attempts and, of course, the proper administration of drugs.

If this observation is correct, we should expect that the best world that is possible is crowded. However, we need not fear that it is a world where we, who are the lucky ones in this world, live lives much worse than the ones we are living right now.

If this is correct, it transpires that the repugnant conclusion is not so repugnant after all. It is an unsought, but acceptable, consequence of hedonistic utilitarianism.

But does not the existence of at least a billion people who starve in today's world mean that it is worse than, say, the world of the seventeenth century, where at least fewer people suffered such hardship? I think not.

In the first place, even if the quality of these poor lives ought to be improved upon (this is the most urgent political task in today's world, I would say), many of these people feel that, after all, their lives are better than no lives at all.

Moreover, in today's world there are four billion people who live lives that are fairly obviously worth living. This does not mean that we should not take action against the misery in the world, but in our value calculus, these four billion people do make a positive entry, probably more weighty than the corresponding negative one, created by the most abject poverty in the world.

My very strong intuition is that it would be very wrong to exterminate the entire population of the world, even if this could be done painlessly and even if there was no other (better) alternative to a continued existence of the world in its present form.

These considerations suggest that, after all, the repugnant conclusion is not that repugnant after all. This vindicates hedonistic utilitarianism as giving a good explanation of the problem of how many people there ought to be. It does not vindicate completely the judgement that hedonistic utilitarianism gives the best moral explanation of the problem here raised, however. In order to show this I ought to show that alternative theoretical approaches face more serious problems than the one that classical hedonistic utilitarianism is facing (the repugnant conclusion). I am convinced that they do. To show this is not possible in the present context, however. It must suffice here to give a brief indication of the problems some of them are facing. They have all been exposed in Derek Parfit's seminal treatment of the subject in *Reasons and Persons*.

To begin with, the person-affecting view suggested by Jan Narveson, according to which we cannot act wrongly unless we act wrongly towards some (timelessly) existing person, faces both moral and theoretical problems.[9]

The main moral problem is that it is far too pessimistic. It allows that Eve and Adam may rightly not conceive any children, even if the children they could have conceived would have been leading extremely happy lives, and would have had, in their turn, children that would have been leading extremely happy lives, and so forth.

The main theoretical problem is that the view implies that the normative status of what we do depends on what we do. If Eve and Adam conceive children who live happy lives, then this is all right. If they do not, then this is all right. The view can even lead to the conclusion that, whatever we do, we act wrongly. This is so if we have two options resulting in either of two states of the world. Either (1) Eve lives and Adam does not. Eve suffers, her life is not worth living. Or (2) Adam lives and Eve does not. Adam suffers, his life is not worth living. If we opt for (1) then this is wrong. Eve has a legitimate complaint to make: her life is not worth living. Since Adam does not exist, he has no say. If instead we opt for (2), then this option is wrong as well. For Adam has a legitimate complaint to make: his life is not worth living. Since Eve does not exist, she has no say. Parfit to the contrary notwithstanding, no real contradiction is involved in this kind of example, but the result is strange indeed.

The average view leads to the conclusion that, in a world where all people lead a terrible life, not worth living, each couple ought to conceive children who live lives that are also not worth living; everybody ought to do so as soon as their children's lives are not quite as bad as their own life. This is morally completely unacceptable.

The idea that additional good lives do not add to the value of the world as soon as the existing population has more than reached a critical level of well-being is completely arbitrary. Where are we to draw the line? Is the important thing how many people live at a certain time, in a certain world? Or is the important thing that enough people live at each place and time in the universe?

Setting the arbitrariness of any answer to these questions to one side, the view faces insuperable moral objections as well. Once the critical number is reached, no addition of lives is permitted, provided that some pain (no matter how slight) goes with it. This is too pessimistic to be acceptable.

The idea that additional good lives do not add to the value of the world unless they are above a critical level of well-being (quality) faces too both theoretical and moral problems.

This view seems, once again, quite arbitrary in where to draw the line.

And the view gives rise to a new version of the repugnant conclusion: we may have to opt for a large population at the critical level, rather than a more restricted population well above it. If we are prepared to accept this, then we may as well accept the repugnant conclusion in its original shape. The gain in simplicity, generality and overall plausibility is considerable.

Finally, the view is too pessimistic. It forbids the creation of new life near (but below) the critical line, as soon as it brings with it some (however small) pain. This is not acceptable.

Killing

It has often been held that hedonistic utilitarianism cannot give an adequate explanation of the wrongness of killing, acknowledged by common sense morality. Is this a fact? It is not. Let us see why.

In its most primitive version the criticism of hedonistic utilitarianism goes as follows: suppose I kill a man when he is asleep and suppose that no one ever notices this. On common sense morality this is morally repugnant. However, on hedonistic utilitarianism this is not objectionable. The victim does not notice any loss, no one else notices any loss, so, on hedonistic utilitarianism, what could there be to object to in my killing? This is a mistake. By killing the man I deprive him of the rest of his life. If the rest of his life would have contained more pleasure than pain, then my action was morally objectionable.

However, this objection to my killing may seem weak. To be sure, if I deprive him of the rest of his life, this may be wrong, but only if it makes the world on the whole worse. Suppose, however, that I compensate for the loss by, for example, creating another person, who experiences at least as good a life as the remainder of the life of the person killed: does this mean that my killing of the person was morally all right?

It does, in this thought-experiment, and this may indeed seem disturbing from the point of view of common sense morality. The reason against killing human beings seems no stronger than that against aborting foetuses or, for that matter, no stronger than the reason for creating new (happy) human beings. Again, appearances are deceptive, however. For it must be remembered that we are not considering an abstract thought-experiment. Common sense morality is not fit to cope with such examples. And in the real world, hedonistic utilitarianism provides us with a strong reason not to contemplate murder. The reason is that, if people were allowed to contemplate and to perform murder, without strong sanctions, this would make people uneasy (and unhappy) while still alive.

How is this possible? If it is not a dramatic loss to die (I do not notice any loss and the loss may well be compensated for, morally speaking, by someone else living in place of me), why do people fear being killed?

The reason is that people have in general a strong wish to go on living (so strong, as a matter of fact, that many people act on this even when it is harmful to them). It is not difficult to see why evolution has provided us with such a wish. In our designing civilised human institutions, we must take this wish seriously.

The hedonistic utilitarian argument against killing is only an indirect one, based on our need for physical security, but it is a very strong one. Furthermore, it is very general in scope. It is hard to conceive of a good society where the ban on murder has been relaxed. This is the explanation why murder should be forbidden, and punished when performed, and why children should be taught not to consider murder a possible solution to any problem they may come to face in life.

The utilitarian (indirect) condemnation of murder may be compared to a more direct one, such as that performed in the name of the sanctity of life doctrine or some theory of absolute and inalienable human rights. The utilitarian condemnation is tempered in a way that the other kinds of condemnation are not. On the utilitarian explanation of the wrongness of killing, wanton killing of adult human beings (against their will) is a very serious crime that should be punished. However, abortion, euthanasia and capital punishment do not fall under the same (categorical) ban. If abortion is allowed, this does not pose any threat to anyone capable of wondering whether he or she will be allowed to go on living. Foetuses may be able to feel pain, but they do not fear death. And if euthanasia is undertaken on the request of people who feel that their lives have lost their point, such a practice need not as such pose any threat to any living person. Those who do not want to have euthanasia should not ask for it. If convicted murderers are executed, this does not mean that people in general must fear that they be executed. If they abstain from murder they will not be executed.

Whether the practices of abortion, euthanasia and capital punishment should be adopted or not depends on the value of the consequences (the side-effects) of adopting them. Will a practice of (free) abortion lead to undesirable sexual behaviour? Will euthanasia take us onto a slippery slope, where people will eventually get killed against their will? Will capital punishment effectively deter people from murder or not? These are controversial matters, where decent people may well come to disagree.

This subtle view of killing, explained in the hedonistic utilitarian manner, is well in line with common sense morality. According to common sense morality, it is obvious that murder is wrong while it is disputable whether abortion, euthanasia and capital punishment are defensible practices or not. So it is the sanctity of life doctrine and the various different ideas about absolute and inalienable human rights, rather than hedonistic utilitarianism, that are at a loss when it comes to explaining the common sense view of the moral status of killing. The claim that abortion, euthanasia and capital punishment are, morally speaking, on a par with murder correctly strikes common sense morality as outrageous.

Justice

Consider the following example: five girls find a doll in the lumber room (where they are not allowed to play). One of them says that she ought to have the doll, since she would benefit most from getting it (she has a collection where only this piece is missing). The second girl protests that she ought to have it, since she is poor. She has no doll. The third protests, in her turn, that she should have it, since she was the one who saw it first. The fourth protests, in her turn, that she is the one who should have it. She deserves to have it since, had she not stolen a key to the lumber room, they would not have found the doll. The fifth, finally, protests that she is the one who should have the doll, since she is the strongest one among them. Unless she gets the doll, she will start a fight, and she is sure to be successful in it.

What does the example show? It shows that all sorts of theories of justice are spread in common sense moral thinking. We tend to rely, in the situation of choice, on the theory that happens to favour our interests. The first girl wants, with Bentham, to have value maximised (this happens to favour her interests); the second goes with Rawls and wants equality (since she is worst off); the third sides with Locke and Nozick for rights (because she is the one who made the original acquisition of the doll, 'she saw it first'); the fourth follows Aristotle and claims that distribution should take place according to merit (since she feels that she has the advantage over the rest in this respect); and the fifth, finally, goes for Hobbes/Gauthier and claims that what the girls find in the lumber room should be distributed according to agreement (she knows that her bargaining position is the strongest).

Does this mean that common sense morality is inconsistent in its view of justice? To some extent I think it does. But also to some extent I think common sense morality can handle the seeming inconsistency itself. Without departing much from common sense morality we can delineate a decision procedure according to which we lean in some situations towards one of the competing ideals, and in other situations towards other ideals. In many situations we accept rationing schemes according to the principle of 'First come, first served.' Few hesitate to pay some extra attention to those who are worst off when the option is what basic structures we should have in society, most people seem to accept that rewards in competitions are given according to merit, most people accept that the governmental economic policy pay at least some attention to the ideal of having value maximised, and, at least in international affairs, many people accept that we must resort to solutions reflecting the different bargaining power of nations. If we wish, we can say that a decision procedure respecting these intuitions is just, and we can say of a person who follows it that he or she is a just person.

Clearly, utilitarianism may well be consistent with common sense ideas of justice. My conjecture is that it is (but since this conjecture is both speculative and empirical, I cannot substantiate it further). However, other putative theories of justice, such as the ones alluded to above, cannot do justice to common sense intuitions. The reason that they cannot do so is, of course, that each of them requires that we should always distribute in accordance with itself. Common sense morality is not prepared to do this. This becomes particularly clear when common sense morality is viewed through the filter set up by the feminist critique, discussed in the previous section.

For example, common sense morality repudiates the libertarian idea that we have no responsibility at all for those who just happen to be worst off. At the same time, common sense morality rejects the idea that we should give everything to them, up to the point where we are all equally badly off. Common sense morality balks at the idea of a society arranged completely along meritocratic principles, and is equally suspicious of the idea that all social relations should be based on agreements between conflicting parties (which is only considered a last resort, when, so to speak, 'morality has failed'). Hence, utilitarianism not only seems to be consistent with common sense ideas of justice, but gives a better explanation of them than does any of the standard competing theories of justice.

Asymmetries in common sense morality

Michael Slote[10] has made us aware of the fact that common sense morality seems to exhibit a strange asymmetry. According to common sense morality, we have special obligations to those who are near and dear to us. The nearer and dearer a person is to me, the stronger my obligation to care for this person. But to the person who is perhaps nearest and dearest to me, myself, I have no moral obligation whatever. How does utilitarianism handle this fact?

In Chapter 9 I have argued that utilitarianism can handle the fact that we seem to have stronger obligations to those who are near and dear to us. It seems responsible for utilitarians to adopt a method of decision making which includes an intuitive level with the normative structure here adumbrated. However, it is more difficult to see why utilitarians should adopt a decision method including an intuitive rule according to which they have no moral obligations whatever to themselves. What could be the rationale behind such a rule?

It might be tempting to argue as follows: people are by nature predisposed to take too much interest in their own well-being. Therefore, no moral rule to this effect is needed. But it is probably also true that people are prepared sometimes to take too much interest in the well-being of those who are near and dear to them. So if the argument works in the one case, it should also work in the other.

I feel at a loss here. Perhaps we should say that, since common sense morality is inconsistent, anyway, we should feel free to improve on it in these respects, and follow the decision method, informed by utilitarianism, that we see fit.

Or, perhaps we could say that the asymmetry does not reflect any inconsistency in common sense morality, after all. For, contrary to what we are prepared to believe is true of ourselves, we are prepared to take care of ourselves, without any help from morality, but we are (often) not prepared to take enough care of those who are near and dear to us. So, in this case, we do need support from morality. Or, the argument could be improved.[11] It might be ideal if we take equal care of everyone, i.e., if we pay the same attention to strangers as we pay to ourselves. However, even if this is something we are taught to do, we will not do it. We are simply not prepared to take equal care of everyone, whatever we are taught about this. With the aid of a Harean two-level morality, a morality where we are taught to take care of everyone but are allowed to take special care of those who are near and dear to us, however, we become disposed to act more decently than we would do if we were educated in any alternative morality. We become disposed to take care of those who are near and dear to us and we become disposed also to take some care of strangers, at least in some circumstances. We become what Peter Railton has called 'sophisticated consequentialists'. This is the best approximation to the ideal that is possible.

In any case, it seems clear that there is no necessary conflict between utilitarianism and a refined version of common sense morality.

Supererogation

The example of supererogation may seem to pose a problem for utilitarianism. Common sense morality allows, but does not require, heroic sacrifices for the sake of others. Utilitarianism, on the other hand, requires exactly these sacrifices. How could utilitarians explain this conflict between their cherished doctrine and common sense?

Some cases where people fail to make great sacrifices for the sake of others are examples of blameless wrongdoing. These actions are wrong, but they are performed because the agent has a good character, and therefore they are blameless. Common sense morality, then, is close to the truth when it claims that they are all right. The actions are not all right, but the agents are. They refuse to sacrifice themselves for the sake of strangers when this would mean a great loss, say, to their families. To be sure, in the situation, they can do the right thing. If they do, though, their action is an instance of blameful rightdoing.

However, there may exist cases where no such excuse is available. Consider the case of a woman without family or other responsibilities, who is capable of rescuing five other persons if she gives up her life. She is not very keen on living but yet, for all that, she refuses to sacrifice her life in the interest of the others. On utilitarianism, not only is she acting wrongly, but we should probably also say that she is doing so; her action has no support in any sound method of decision making informed by utilitarian thought. Common sense morality does not blame her, however. According to common sense morality, it would be great if she sacrificed her life but, when she does not, she acts rightly all the same. What are utilitarians to say of this conflict between their cherished doctrine and common sense morality?

We have seen above that, in our dealing with remote effects of our actions, we have reasons to give up common sense morality. It is too lenient to us in those contexts. We have now come across another place where I think it would be wise to give up common sense morality. It is difficult to find a rationale behind common sense morality in these circumstances.

It might be thought that unless utilitarianism be relaxed to allow for people not sacrificing themselves for others, and unless we allow in moral education that people be taught that they need not sacrifice themselves, then morality will lose its grip on us. The same objection can be made, as we have seen, against the claim that we ought to act truly altruistically in prisoner's dilemma situations, where common sense morality gives us different and conflicting moral aims. A common sense morality making such heavy demands will not be taken seriously. This line has been taken by John Mackie, who stresses that it is not likely that people will live in accordance with utilitarian demands: 'To identify morality with something that certainly will not be followed is a sure way of bringing it into contempt, practical contempt, which combines all too readily with theoretical respect.'[12] I think we ought to resist this line of thought. In the first place, note that even if it is true that people will certainly not follow a recommendation that they sacrifice themselves for others, it may well be true that this sacrifice is something that people can make. Now, I am not convinced that people are not at least sometimes capable of making heavy sacrifices, in particular in cases where only their own interests are at stake (they do not have to sacrifice the interests of people who are near and dear to them in order to profit strangers).

Secondly, I think that people, even when they fail to live up to such demands, are capable of countenancing them in their moral thinking. They are capable of admitting that, when they did not abide by them, what they did was the wrong thing.

When is a heavy requirement brought into contempt? It is brought into contempt when it is too heavy and without any good point. If we can see a point to it, we do not feel any contempt for it. So it is probably not true that we are not capable of taking heavy moral demands seriously (even if, now and then, we fail to live up to them). We do take them seriously when we can see a rationale behind them.

People are prepared to make, or at least allow that they ought to make, all sorts of sacrifice in order to avoid contagious diseases spreading, say, and in times of war, many people do not hesitate to give their lives for what they consider higher purposes. But a moral (or legal) requirement loses its grip on us, no matter how light a demand it makes on us, if the rationale is wanting. Unless we are presented with good reasons to comply, we are not even prepared to respond to innocuous inquiries about our whereabouts from governmental authorities.

The asymmetry mentioned in the previous section speaks too in favour of the decision to revise common sense morality when it comes to supererogation. It is true that utilitarianism makes heavier requirements on us with respect to what common sense speaks of as 'supererogation', but, on the other hand, common sense is too lenient when it allows that a person may rightly sacrifice his or her life even for the minor benefit of others. Utilitarianism strikes a reasonable balance between these two extremes.

Pace common sense morality, we ought to sacrifice our lives in situations where this benefits other persons more than it thwarts our own interests. But, once again, *pace* common sense morality, it would be wrong to sacrifice one's life when other persons have very little to gain from this. Utilitarianism substitutes consistent and plausible theory for schizoid, or even inconsistent, common sense beliefs. A modified common sense morality should be informed by this theory.

The reason why the utilitarian can publicly countenance the conclusion that it is wrong not to perform supererogatory acts, when this does not exhibit any deficiency in the character of the agent (such as neglect for those who are near and dear to him or her), has been stated by John Mackie himself, although he does not fully appreciate its strength:

> But why have moralists and preachers thought it worthwhile to propound rules that obviously have so little chance of being followed? They must surely have thought that by setting up such admittedly unattainable ideals they might induce at least some movement towards them, that if men were told to let universal beneficence guide all their conduct, they would not indeed do this, but would allow some small admixture of universal beneficence to help to direct their actions.[13]

Notes

1 Cf. D. Parfit, *Reasons and Persons*, p. 102.
2 Parfit, *Reasons and Persons*, p. 102.
3 To be sure, there exist some feminist moral philosophers who have endorsed a relativistic metaethics, but these thinkers have not gained much support. And the reason for this is, I believe, that the view that women are and have been systematically wronged in most (perhaps all known) societies is really a defining characteristic of the feminist stance. For a discussion about feminism and relativism, see Jean Grimshaw's classical *Feminist Philosophers: Women's Perspectives on Philosophical Traditions*, Ch. 4.
4 As was observed in Ch. 2, there exist some particularist feminist moral philosophers. There I mentioned Margaret Urban Walker and her 'Moral Understandings: Alternative "Epistemology" for a Feminist Ethics'. However, if the main thrust of the argument of that chapter is correct, then particularism is not a sound strategy for a feminist moral philosopher to adopt.
5 Cf. my *Moral Realism*, Chs 3 and 5, about this.
6 C. Gilligan, *In a Different Voice: Psychological Theory and Women's Development*, p. 104.
7 Cf. for example Lea Campos Boralevi, 'Utilitarianism and Feminism', for a discussion of the connections between early utilitarianism and early feminism.
8 Parfit, *Reasons and Persons*, p. 392.
9 Cf. J. Narveson, 'Utilitarianism and New Generations'.

10 Cf. for example M. Slote, *From Morality to Virtue*, pp. 39–40.
11 This improvement was suggested to me by Ragnar Ohlsson.
12 J. L. Mackie, *Ethics: Inventing Right and Wrong*, p. 132.
13 Mackie, *Ethics*, p. 131.

Chapter 12

Conclusion and remaining concerns

In this book I have given what I hope is a clear and comprehensive statement of a doctrine known as classical hedonistic utilitarianism. I have contended that it should be considered a live alternative in the ongoing search for a viable moral theory. And I have defended the claim that we need such a theory. I have argued that even if many of the implications of hedonistic utilitarianism may at first strike us as counter-intuitive, the theory still presents us with the most plausible moral theory hitherto developed. It is also less at variance with common sense morality than has often been assumed, I have argued. This becomes even more clear when common sense morality is viewed through the perspective of the modern feminist moral critique.

I will now briefly sum up some of the most salient features of the doctrine put forward in this book.

Main results

First of all I have argued, then, that we need a moral theory. Not only do we need it to fill in gaps in our common sense moral thinking, to solve dilemmas where our common sense notions provide us with conflicting pieces of advice, and so forth, but we need it in order to escape the spectre of moral scepticism. The main rival to the theoretical moral approach, to wit, moral particularism, does lead to scepticism. This was the message of Chapter 2. A remaining concern in this chapter is, however, that it is not easy to ascertain that the utilitarian criterion of rightness itself faces up to the requirement put forward in the chapter. The defence of the utilitarian criterion of rightness, with respect to the decision methods it rationalises, is quite indirect and somewhat shaky. I feel that more work should be done in this field.

In Chapter 3 I made a simple statement of the utilitarian criterion of rightness of actions. According to this criterion, an action is right if, and only if, in the situation, there was nothing the agent could have done instead such that, had the agent done it, the world, on the whole, would have been better. In the chapter I distinguished between act utilitarianism and rule utilitarianism and I put forward some reasons why act utilitarianism is the more plausible view. I also distinguished between objective and subjective rightness and between criteria of rightness, on the one hand, and methods of responsible decision making on the other. A remaining concern in this chapter is that the principle of counterfactual act-determinism, so desperately needed not only by my approach but by all kinds of sensible moral theory, lacks a foundation. The principle has a strong intuitive appeal, but it is not validated in existing systems of possible world semantics. One possible reaction (my reaction) to this fact is to claim that no reductive analysis can be given of the meaning of counterfactual utterances. We may look upon the systems of possible world semantics as heuristic devices rather than as explications of the meaning of counterfactual utterances. A concern remains, however. It would be nice to have a system of possible world semantics validating the principle of counterfactual act-determinism.

In Chapter 3 I also defended two important principles, to wit, the principle of counterfactual dependence, used in my statement of the criterion of rightness, and the total state principle. These principles, roughly to the effect that it does not matter how a state of affairs is brought about and that past and future are of equal moral importance, seem innocent, but in subsequent chapters they turn out to have unexpected moral implications.

In Chapter 3 I also argued that my simple statement of the utilitarian criterion of rightness does not give rise to any deontic paradoxes.

In Chapter 4 I extended the utilitarian formula to cover not only the actions of individuals, but also collective actions. By so doing I became able to defend the thesis that if everyone (and each collectivity too) is always doing what he, she or it ought to do, things go as well as possible. If I am right about this, the most important argument against act utilitarianism and for rule utilitarianism falls. A remaining concern here, however, is that some such collectivities, taken to be moral agents in this chapter, may seem, to some at any rate, to be gerrymandered.

In Chapter 5 I presented the classical hedonistic idea that pleasure possesses intrinsic value. I defended a version of this view according to which subjective time, not objective time, is what matters morally, and I constructed a unit in our measurement of well-being (pleasure), namely the least sub-noticeable difference of well-being. My introduction of sub-noticeable difference of well-being into hedonistic utilitarianism pushed me to the conclusion that in order to increase the well-being of many already very happy sentient beings in a sub-noticeable manner, we might have to torture one sentient being. I argued that, although this was an unsought consequence of hedonistic utilitarianism, it is one that we can live with. A remaining concern in this chapter is that, in principle, there may exist even smaller differences of well-being than the ones acknowledged by me. It must remain a conjecture that all sub-noticeable differences of well-being can be brought to the surface as indirectly noticeable, if only we bring in new comparisons. This conjecture is empirical in nature, but it can never be put to the empirical test. If intransitivities cannot be explained away by the introduction of sub-noticeable differences that are indirectly noticed, the reason may be that the experience machine is not good (sensitive) enough. I feel pretty confident in my conjecture that all sub-noticeable differences of well-being are indirectly noticeable (in principle), but I am concerned that this must remain a conjecture.

In Chapter 6 I argued against the view that preference satisfaction is of intrinsic value. I noticed that few accept preferentialism in its 'raw' version, where actual preferences are what count. Most adherents of the view tend to tamper with the preferences before they are prepared to say that the more satisfaction of preferences the better. I claimed that such tampering tends to lead out of preferentialism altogether and into either hedonism or a perfectionist view of value. I argued too that while it seems odd to claim that we ought to choose something since we prefer to have it, it is plausible to say that we ought to choose something since it would make us happy or make us prosper. Therefore, among the three views of intrinsic value – (1) the preference satisfaction view, (2) hedonism and (3) perfectionism – the first one has to yield.

In Chapter 7 I argued against a perfectionist view of value and against those who claim that personal autonomy is of moral importance as such, and I rebutted the arguments of both J. S. Mill and Robert Nozick (his experience machine argument) against hedonism. This brought me closer to a complete defence of hedonism.

In Chapters 5–7 I took it for granted that intrinsic value is individual, however. When something is good, it must be good for someone. This claim is, of course, debatable. G. E. Moore, for example, has argued that there are, besides pleasure, many things that possess intrinsic value. In Chapter 8 I rebutted this claim and completed my defence of hedonism. Impersonal values are merely speculative, I argued. There are no good reasons to the effect that they are real (nor are there any good reasons to the effect that they are not real). But then we ought not to believe in them, I argued. At least we ought not to sacrifice known, individual values in order to further them. This conclusion was based on the principle of known values taking precedence over merely speculative ones.

In Chapter 9 I defended the claim that a consequentialist theory such as hedonistic utilitarianism can account successfully for agent-relativity, i.e., the putative fact that different moral agents may have different moral goals. For example, an agent may have special obligations towards those who are near and dear to him or her. A moral agent may feel, with some right, that, although she or he can help a stranger more, she or he ought rather to help her or his own child slightly less. For consequentialist reasons, it is a good thing that we are people of a kind who behave like this. However, this does not mean that, when acting on our character, our actions are right. We can act against our characters, and should do so in particular situations. However, since our moral mistakes are due to a correct choice of character, they are yet, for all that, blameless.

This insight means that the notion of a moral character, a moral virtue, if one prefers that phrase, has a place within utilitarian moral reasoning. And this means in turn that hedonistic utilitarianism is less at odds with our common sense morality than might at first be assumed.

In Chapter 10 I discussed free will and determinism, and I defended the claim that, in performing actions, we become responsible not only for the future, but also for what went on in the past. This is the result of the principle of counterfactual dependence and the total state principle being put together and wedded to a plausible view of modality in my statement of hedonistic utilitarianism. This is an unexpected consequence of hedonistic utilitarianism in its most plausible form, a consequence of the utmost theoretical importance. It is at odds with some of our strongest unreflected-on moral sentiments, but it is a consequence that, upon reflection, we can live with. Or can we not? A concern remains that there may be something very problematic with the idea of free will as such. However, this enigma pertaining to the idea of free will pertains not to utilitarianism in particular, but to any moral theory paying any attention to what would have happened had the agent acted otherwise.

Be that as it may, it should be noted that my result in this chapter has little practical importance. For, to be sure, we never know of any way of acting such that, were we to embark on it rather than on the action we have chosen, the future would be worse but the past much better. So the real impact of my result is that some doubt is cast upon the notion of free will as such. And this should be grounds for concern for anyone interested in moral philosophy of any variety.

In Chapter 11, finally, I discussed what could be meant by the phrase 'common sense morality', and I examined to what extent hedonistic utilitarianism is consistent with it. I had already in Chapter 9 observed that some common sense moral notions (such as those of a moral character and a moral virtue) are compatible with hedonistic moral reasoning. The upshot of the discussion in Chapter 11 is even more optimistic: hedonistic utilitarianism does explain, in a satisfactory manner, those parts of our common sense morality that we want, upon critical reflection, to hold on to. I am thinking of basic notions of justice, of duties to future generations, of asymmetries between duties to ourselves and to others, and of the notion of supererogation. In particular, utilitarianism satisfies desiderata put forward as a point of departure for the core of a recent feminist critique.

Conclusion

I conclude my book without any firm conviction that those who were critical of hedonistic utilitarianism when they started to read it will have given up their criticism when they finished. It might even be the case that some of them feel that they have found new and strong arguments against the acceptability of the doctrine. It is often difficult to predict the impact of an argument upon critical and reflecting people. However this may be, my hope is that, at least, they will feel that they have reached a deeper understanding of the view and found that, perhaps to their surprise, it is surely worth taking more seriously than has been the case recently. In particular, even those readers who do not concur in my polemical thesis, defended in Chapters 6–8, that hedonistic utilitarianism covers the entire moral field (these readers believe that things other than happiness may be of value in themselves too) should have learned from the rest of the book that hedonistic utilitarianism does at least present us with a bold, systematic, consistent and fruitful candidate for a moral principle of some scope.

Classical hedonistic utilitarianism is a bold conjecture in Karl Popper's[1] slightly technical sense: it contradicts earlier theories while at the same time, through the two level approach, explaining their relative success.

Classical hedonistic utilitarianism has proved to be fruitful in the obvious manner that it has played a major role in the development of modern moral philosophy. It has given rise to many interesting problems and engendered diverse and subtle philosophical discussions and debates.

I hope for a revival of interest in the hedonistic utilitarian doctrine. The various different concerns voiced in this book should indicate that hedonistic utilitarianism is a research project rather than a clear-cut theory. So there remains much to be said about it. I feel confident that the day when we hear no more about utilitarianism is far off in the distant future.

Note

1 Cf. for example K. Popper, *Objective Knowledge*, p. 16.

Bibliography

Alston, W. P., 'Pleasure', in Paul Edwards (ed.), *The Encyclopedia of Philosophy*, London and New York: Macmillan, 1967

Aristotle, *Ethics*, Harmondsworth: Penguin, 1953

Armstrong, D., *A Combinatorial Theory of Possibility*, Cambridge: Cambridge University Press, 1989

Arrow, K. J., *Social Choice and Individual Values*, 2nd edn, New York: Wiley, 1963

Arrow, K. J., 'Extended Sympathy and the Possibility of Social Choice', American Economic Association, 1977

Bales, R. E., 'Act-Utilitarianism: Account of Right-Making Characteristics or Decision-Making Procedure?', *American Philosophical Quarterly*, Vol. 8, 1971, pp. 257–65

Bales, R. E., 'Review of Bergström's *The Alternatives and Consequences of Actions* and Other Works', *Theoria*, Vol. 40, 1971, pp. 35–57

Bennett, J., 'Counterfactuals and Temporal Direction', *Philosophical Review*, Vol. XCIII, 1984, pp. 57–91

Bentham, J., 'Value of a Pain or Pleasure', in Bhikhu Parekh (ed.), *Bentham's Political Thought*, London: Croom Helm, 1973

Bentham, J., *An Introduction to the Principles of Morals and Legislation*, eds J. H. Burns and D. L. A. Hart, London and New York: Methuen, 1982

Bergström, L., *The Alternatives and Consequences of Actions*, Stockholm: Almqvist and Wiksell, 1968

Bergström, L., 'On the Formulation and Application of Utilitarianism', *Nous*, Vol. 10, 1976, pp. 121–44

Bergström, L., 'Utilitarianism and Future Mistakes', *Theoria*, Vol. 43, 1977, pp. 84–102

Bergström, L., 'Vad är nyttomoral?' ('What is Utilitarianism?'), in Gunnar Andrén, Giuliano Pontara and Torbjörn Tännsjö (eds), *Filosofi och samhälle*, Bodafors: Doxa, 1978, pp. 49–52

Bergström, L., 'Interpersonal Utility Comparisons', *Grazer Philosophische Studien*, Vol. 16/17, 1982, pp. 283–312

Berlin, I., 'Two Concepts of Liberty', reprinted in *Four Essays on Liberty*, Oxford: Oxford University Press, 1969

Blackburn, S., *Spreading the Word*, Oxford: Oxford University Press, 1984

Bohm, P., *Social Efficiency: A Concise Introduction to Welfare Economics*, London: Macmillan, 1973

Boralevi, L. C., 'Utilitarianism and Feminism', in Ellen Kennedy and Susan Mendus (eds), *Women in Western Political Philosophy*, Brighton: Wheatsheaf, 1987

Brandt, R. B., *A Theory of the Good and the Right*, Oxford: Clarendon Press, 1979

Brandt, R. B., 'The Explanation of Moral Language', in David Copp and David Zimmerman (eds), *Morality, Reason, and Truth: New Essays on the Foundations of Ethics*, Totowa, N.J.: Rowman and Allanheld, 1985

Broad, C. D., 'The Doctrine of Consequences in Ethics', *International Journal of Ethics*, Vol. 24, 1913–14, pp. 293–320

Brock, D. W., 'Recent Work in Utilitarianism', *American Philosophical Quarterly*, Vol. 10, 1973, pp. 241–69

Buchanan, J. M., 'Positive Economics, Welfare Economics, and Political Economy', *Journal of Law and Economics*, 1959

Carlson, E., *Some Basic Problems of Consequentialism*, Uppsala University, 1994

Conee, E., 'Review of Donald Regan's *Utilitarianism and Co-operation*', *Journal of Philosophy*, Vol. 80, 1983, pp. 415–24

Dancy, J., *Moral Reasons*, Oxford: Blackwell, 1993

Danielsson, S., *Filosofiska utredningar*, Stockholm: Thales, 1988

Danielsson, S., 'Hur man inte kan mäta välmåga' ('How One Cannot Measure Well-being'), in *Filosofiska invädningar*, Stockholm: Thales, 1989

Davidson, D., *Actions and Events*, Oxford and New York: Clarendon Press, 1980

Dworkin, G., 'The Concept of Autonomy', in Rudolf Haller (ed.), *Science and Ethics*, Amsterdam: 1981

Dworkin, R., 'What is Equality? Part I: Equality of Welfare; Part II: Equality of Resources', *Philosophy and Public Affairs*, Vol. 10, 1981, pp. 185–246, 283–345

Edgeworth, F. Y., *Mathematical Psychics*, London: Kegan Paul, 1881

Eriksson, B., *Heavy Duty: On the Demands of Consequentialism*, Stockholm: Almqvist and Wiksell, 1994

Feinberg, J., 'Physics and the Thales Problem', *Journal of Philosophy*, Vol. 63, 1966, pp. 5–17

Feinberg, J., 'Interest in Liberty on the Scales', in Alvin I. Goldman and Jaegwon Kim (eds), *Values and Morals*, Dordrecht: Reidel, 1978

Forrest, P., 'Backward Causation in Defence of Free Will', *Mind*, Vol. 95, 1986, pp. 210–17

Frankena, W., 'Obligation and Value in the Ethics of G. E. Moore', in P. A. Schilpp (ed.), *The Philosophy of G. E. Moore*, Library of Living Philosophers, La Salle, Ill.: Open Court, 1942

Frankfurt, H. G., 'Freedom of the Will and the Concept of a Person', *Journal of Philosophy*, Vol. LXVIII, 1971, pp. 5–20

Gauthier, D., *Morals by Agreement*, Oxford: Oxford University Press, 1986

Gibbard, A., 'Interpersonal Comparisons: Preference, Good and the Intrinsic Reward of a Life', in J. Elster and A. Hylland (eds), *Foundations of Social Choice Theory*, Cambridge: Cambridge University Press, 1986, pp. 165–93

Gibbard, A., *Wise Choices, Apt Feelings: A Theory of Normative Judgement*, Oxford: Clarendon Press, 1990

Gilligan, C., *In a Different Voice: Psychological Theory and Women's Development*, Cambridge, Mass.: Harvard University Press, 1982

Glover, J., 'It Makes No Difference Whether or Not I Do It', *Proceedings of the Aristotelian Society*, Suppl. Vol. 49, 1975

Glover, J., *Causing Death and Saving Lives*, Harmondsworth: Pelican, 1977

Glover, J., *What Sort of People Should There Be?*, Harmondsworth: Penguin, 1984

Griffin, J., 'Modern Utilitarianism', *Revue Internationale de Philosophie*, Vol. 36, 1982, pp. 331–75

Griffin, J., *Well-being*, Oxford: Clarendon Press, 1986

Grimshaw, J., *Feminist Philosophers: Women's Perspectives on Philosophical Traditions*, Brighton: Wheatsheaf, 1986

Hare, R. M., *Moral Thinking*, Oxford: Oxford University Press, 1981

Hare, R. M., 'What is Wrong With Slavery?', in Peter Singer (ed.), *Applied Ethics*, Oxford: Oxford University Press, 1986

Harman, G., 'The Inference to the Best Explanation', *Philosophical Review*, Vol. 70, 1965, pp. 88–95

Harman, G., *The Nature of Morality: An Introduction to Ethics*, New York: Oxford University Press, 1977

Harman, G., *Change in View: Principles of Reasoning*, Cambridge, Mass.: Bradford, 1986

Harsanyi, J. C., *Rational Behaviour*, Cambridge: Cambridge University Press, 1977

Harsanyi, J. C., 'Rule Utilitarianism and Decision Theory', *Erkenntnis*, Vol. 11, 1977

Harsanyi, J. C., 'Morality and the Theory of Rational Behaviour', in A. Sen and B. Williams (eds), *Utilitarianism and Beyond*, Cambridge: Cambridge University Press, 1982

Hodgson, D. H., *Consequences of Utilitarianism: A Study in Normative Ethics and Legal Theory*, Oxford: Clarendon Press, 1967

Horgan, T., 'Counterfactuals and Newcomb's Problem', *Journal of Philosophy*, Vol. LXXVIII, 1981, pp. 331–56

Hume, D., *A Treatise of Human Nature*, ed. L. A. Selby-Bigge, second edition (with text revised and notes by P. H. Nidditch), Oxford: Clarendon Press, 1978

Jackson, F., 'Group Morality', in Philip Pettit, Richard Sylvan and Jean Norman (eds), *Metaphysics and Morality*, Oxford: Blackwell, 1987

Jonsen, A. R., and Toulmin, S., *The Abuse Of Casuistry: A History of Moral Reasoning*, Berkeley, Los Angeles and London: University of California Press, 1988

Kagan, S., *The Limits of Morality*, Oxford: Clarendon Press, 1989

Kant, I., *Critique of Judgement*, Oxford: Clarendon Press, 1952

Leibniz, G. W. 'Correspondence with Arnauld, 1686–87', in Leroy Loemker (ed.), *Goffried Wilhelm Leibniz: Philosophical Papers and Letters*, Dordrecht: Reidel, 1969

Lewis, D. K., *Counterfactuals*, Oxford: Blackwell, 1973

Lewis, D. K., 'Are We Free to Break the Laws?', *Theoria*, Vol. 47, 1981, pp. 113–21

Lewis, D. K., *Philosophical Papers*, Vol. 2, Oxford: Oxford University Press, 1986

Lyons, D., *Forms and Limits of Utilitarianism*, Oxford: Oxford University Press, 1965

Mabbott, J. D., 'Moral Rules', *Proceedings of the British Academy*, Vol. XXXIX, 1953, pp. 97–117

MacIntyre, A., *After Virtue: A Study in Moral Theory*, London: Duckworth, 1981

Mackie, J. L., *Ethics: Inventing Right and Wrong*, Harmondsworth: Penguin, 1977

McDowell, J., 'Virtue and Reason', initially *Monist*, Vol. 62, 1979, pp. 331–50, here quoted from Stanley G. Clarke and Evan Simpson (eds), *Anti-Theory in Ethics and Moral Conservatism*, New York: State University of New York Press, 1989

Mill, J. S., 'Mill on Bentham', reprinted in *Utilitarianism*, ed. Mary Warnock, London and Glasgow: Collins, 1962

Mill, J. S., 'On Liberty', reprinted in *Utilitarianism*, ed. Mary Warnock, London and Glasgow: Collins, 1962

Mill, J. S., 'Utilitarianism', reprinted in *Utilitarianism*, ed. Mary Warnock, London and Glasgow: Collins, 1962

Mill, J. S., *Utilitarianism*, ed. Mary Warnock, London and Glasgow: Collins, 1962

Moore, G. E., *Principia Ethica*, Cambridge: Cambridge University Press, 1903

Moore, G. E., 'A Reply to My Critics', in P. A. Schilpp (ed.), *The Philosophy of G. E. Moore*, Library of Living Philosophers, La Salle, Ill.: Open Court, 1942

Naess, A., 'The Shallow and the Deep: Long-range Ecological Movement. A Summary', *Inquiry*, Vol. 16, 1973, pp. 95–100

Naess, A., *Ökologi, Samfunn og Livsstil*, Oslo: Universitetsforlaget, 1976

Nagel, T., *The View from Nowhere*, Oxford, New York and Toronto: Oxford University Press, 1986

Narveson, J., *Morality and Utility*, Baltimore: Johns Hopkins University Press, 1967

Narveson, J., 'Utilitarianism and New Generations', *Mind*, Vol. 76, 1967, pp. 62–72

Ng, Y.-K., 'Bentham or Bergson? Finite Sensibility, Utility Functions and Social Welfare Functions', *Review of Economic Studies*, Vol. 42, 1975, pp. 545–69

Nozick, R., *Anarchy, State, and Utopia*, Oxford: Blackwell, 1974

Nozick, R., *The Examined Life: Philosophical Meditations*, New York: Simon & Schuster, 1989

Ohlsson, R., *The Moral Import of Evil*, Filosofiska studier, Stockholm, 1979

Parekh., B. (ed.), *Bentham's Political Thought*, London: Croom Helm, 1973

Parfit, D., *Reasons and Persons*, Oxford: Clarendon Press, 1984

Popper, K., *Objective Knowledge*, Oxford: Clarendon Press, 1972

Postow, B. C., 'Generalized Act Utilitarianism', *Analysis*, Vol. 37, 1977, pp. 49–52

Prichard, H. A., 'Does Moral Philosophy Rest on a Mistake?', *Mind*, Vol. 21, 1912, pp. 21–37

Prichard, H. A., *Moral Obligation*, Oxford: Clarendon Press, 1949

Railton, P., 'Alienation, Consequentialism, and the Demands of Morality', *Philosophy and Public Affairs*, Vol. 13, 1984, pp. 134–71

Rawls, J., *A Theory of Justice*, Oxford: Oxford University Press, 1971

Regan, D., *Utilitarianism and Co-operation*, Oxford: Clarendon Press, 1980

Resnik, M. D., *Choices: An Introduction to Decision Theory*, Minneapolis: University of Minnesota Press, 1987

Ross, W. D., *The Right and the Good*, Oxford: Clarendon Press, 1930

Russell, B., 'On the Notion of Cause', first printed in *Mysticism and Logic*, reprinted in H. Feigl and M. Brodbeck (eds), *Readings in the Philosophy of Science*, New York: Appleton Century Crofts, 1953

Scanlon, T. M., 'The Moral Basis of Interpersonal Comparisons', in Jon Elster and John Roemer (eds), *Interpersonal Comparisons of Well-being*, Cambridge: Cambridge University Press, 1991

Scheffler, S. (ed.), *Consequentialism and its Critics*, Oxford: Oxford University Press, 1988

Schelling, T., *The Strategy of Conflict*, Cambridge, Mass.: Harvard University Press, 1960

Sen, A. and Williams, B. (eds), *Utilitarianism and Beyond*, Cambridge: Cambridge University Press, 1982

Sidgwick, H., *The Methods of Ethics*, New York: Dover Publications, 1966

Singer, P., *Practical Ethics*, Cambridge: Cambridge University Press, 1979

Slote, M., *From Morality to Virtue*, Oxford: Oxford University Press, 1992

Smart, J. J. C., 'An Outline of a System of Utilitarian Ethics', in J. J. C. Smart and B. Williams (eds), *Utilitarianism: For and Against*, Cambridge: Cambridge University Press, 1973

Smart, J. J. C., 'Hedonistic and Ideal Utilitarianism', *Midwest Studies in Philosophy*, Vol. III, 1980

Smart, J. J. C., *Ethics, Persuasion and Truth*, London: Routledge and Kegan Paul, 1984

Smart, J. J. C., and Williams, B. (eds), *Utilitarianism: For and Against*, Cambridge: Cambridge University Press, 1973

Smith, H. M., 'Moral Realism, Moral Conflict, and Compound Acts', *Journal of Philosophy*, Vol. 83, 1986, pp. 341–5

Stalnaker, R., 'A Theory of Counterfactuals', in Nicholas Rescher (ed.), *Studies in Logical Theory*, Oxford: Blackwell, 1968

Stevenson, C. L., *Facts and Values*, New Haven: Yale University Press, 1963

Sturgeon, N., 'Moral Explanations', in David Copp and David Zimmerman (eds), *Morality, Reason, and Truth: New Essays on the Foundations of Ethics*, Totowa, N.J.: Rowman and Allanheld, 1985

Tännsjö, T., *The Relevance of Metaethics to Ethics*, Stockholm: Almqvist and Wiksell, 1976

Tännsjö, T., 'The Morality of Abstract Entities', *Theoria*, Vol. XLIV, 1978, pp. 1–18

Tännsjö, T., 'Responsibility and the Explanatory View of Consequences', *Philosophical Studies*, Vol. 42, 1982, pp. 151–61

Tännsjö, T., 'Moral Conflict and Moral Realism', *Journal of Philosophy*, Vol. LXXXII, 1985, pp. 113–17

Tännsjö, T., 'The Morality of Collective Actions', *Philosophical Quarterly*, Vol. 39, 1989, pp. 221–8

Tännsjö, T., *Conservatism for Our Time*, London and New York: Routledge, 1990

Tännsjö, T., *Moral Realism*, Savage, Md.: Rowman & Littlefield, 1990

Tännsjö, T., 'Morality and Modality', *Philosophical Papers*, Vol. XX, 1991, pp. 139–53

Tännsjö, T., 'Who are the Beneficiaries?', *Bioethics*, Vol. 6, 1992, pp. 288–96

Tännsjö, T., 'The Expressivist Theory of Truth', *Theoria* (forthcoming)

Taylor, B. M. (ed.), *Michael Dummett: Contributions to Philosophy*, Dordrecht: Martinus Nijhoff, 1987

Taylor, R., 'Agent and Patient', *Erkenntnis*, Vol. 18, 1982, pp. 224–5

Tersman, F., 'Utilitarianism and the Idea of Reflective Equilibrium', *Southern Journal of Philosophy*, Vol. XXIX, 1991, pp. 395–406

Tersman, F., *Reflective Equilibrium*, Stockholm: Almqvist and Wiksell, 1993

Urmson, J. O., 'The Interpretation of the Philosophy of J. S. Mill', *Philosophical Quarterly*, Vol. III, 1953, pp. 33–40

van Inwagen, P., *An Essay on Free Will*, Oxford: Clarendon Press, 1983

Walker, M. Urban, 'Moral Understandings: Alternative "Epistemology" for a Feminist Ethics', in Eve Browning Cole and Susan Coultrap-McQuin (eds), *Explorations in Feminist Ethics: Theory and Practice*, Bloomington: Indiana University Press, 1992

Williams, B., 'A Critique of Utilitarianism', in J. J. C. Smart and B. Williams (eds), *Utilitarianism: For and Against*, Cambridge: Cambridge University Press, 1973

Williams, B., 'Ethical Consistency', in *Problems of the Self*, New York and Cambridge: Cambridge University Press, 1973

Williams, B., *Ethics and the Limits of Philosophy*, London: Fontana, 1985

Wolff, R. P., *In Defense of Anarchism*, New York: Harper and Row, 1970

Index